THE
URBAN
BESTIARY

THE URBAN BESTIARY

Encountering the Everyday Wild

Lyanda Lynn Haupt

Little, Brown and Company
New York Boston London

Little, Brown and Company
Hachette Book Group
237 Park Avenue, New York, NY 10017
littlebrown.com

First Edition: September 2013

Little, Brown and Company is a division of Hachette Book Group, Inc. The Little, Brown name and logo are trademarks of Hachette Book Group, Inc.

Illustrations by Tracie Noles-Ross

The publisher is not responsible for websites (or their content) that are not owned by the publisher.

The Hachette Speakers Bureau provides a wide range of authors for speaking events. To find out more, go to hachettespeakersbureau.com or call (866) 376-6591.

Library of Congress Cataloging-in-Publication Data
Haupt, Lyanda Lynn.
    The urban bestiary : encountering the everyday wild / Lyanda Lynn Haupt.—First edition.
      pages cm
    Includes bibliographical references and index.
    ISBN 978-0-316-17852-5
  1. Urban animals—United States.   2. Urban animals—Ecology—United States.
3. Wildlife watching—United States.   4. Human-animal relationships—United
States.   5. Philosophy of nature.   I. Title.
    QH541.5.C6H38 2013
    591.75'6—dc23   2013014205

10 9 8 7 6 5 4 3 2 1

RRD-C

Printed in the United States of America

FOR MY SISTER, KELLY—

A HIGH SCHOOL SCIENCE TEACHER
WHO HAS INSPIRED THOUSANDS OF STUDENTS
WITH HER LOVE OF NATURE

Contents

CONTENTS

The Bestiary's Bestiary
A Note on Process

Though I always like to write outdoors, I made it a point with this book in particular to work outside whenever possible, to immerse myself in the world I was writing about. This meant constant interruptions — crows alerting me to the presence of a sharp-shinned hawk, bugs in my hair, squirrels that required chasing before they ate every last cherry on the tree. And from these interruptions came observations and ideas that needed to be in the book — not in the chapter I was working on, but somewhere else altogether. I would pause, and then quilt the new thoughts into my notes.

Writing outdoors also meant a fair bit of thermoregulation. I commonly needed another sweater, or more shade, or, since I write in Seattle, a big umbrella. In the cooler months, I often built a fire in the backyard fire pit, extending the season of the outdoor writing studio (and providing the opportunity to fortify myself with the perfect lunch: s'mores). Though it wasn't my initial intent, I believe all of this helped to deepen my empathy with the creatures in my neighborhood, most of whom contrive some kind of shelter but none of whom (excepting the pair of squirrels that have taken up in my attic cornice) have access to anything as stalwart as my own heated wooden house. The most disconcerting thing about writing the bestiary in this manner was that it completely upset my normal writing process, which is to write a chapter, tidy it up, write another. This book seemed to me entirely haphazard, with all the chapters being written at pretty much the same time. This offended my sense of calm order and made me worry that in all of these disheveled words there would never be a book at all. But I started to realize that this rangy form mimicked its subject: the ambling, lateral knowledge of the wild — unfolding constantly, simultaneously, and without any regard at all for my own insistence on what is best for it or for me.

One of the things that emerged from my unorthodox writing studio was a kind of sub-bestiary, what I think of as the Bestiary's Bestiary — a list of animals that I observed while writing these pages. And not the animals I saw over the course of time during which I worked on the book or sighted while camping or hiking or birding, but the animals I spotted while actually putting pen to paper, or fingers to laptop, and without getting up from my desk at the window/patch of grass/perch on a cozy tree limb in my back-yard or urban park. I love that these animals reflect both the typical urban generalists (eastern gray squirrel, American robin) and those particular to my place here in Seattle, with park benches along the Puget Sound shoreline (Pacific harbor seal, osprey). I list them here in part to acknowledge with gratitude the role they played in this project by way of inspiration and holy distraction, and because I hope that they may inspire others to create their own working bestiaries—an increased attentiveness to the animals that cross our paths daily. While writing this book I was visited by:

MAMMALS
Eastern Gray Squirrel
Pacific Harbor Seal
California Sea Lion

BIRDS
Common Loon
Western Grebe
Horned Grebe
Double-crested Cormorant
Great Blue Heron
Gadwall
Mallard
Surf Scoter
Red-breasted Merganser
Canada Goose
Bald Eagle
Red-tailed Hawk
Cooper's Hawk
Sharp-shinned Hawk
Osprey
Domestic Chicken
Killdeer

Glaucous-winged Gull
Caspian Tern
Rock Pigeon
Anna's Hummingbird
Rufous Hummingbird
Belted Kingfisher
Red-breasted Sapsucker
Northern Flicker
Pileated Woodpecker
Steller's Jay
American Crow
Violet-green Swallow
Black-capped Chickadee
Chestnut-backed Chickadee
Red-breasted Nuthatch
Bewick's Wren
Pacific Wren
Golden-crowned Kinglet
Ruby-crowned Kinglet
Varied Thrush
American Robin
Hermit Thrush
Cedar Waxwing
Yellow-rumped Warbler
Townsend's Warbler
Orange-crowned Warbler
Wilson's Warbler
Western Tanager
Spotted Towhee

Dark-eyed Junco
Song Sparrow
House Finch
House Sparrow

BUTTERFLIES AND DRAGONFLIES
Lorquin's Admiral
Western Tiger Swallowtail
Mourning Cloak
Painted Lady
Cabbage Butterfly
Common Green Darner
Cardinal Meadowhawk
Eight-spotted Skimmer

A singular awareness never abandoned me: though these were the animals I chanced to see, there were far more creatures across the taxa *seeing me.*

One of the most difficult tasks for this project was choosing what animals to feature in the chapters. An exhaustive coverage of even the most common urban animals in my rambling essay form would result in a biblically proportioned volume, far beyond the scope of this small book. My intent was not to be all inclusive, but rather to treat species that are common in most urban places and those that have a particular lesson for coexisting with wildlife that can be extrapolated to other species, including the many that are not directly considered here. I tended not to include animals with strongly overlapping natural histories or similar ecological lessons/ strategies. Thus I included squirrels as the representative small rodent (rats are considered alongside squirrels, but without their own chapter), moles as the subterrestrial mammal (rather than the more geographically limited pocket gopher), and coyotes as the top urban-wild predator-trickster (rather than foxes, which are also present in many places). The struggle over what to include and what to leave out was especially problematic for birds — not only my area of expertise (so I was inclined to get carried away), but a group with nearly a thousand species in North America, hundreds of which are present in urban areas, far more than mammal species. Again, I did some generalizing and chose a few common, widespread, wonderful species that challenge our everyday perceptions of city birds. I know that nearly everyone reading this book will be able to say, "I wish she'd written about _____." But my goal, my *dream,* actually, is that this is just the start of a huge, earthen bestiary, an invitation to wild intimacy, written daily by all of us, through attention to the creatures in our midst.

PART I

Entering the Bestiary

A New Nature, a New Bestiary

t sounds like an urban myth, but it isn't. One day a lost coyote wandered into downtown Seattle. It was promptly discovered by a group of crows, who hate coyotes for their habit of preying on crow fledglings. The crows began to chase and dive-bomb the coyote, who, increasingly confused and disoriented, attempted to escape his tormentors by scampering, no one quite knows how, through the front doors of the Federal Building. From there, things got even worse for the young coyote, who had never been indoors and, horribly frightened, began running blindly about, slamming his thin, gangly body into the glass walls until he spotted the refuge of an open elevator and quickly slipped in. The doors closed, and the coyote was caught inside. Not knowing what to do, the building officials rang the police and the local wildlife officers, but help was delayed because no one would believe that there really was a coyote stuck in the downtown Federal Building elevator. Nearly three hours later, state fish and wildlife officers managed to trap the coyote — who was found to be a healthy male, probably just eight months old — and then relocated him unharmed to a suburban forested area.

Of course, no one was able to see the coyote inside the elevator. At first, I imagined him relieved. No people, no crows, a chance to draw a breath. But it is much more likely that his terror only increased in a cramped space with no exit, no glimpse of sky or earth.

So many of us are seeking gracious, creative ways of inhabiting our urban homes in this time of ecological upheaval. We want to respect the wild animals that make their homes alongside us and help them to flourish. But what does this really mean? The downtown-coyote incident, and so many others like it, unleash a tangle of questions that force us to revisit the depth, complexity, and necessity of these interrelationships, questions that are deeply relevant to all of us, whether we keep urban chickens and a garden, or live in a tiny, rented studio apartment: What is that coyote doing here, out of its forest? Whose "home" is this? Where does the wild end and the city begin? And what difference does it make to us as humans living our everyday lives?

As human habitations cut more deeply and rampantly into open space, wild animals are left with smaller, more fragmented areas in which to live, eat, and breed. The rural buffer that once separated cities from wilderness in the past is disappearing as small farms are overrun by big agriculture and urban sprawl. The tidy divisions once labeled, respectively, *urban, rural,* and *wild* are breaking down as animals that once lived well beyond urban edges are now turning up in city neighborhoods with some regularity, and human-wild encounters of all kinds are increasingly frequent, startling, and confusing. Some of these animals have long coexisted with humans, and we simply see them more often now because there are more of us living in close quarters: many songbirds, hawks, raccoons, skunks, squirrels, and opossums. But a few of these animals are unsettlingly wild: Coyotes. Even bears and cougars. Seeing them, we have conflicting thoughts rush through our heads. We can almost glimpse the fresh mountain streams, the images of bright, clean wilderness these creatures signify within our psyches. We want to run toward them. We want to run the other way. We notify the media. We protect our cats and shield our children. We hope that they thrive. We wish they would leave. "It's the city, they don't belong," some suggest, and argue for eradication. "They were here first," others say generously, but far, far too simplistically. And when they do leave, we crane our necks for the last glimpse of fur, tail, paw.

The practice of assembling written bestiaries—compendiums of animal lore and knowledge—began in medieval times. They were often lavishly illustrated volumes, lettered by monastics on vellum, edged with hand-mixed colors and gilt. The medieval bestiaries were wonderful in that they blended the best of medieval science— what was believed to be factually true about each animal—with unreservedly fanciful descriptions. These were not meant to be fantastical, and they were based on a combination of observation, conjecture, and pure imagination. All of this was presented as equally objective, with no teasing out of the observed, the assumed, and the conjured. This is in line with a broader reluctance in the highly superstitious medieval culture to distinguish the real from the fabulous in daily life. In *The Time Traveler's Guide to Medieval England,* historian Ian Mortimer writes, "At times it seems that medieval people pride themselves on the *quantity* of their knowledge, not its quality or correctness." While there were scientists and rationalists, Mortimer suggests that you "will find their writings even more outlandish than the prophecies." All of these medieval tendencies are recapitulated in the extant bestiaries, and in them we also glimpse the ray of light that Mortimer finds in such scientific murkiness: "It is from the same belief that *anything* is possible that the greatest discoveries are made."

Perhaps the most famous and beautiful extant bestiary is the gilt-edged *Aberdeen Bestiary,* penned in the twelfth century. The *Aberdeen Bestiary* spent much of its circuitous history in ecclesial or monastic settings, but we know that for a time it resided with the English royal family. The manuscript entered the library at Westminster under Henry VIII, and it bears his royal shelf mark. It is unclear how the book came into royal keeping, but Aberdeen history of arts professor Jane Geddes suggests that it was likely "plucked" during the dissolution of a monastery's assets. We don't know whether Henry himself had any personal interest in the volume, though some members of the royal family were captivated by the subject of wild creatures. That the book was thoroughly studied and not just an objet d'art like many of our own coffee-table volumes is revealed in the well-thumbed corners of the vellum pages. In the early seventeenth century, when the Scottish king James VI became King James of England, the *Bestiary* passed from the royal collection to Marischal College in Aberdeen, and it is housed today in the Aberdeen University Library.

The *Aberdeen Bestiary*'s entry for beavers exhibits the classic medieval bestiary components of observation, imagination, and allegory. The beaver is accurately described as possessing a tail that is flat like a fish's and fur that is soft like an otter's; it was prized for its testicles, which were said to contain a medically potent liquid that could cure headache, fever, and "hysteria" (this liquid would have been castoreum, located in a small glandular sac at the base of the tail on both male and female beavers). It is noted, impossibly, that to keep from being killed by a hunter, a beaver would castrate itself and toss its testicles in the hunter's path, and if it encountered another hunter, it would lift its tail to demonstrate its useless, testicle-less condition. Morality-laden allegory is woven throughout the *Bestiary*. Here, like the beaver, men should castrate their vices and toss them away to avoid the devil. Elsewhere, the jay is "the most talkative species of bird and makes an irritating noise." Just as we try to close our ears to such chatter, so should we avoid the "empty prattle of philosophers or the harmful wordiness of heretics." Less often, an animal's behavior is held up as a model of virtue rather than vice, as with the dove, who rests near flowing water so that it can spot the reflection of an overhead hawk and flee to safety, just as we should study scripture to "avoid the plotting devil." With more dovelike qualities, we, too, might "assume the wings of contemplation and fly to heaven." But it's not all moralizing. There are hundreds of sweet, earthen moments in the *Bestiary*, evidence of quiet and humble observation:

> The ant has also learned to watch out for periods of fine weather. For if it sees that its supplies of corn are becoming wet, soaked by the rain, it carefully tests the air for signs of a mild spell, then it opens up its stores, and carries its supplies on its shoulders from its vaults underground out into the open, so that the corn can dry in the unbroken sunshine.

We may chuckle over the misguidedness of beaver-testicle tales, but despite the scientific strides that have brought us to the current moment, our own cultural/zoological mythology is fraught with misinformation every bit as false as the beaver-castration story. Nature books, television shows, and conservation organizations educate us about the remote wild and endangered species. Certainly knowledge about all earthen creatures is wonderful and essential, but very often we know a great deal more about the Chinese giant panda or the lowland mountain gorilla than we do about the most common of local creatures, say the eastern gray squirrels in our backyards.

It is time for a new bestiary, one that engages our desire to understand the creatures surrounding our urban homes, helps us locate ourselves in nature, and suggests a response to this knowledge that will benefit both ourselves and the more-than-human world. We were born for this knowing, for a quick, innate sensitivity to other animals. We are evolutionarily formed to be attuned to the presence and habits of animals. Studies show that we register the movement of biological things more rapidly than we do those of mechanical things. If two entities about the same size, say a Mini Cooper and a bison, are positioned at the same distance in our peripheral vision and both of them suddenly and simultaneously move a foot forward, our precognitive nervous systems will more quickly recognize the movement of the bison. (Naturalist and entomologist E. O. Wilson coined the term *biophilia* to refer to the innate human affinity for the natural and biological dimensions of earthly life. Thinking to borrow the notion to speak to our particular bond with animals for the purposes of this project, I invoked the Google Oracle to see whether anyone had thought of it already: I naively typed *zoophilia* into the search bar. Mistake. I was immediately directed to dozens of sites featuring man-on-sheep sex acts.)

Why a new bestiary? There is much available on the interwebs. Everything you need to know about how to identify urban animals and keep them out of your house is a click away. But a bestiary is another matter altogether — entering a bestiary, we cross the threshold into a world in which our imaginations, our art, our bodies, our science, our mythology, all have an exuberant place. Mythology in particular is underrepresented in our modern ways of knowing; it has become suspect, synonymous with the primitive, the irrational, the unscientific, or simply the untrue. But myths have always given our meaning-seeking species a way to find the thread of pattern, significance, and timelessness underlying our chaotic and unpredictable daily lives. Karen Armstrong writes in *A Short History of Myth* that "mythology and science both extend the scope of human beings." Myth invites us to decouple our modern conflation of truth and fact. Armstrong considers it "a mistake to regard myth as an inferior mode of thought, which can be cast aside when human beings have attained the age of reason. Mythology is not an early attempt at history, and does not claim that its tales are objective fact. Like a novel, an opera or a ballet, myth is make-believe; it is a game that transfigures our fragmented, tragic world, and helps us to glimpse new possibilities." In this bestiary, as in its medieval precursors, mythology is among the many lovely paths toward human knowing: science, natural history, personal observation, everyday storytelling.

In a recent *New York Times* article, Jane Brody wrote about the increasing frequency of human-wild encounters from the standpoint of possible threats to humans. While the sighting of coyotes and other beasts might thrill, she writes, these animals can "wreak havoc on human health and safety." Like much of the media's coverage of wildlife, this article focuses on pathology and the possibility of disaster. Brody cites coyote-child encounters, raccoons ransacking homes they enter through pet doors, and the potential slipperiness of goose excrement. She outlines ways to protect our bodies, our health, and our property from the impacts of wild run-ins. Everything she writes is true. But I want to reframe the issue. While limiting conflict is absolutely essential for coexistence with wildlife (and a good part of *The Urban Bestiary* will address this very thing), it is time to evolve from the basic stance that "wild animals can hurt us, and we need to fear and contain them," to the more expansive idea that we exist as a community of beings — a creative, enlivening, and complex recognition. Care is required, but fear is almost always misguided and undermining. It is time to redress our knowledge imbalance regarding common wildlife, where potential harms are hyped, fear is heightened, good natural history information is missing, and the benefits of living alongside wild creatures are unmentioned. If there is a moral to the modern bestiary, it is this: *The more we understand the wild animals that share our home places, the better we can coexist in safety, wisdom, conviviality, and delight.*

Like many urban chicken keepers, I find that a good part of me longs for a rural existence. I never meant to live in a city. I always imagined growing my family and garden on a remote expanse of rural land at the end of a tree-lined dirt road. I would keep a cow, write nature books, send my daughter to some hippie Waldorf school, make goat cheese, bake bread. Mornings, I would watch the deer gather at the edge of our meadow; evenings, I would be on the lookout for rangylimbed coyotes disappearing into the woods. Instead, I took a job with an urban environmental organization and married a man who works in global health for the University of Washington, and we're raising our daughter in a Seattle neighborhood, where we will be for the foreseeable future. And as much as a corner of my mind still dreams of a farmy, rural life at the forest's edge, I realize more each day that modern times have thrown us into a curious paradox: For those who love nature and hope to conserve wild places, urban homes are in many ways the most appropriate places to live.

City dwellers often cite the cultural advantages of urban life. Cities are where the people are. They are where we gather to live, raise our families, build our schools and libraries, make music, produce theater. If cities are places where we incite one another to heightened material desires and rampant consumerism, where we are blinded to the needs, rhythms, and even existence of nature, they are also places that invite collaboration in the highest arts and the richest community endeavors. But there is also an unexpectedly profound ecological element to the human density that characterizes urban sites. Cities, ill-planned messes as they might currently be, are the places that the bulk of us will have to live if earthly life — both human and wild — is going to have any chance of flourishing. As inviting as the notion of a rural existence might be for many of us, the remaining open spaces in our country and beyond simply cannot accommodate a modern back-to-the-land movement, no matter how well intentioned. Well-planned urban density is the most ecologically promising mode of human habitation, allowing our homes to cluster, to be built alongside and on top of one another. This clustering encourages a sharing of resources, tools, energy, ingenuity, transport, and pavement that keep humans in one walkable/bikeable/

busable place instead of sprawling out and further fragmenting the open spaces, wetlands, and woodlands that support wild creatures and systems. No matter how much I might yearn for a sweet Jersey cow on the back forty (and at this point, I'd settle for a pair of dwarf Nigerian goats on a shy half acre), I have come to realize that the most ecological life I can live begins with a new understanding of my urban home.

We are in the midst of a vital thrust toward urban and earthen sustainability, changes in food practices, and conservation imperatives. We inhabit what I call a new nature, where the romantic vision of nature as separate from human activity must be replaced by the realistic sense that all of nature, no matter how remote, is affected by what we do and how we live. But at the same time, while enthusiasm and good intentions run high, as urban dwellers, we find ourselves unmoored — bereft of the folklore; naturalist practices; knowledge of local creatures, plants, and soil that were a necessity of life just a couple of generations ago. In this decade, for the first time in the history of the earth, more humans live in urban places than rural. Simultaneously, there is more popular interest in nature, wildlife, conservation, and natural living than there has ever been. As a new urban culture emerges, we are seeking to reclaim, and in many ways create anew, a body of knowledge that ties us to the natural world and that engages all dimensions of human knowing — intellectual, spiritual, philosophical, and deeply practical — informing a connection to the natural world that is creative, intelligent, earthy, wild, and beautiful.

This unfolding vision of a new urban ecology has everything to do with rethinking nature more broadly. The concept of a new nature solidified for me while I was reading a recent essay by Jason

Cowley, editor of the Cambridge-based journal *Granta,* about the changing face of nature writing. Gone are the days when "man" — typically a bearded, poorly dressed, lone semi-misanthrope in the shape of a Thoreau, or an Emerson, or a Muir — wanders into the woods in search of meaning and purpose through a romantic communing with nature. Nature was, in the history of the genre, a kind of cipher against which the writer/thinker could, through his own longings, desires, studies, and raptures, create a meaningful sense of self. The perceived inauthenticity of conventional society was renounced for something real, true, and — always — separate from the everyday life in town that the writer left behind. New nature writing, Cowley argues, is different. The "lyrical pastoral tradition of the romantic wanderer" and even the descriptive natural history essay are being replaced by first-person narratives in which the writer places herself, *along with* nature, in a vital, urgent, and highly practical exploration of the human place in an ecological world. Humans are not observers of an untouched beauty; we are present, involved, touched *and* touching, in a journey of reconnection between daily life and wilder earth.

But this notion of a new nature writing invites a question: Are writers changing, or is nature? *Nature* has never been securely defined. Our use of the word in an everyday sense is extremely broad. "I need some time in nature," a friend might say colloquially, and we nod, knowing what is meant. A camping trip, a walk in the park, something to do with trees, perhaps just a foray into the backyard garden. This is a perfectly good and useful interpretation of the word, but beyond this colloquial meaning, it serves us now to be more specific. In the past, nature has been romanticized into an untouched place beyond human civilization. We love this vision and long, at times, to find ourselves immersed in wild, pristine nature. But finding untouched nature is almost impossible. Not only are the wilderness areas and parks carved with roads, trails, noise pollution, and car exhaust, but the ramifications of human-caused climate change for wild places and animals are unrelentingly global. We know that the human footprint covers the entire planet, with no place left unaltered. I would reluctantly argue that there is indeed a new nature, a sense of the earth in which we understand that humans are entangled with all of wild life, what we see and what we don't, whether we wish this to be so or not. (*Wildlife,* one word, refers to wild animals, but I like to use *wild life,* two words, to refer to the expansive sense of biological life that throws humans into the mix alongside all things animal, botanical, geological, and atmospheric.)

This understanding is both disheartening and inviting. I for one would rather hold fast to the notion of a remote wild earth. I want wild nature to have nothing to do with my little human plans and wants and travails and foibles. I want there to be a "big wild" that inspires my days and my writing and my home life. But coming to terms with the fact that even the wildest places are now tied to the way we create our human lives, I try to find the poetry in this view — to know that how I live and how I focus my attention, even (*especially*) in my urban home, can be of benefit to wild places that I will never see but for which I have a deep passion and with which I am constantly, intimately connected. The earth is small. My life and wild life twine together. I come to this understanding by exploring wilderness with a pack on my back and with my ear to the wind, yes, but also by observing a migratory warbler in my backyard and by joining my daughter in watching a nonnative house sparrow gather nest material in the backyard garden while allowing myself to recognize fully that these activities are all of a piece.

On our living room table lies a nest made, literally, out of our household — chicken feathers, bark from the front yard, moss from the garden stones, string from a woven rice bag that was in the garbage, bits of yarn from a scrap of carpet. It was woven by house sparrows, birds whose ancestors, like mine, came from Europe, and its loose form tells a perfect story of what I've come to think of as the lost boundary: the walls of our homes, our urban planning and map drawing, our workday distractions do not, and cannot, separate us from the lives and needs of a more-than-human world. We are part of a great conversation. As we pay attention, we'll find the tracks, the script of our wild neighbors, to tell us so; we'll begin to answer the essential question of how to live on a changing earth, where humans and nature are tangled so messily and so wondrously.

The Lost Art of Urban Tracking

*T*racking *has traditionally been considered a practice for hunters, but* in the past few years, wilderness-tracking classes have become terrifically popular across the country among people with a general interest in nature, and one of the nation's preeminent trackers, Paul Rezendes, has been a vegetarian for more than thirty years. Before that he was a leader in the Devil's Disciples, a notoriously violent motorcycle gang. In his memoir, he speaks with raw honesty of the part he played in a shocking act of abuse against a young woman, one of the Disciples' hanger-on "mamas." After leaving the gang, he spent a decade in self-imposed atonement, literally crawling on his hands and knees in spiritual pilgrimage, a period that healed his psyche while attuning him very literally to the details of the earth.

Rezendes's book *Tracking and the Art of Seeing* is one of the best tracking books I know. We think of tracking as something done in the forest, or perhaps in the sandy desert wilderness, but of the forty-four mammals Rezendes teaches us to follow, covering all of the country's diverse habitats, fourteen species typically occur in urban and suburban areas, and the trackable birdlife in cities is even greater. There is more than enough, right in the places we dwell, for a lifetime of animal study.

Tracking often has very little to do with actual tracks. In concretized urban settings, this is good news. Certainly we can watch for real tracks, searching especially garden perimeters, the muddy edges of sidewalks, the unwalked sides of park trails, the swampy mouths of culverts. We can celebrate a tracking heyday after a snow. But we learn as much, or more, from what is called *sign*. The word used in the singular is often seen as a typo (shouldn't it be *signs?*), but *sign* is the all-encompassing official tracker's noun, referring to the almost endless observable clues that animals leave behind in their daily lives. It's wonderful to see in body the actual creatures that dwell among us, but often they are wary, or hiding, and their behavior might change when they discover they are under observation. Sign is the true story of a secret, ever-present, insistent world. In sign, animals offer their own stories, told in an expansive alphabet that might include trails, feathers, broken nuts, dismantled pinecones, nests, droppings, pellets, scratched bark, clipped branches, middens, piles of shells, holes in trees, hollows in earth, bits of bird leg or head, the strewn fur or feathers of a kill site, sometimes entire dead creatures, their presence advertised by a gathering of crows. It takes study and practice to read animal sign skillfully, but it takes only a slender mental shift to attune our minds and bodies to the presence of sign, to be more watchful, more aware, and, through all of this, more connected to the wild life of our home places.

Observation is a lovely, overlooked word. It seems to indicate separation: one thing (the human animal) observing another thing (the raccoon, the thrush, the fern frond, the dragonfly). But observation can become more than mere watching, more than looking across our noses at the Other, through, perhaps, the mediation of a notepad or binoculars. The word evolved from the Medieval Latin *observare,* which means not just "to watch" (*ob-*), but also "to attend" (*servare*). And to attend to something is an uncommon thing. It implies a kind of service, a graced allowing, a room for the movement of the observed in its own sphere—a sphere that, as attendants, we are invited to enter. With practice, our attendance deepens, becomes more astute, and also easier, more natural, part of our lives, our days, our intellects, our bodies. Observing, we grow wild, in the loveliest sense. It takes just a momentary shift in attention to turn any walk, any time spent outdoors (or even indoors, if you have a view out the window or a moth on the door frame), into a moment of natural attunement, a time in which we allow the nonhuman life among us to show itself, to have presence, to speak for itself. This manner of observation, of *tracking,* involves science, natural history, conservation issues, even politics—all of which are important. But it requires in equal measure contemplation, curiosity, art, wonder, poetry, play, and love.

When I talked with David Moskowitz, one of our nation's top trackers, he agreed that urban neighborhoods are great places for tracking. We are wired for this kind of observation, he says, to be alert to our surroundings as a condition for survival, to be active daily participants in the places we live. "In any hunter-gatherer culture," he writes, "a detailed understanding, respect, and appreciation

Feline or Canine?

In the muddy edges of our urban lives, the most common mammal tracks we see will be from cats and dogs; knowing feline from canine tracks is a good starting place in the urban tracker's art. They are similar in shape, each paw with four toes and a heel pad, so they can be confusing initially, but there are several simple ways to tell them apart. Experienced trackers can determine individual species of canines and felines, but there are generalizations that are true for most species in each group.

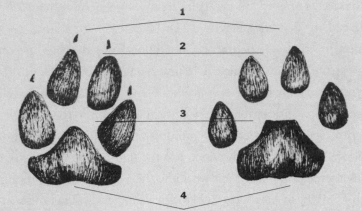

Canine front track (domestic dog, coyote, fox, or wolf)

Feline front track (domestic cat, bobcat, or cougar—lynx are unique and don't conform to these norms)

Canine tracks typically show claw marks, while a feline's do not (1). If a cat is running after prey or pouncing, claw marks might be visible.

The front two toes are side by side on a canine, and their tips are nearly parallel. On a feline track, one toe is discernibly farther forward (the inner toe, so this trait will also tell you whether the track is from the right or left paw) (2).

On a dog, the top of the heel pad shows a clear arched, bell shape. On a cat, the top of the heel pad is dipped (3).

The back of the canine heel pad is arched upward; the feline's has three lobes (4).

For both cats and dogs, front tracks are normally smaller than hind tracks. Remember, "Think horses, not zebras": while such prints might be left by a coyote, fox, or even cougar, in our neighborhoods, the majority of these tracks will be from domestic pets.

for wild creatures is integral to the material survival and safety of its people. Though we may think that we in this modern world have moved far from our roots in subsistence cultures, in actuality our survival and safety still depend on understanding, respect, and appreciation for our natural environment." It is in this spirit that tracks and sign are illustrated for most animals featured in this bestiary. Tracking is a forgotten element of our innate human intelligence, one that we can practice and reclaim no matter where we live.

I have always loved the romantic notion of "the field" and have cultivated a sense of myself as a naturalist by the ever-ready presence of my field bag, which carries field guide, field glasses (a much more romantic word than *binoculars*), and my endless field notes. The notion of the field as a place for natural history exploration and scientific study came into common usage near the end of the nineteenth century, alongside the explorations of Charles Darwin, Alfred Russel Wallace, and Henry Walter Bates, all of whom set off to distant lands and returned with journals and specimens through which we furthered our understanding of biological life. Field science as a discipline was honed in the first part of the twentieth century, and along with it came the idea that the field was a place, in fact, *afield,* away from the home or the lab, a place at least somewhat remote, awaiting exploration, with secrets to be studied and brought back. But as Michael Canfield wrote in his study of field notes in science, *the field* has no specific scope, no "geographical or physical bounds"; it is defined instead "by those who go there to investigate, study, or commune with nature." In this light, the naturalist's or tracker's attitude allows us to reframe our home places as a version of the field, full of wild possibility, never wholly explored.

Sweeping up the patio yesterday, I discovered a clump of striped fur. Raccoon. Raccoon-tail fur is singular; while we might think that the striped tail is created by alternating rings of light gray and darker black-brown fur, in actuality, each individual fur strand is itself also striped. I picked up the bit of fur and set it on a ledge. Sweeping more, I found another clump of fur, this one attached to three slender vertebrae — the bones from the end of the tail. Dear me! Here was a story. Another clump (no bone), and another. I did not discover the sorry reason for the tail-snipping, but I am now on the lookout for a blunt-ended, ratty-tailed raccoon.

The deepened intimacy that tracking yields is a kind of modern survival knowledge. The connection might be lightly perceived at first — here are two animals, one human, one not, sharing the same sounds, sky, smells. But as we come to follow an animal's story more deeply, we realize that, in a sense, its trail is our trail. As an animal moves through its life, it affects the place where it lives, the place where we also live. There can be no absolute separation between us. With this frame of mind, we enter the bestiary as true observers — as participants and inhabitants among the unfolding stories of wild life.

Collecting Tracks: A Wild Guest Book

A tracking box can help you learn to identify tracks in your backyard or even inside your house. Make a wood frame out of four-by-sixes (tracking schools recommend a minimum of four feet by eight feet for an instructive box), and fill it with sand. Play sand is great—it is light and lump-free, and especially good for small birds. Construction sand or beach sand works too. Dampen the sand enough so that it holds a shape without becoming runny. You might want to put a little food bait (peanut butter or raisins are classic) in the middle to attract nocturnal creatures. Besides framing a unique window into the at-home wild, such a box can enhance tracking skills in other ways. Try visiting tracks as they age, as they fill with debris, as they are affected by weather. If no wild animals come, then practice with domestic ones. Try walking your dog through the box when he is hungry, when he is full, when he has to pee, when he doesn't. Try getting him to prance or to run, or do these things yourself—see how the imprints are affected. I know of one naturalist who set up such a box in her New York apartment and tracked her cat as well as visiting ants and roaches!

A box is best, because it offers a controlled, contained substrate, but if you are like me and possess unreasonable aesthetic tendencies that keep you from setting up wooden boxes of sand in your garden, then you can still benefit from the idea by leaving damp sand or soil edges around your yard. I have experimented with these loose-form tracking boxes, sometimes baited, sometimes not, at the borders of our koi pond (sprinkled wildly with raccoon tracks) and our vegetable garden (mouse, squirrel, rat, opossum) and beneath our cherry tree (more of all of the above)—all of them small wild entries into the loveliest guest book I have ever kept.

PART II

The Furred

Coyote

Urban-Wild Trickster

Dominic and Crystal's border collie, Earnhardt, rules the world — he rules the sofa, the sidewalk, the upscale Seattle neighborhood in which he lives, and all the neighborhood's dogs. Earnhardt likes to bark. He barks at children, moms with strollers, the postal carrier, the UPS guy, dogs he likes, dogs he doesn't like; he barks when he is crabby, when he is playful. He prances, struts, plays, eats, and barks; that is the sum of Earnhardt's favorite life activities. But one day when Dominic and Crystal and Earnhardt were all out walking, a coyote appeared on the sidewalk. When Earnhardt saw the coyote, he did not bark. He yelped. A high-pitched, feral yelp that his owners had never heard before and would not even have believed him capable of. After the yelp, Earnhardt hid behind Crystal's legs, refusing to continue on the walk, even though he hadn't pooped like he was supposed to. The coyote was thin and light, not much bigger than Earnhardt, certainly not as big as the dogs Earnhardt liked to bark at. The coyote was shaped like a dog, was in fact a member of the genus *Canis,* just like Earnhardt. The coyote trotted away quickly, almost running, as if he'd accidentally gotten himself into this overly urban area and was anxious to get out of it; he did not threaten Earnhardt or even take much notice of him at all. What is this? This wildness that is so obvious, so true, so beyond language and cultural conditioning that it is primally recognizable in less than an instant, even to the utterly domestic cock of the walk Earnhardt? The coyotes among us open the door to such questions, pad through, then glance over their shoulders to make sure we are following.

Coyotes are slender, sinewy, more fur than flesh. Their snouts are long; their fur is mixed goldens and browns, like the prairie grasses of their native habitat; their bushy tails are tipped with black and usually hang down, never wagging upright like pet dogs' tails; their ears seem a little too big for their heads, funnels for the minute sounds they must sift through in their lives as hunters; their eyes, close-set on the fronts of their heads in classic predator fashion, are striking yellow with round black pupils (domestic dog pupils are browner, fox pupils vertical and narrow); their toenails are worn smooth and blunt and are not used much in capturing prey — coyotes catch smaller animals in their jaws, which are lined with forty-two sharp teeth.

Stories of human-coyote interactions in urban areas are increasing. As urban and suburban sprawl encroaches on woodland areas, coyote habitat morphs into a complicated blend of forest and neighborhood edges. There was a coyote on the Golden Gate Bridge this spring, and coyotes in Central Park. We don't really know how many coyotes live with us — just a couple of decades ago, there was no perceived need for studies on urban coyote habits and populations (there were both fewer coyotes *and* fewer humans living in urban haunts), and wildlife biology is just beginning to catch up with the changing face of the urban ecosystem. Even in cities where coyote populations have been studied extensively, like Chicago and Los Angeles, no one is sure exactly how many coyotes are really there, but it is likely to be far more than we imagine. Once the ghosts of the plains, coyotes have become the ghosts of the cities, living among us, watchful, quiet, and largely unseen. The ones we happen to glimpse are just the ones we happen to glimpse. Stan Gehrt of Ohio State University has studied urban coyotes as much as any wildlife researcher. Over the course of his decade-long study of coyotes in urban Chicago, he and his colleagues radio-collared more than two hundred individuals that they then monitored day and night, giving unprecedented insight into the activities of urban coyotes. One of the biggest surprises to Gehrt was that there were so many coyotes living right in the urban matrix. Whereas at the beginning of his study he thought there might be just a hundred or so, he now estimates there are somewhere between several hundred and two thousand (even after years of research, precision is elusive). There are thriving coyote populations in Chicago, Los Angeles, San Francisco, New Jersey, Seattle, New York, and many other metropolitan places. There was also, this week, coyote scat on the sidewalk just a few doors down from my house.

Coyote Tracks and Sign

Coyote scat is one of the easiest wild-mammal droppings to recognize, especially in winter. In summer and early autumn, coyotes enjoy so many fruits and insects in their diets that the scats become seedy and crumbly, resembling that of many other creatures. But in winter, the scats are wide, tidy twists of fur and bone, nearly an inch around (real trackers carry calipers for accuracy in such measurements; I am perfectly happy to eyeball), and typically taper to a thin, curling point on each end.

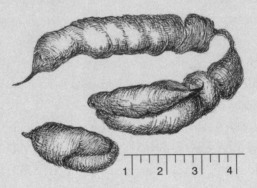

Of course, you shouldn't go around picking up coyote poop with your bare hands, but with a stick or gloves, it is perfectly safe to inspect it. Unlike dog poo, it doesn't stink.[*] Using two sticks, you can pull the scats apart and see what the coyote has been up to. In urban places, the fur is usually short rodent fur, and it includes lots of rat. There are typically crunched-up little bones and some whole ones—tiny mouse or shrew jaws and femurs are the most likely to survive the digestive tract intact. Berries

---

[*] This is because the coyote has an efficient carnivore's digestive tract and, even in cities, a natural diet that leaves little waste. The scats are simply clean indigestibles.

in the coyote diet are easy to identify by seed and color, as are the shimmering exoskeletons of beetles and grasshoppers.

Coyote   **Domestic dog**

Coyote tracks are very similar to domestic dog tracks, but notice the more circular shape of the dog track. Size is not a good indicator, as both dogs and coyotes vary in size with breed (in the case of dogs) and age, though a very large canine track is likely a big dog. The pattern of the tracks, their trail, is worth investigating. If you've ever walked a dog, you know that dogs are not much interested in going anywhere efficiently—they wander, and investigate, and backtrack. Coyotes, and foxes too, will leave trails that are far more direct, pretty much a straight line; this is particularly true in urban settings, where they are wary of the environment.

As I was enjoying my examination of this curbside coyote scat, the couple in the neighboring house came outside. I forgot to worry that I might look a bit odd, picking through sidewalk poop, and stood up to say excitedly, "This is coyote, right here outside your house!" Thankfully, they were game for such a discussion. "We thought that might be what it was," the woman said. "That's so cool!" We all turned to look as their little Jack Russell terrier trotted brightly out the door. "Yeah." She nodded. "We keep him in at night." There is a chain-link fence around their house, which might inspire a sense of safety, but coyotes can leap fences up to six feet high. They don't bound over them like, say, a deer. They jump up and hang from the very top of the fence by the tips of their front paws, then climb up with their back feet and push themselves over. People serious about coyote deterrence install rollers along the tops of their fences, which keep the coyotes from grabbing on with their toes.

Not everyone is as sanguine as this nice couple about sharing the neighborhood with coyotes. In general, though most of us enjoy the idea that "the wild" somehow surrounds our neighborhoods, we tend to like our urban wildlife somewhat smaller, more predictable, and less carnivorous. We prefer that it have smaller teeth, or none at all. We have deliberately built orderly perimeters of physical and cultural civilization from which we can delight comfortably in the ideas of wilderness and wildness. How did this animal cross these boundaries, more or less uninvited? More than any other animal, the coyote represents the urban-wild trickster—a creature that inhabits our imaginations as richly as it does the edges of our neighborhoods. Trickster figures regularly turn up in the narrative mythology of native cultures in North America and around the world. Part of the trickster mystique lies in a refusal to be defined, but typically tricksters are animals (often ravens, hares, coyotes, or raccoons—Br'er Rabbit and Bugs Bunny are modern tricksters) that take on some human capacities as they dance through life and do their primary work: turning our preconceived social norms upside down. Tricksters dwell in a self-made amoral world, neither good nor bad, and in a tangle of contradiction: footloose, irresponsible, callous, but also funny, lovable, clever, and, as we will see in the case of coyotes, irrepressibly sympathetic. They create a "margin of mess," writes folklorist Barbara Bannick, the chaos that contains all possibility.

No matter what we know of native mythology, all of us know on some inner level (just like Earnhardt does) something about Coyote. Coyote represents a sensibility that does not stay neatly inbounds. Coyote is both wholly other and an intricate part of our human story. Coyote will inspire our poems. Coyote will eat our cats. Coyote's life is messy, wary, prancing, a life that cannot avoid pain, or death, or dirt, but is nevertheless enlivening: ears pricked, alert, lean, wild, delighted.

There are many reasons that we are seeing coyotes more regularly in the city these days. The main one is that buildings and roads and malls and homes sprawl farther and farther into semirural habitat that was once the coyote's favorite haunt. Though historically, coyotes have been wary of living too close to humans, there are simply lots of coyotes, and they need someplace to live—they are scrappy, adaptive, opportunistic, omnivorous, and smart. They are making do with changing circumstances. So it's not just a perception and the hype of social media—humans and coyotes really *are* living in closer proximity, and consequently, we see more of them.

Coyotes have lived on the edges of our neighborhoods for decades, and in this time, they have remained largely nocturnal. In wilder places, this is generally not the case; coyotes are more crepuscular—that is, active in rhythmic cycles throughout the day and night. In urban places, they adapted to the presence of humans by avoiding us—denning or sleeping during the day (like bird nests, dens are used for whelping and protecting young pups, not for year-round sleeping—coyotes sleep aboveground) and coming out at night for hunting and all the other coyote-life essentials. We have lived this way for years, the coyotes and us, avoiding what wildlife biologists call the human-wildlife spatiotemporal interface. But now we are seeing coyotes during the day, mostly in the early morning or after dusk, but sometimes at bright stark noon. As my husband, Tom, and my daughter, Claire, and I were walking in the wooded periphery of a golf course the other day, we saw two handsome coyotes prancing about, loping, sniffing, playing. When golfers approached, we thought the coyotes would disappear into the woods, but they didn't. They barely registered the people's presence. Coyotes are learning several things: that most people don't hurt them; that people often feed them, either intentionally (yes, many people, enthralled by the presence of coyotes, leave food outside for them at night or toss a leg of fried chicken from the picnic basket in a woodland park) or inadvertently (in the way of pet food left on the porch, messy birdfeeders, rats attracted by these same birdfeeders, garden fruit, and fat outdoor cats); and that human habitations are typically home to refuse cans with ill-fitting lids, full of all manner of coyote-worthy foodstuffs: peaches, pizza, the fat from a filet mignon.

We have coexisted alongside coyotes with very few incidents for a long time, but there is concern over what appears to be an increase in daylight sightings of less wary coyotes in urban places. When I talked with Stan Gehrt about this, he agreed that it would be best for everyone (humans and coyotes) if urban coyotes continued their general habit of staying out of sight between dawn and dusk, but he cautioned against interpreting daylight sightings as a trend to worry over. "With more coyotes around," he tells me, "exceptions become more prevalent." We see the few individuals that are bolder, and with such animals we are right to be cautious, but that doesn't mean urban coyotes on the whole are becoming less watchful.

Our perception of coyotes is distorted in part by the proliferation of social media. Just a few years ago, if someone saw a coyote, she might get really excited and tell her friends. Now she posts it on Facebook accompanied by a photo, then, for good measure, sends the photo and story to the neighborhood blog. All of this can be immensely positive. Sharing of wild stories is a lovely and ancient human practice, one that evolved with our cultural habits. Evening tales around the campfire after a day's gathering and hunting are now stories of neighborhood wildlife sightings posted on the interwebs; we participate in the storyteller's art and lineage by spinning our "everyday" wild tales. Most neighborhood blogs pair sightings of animals like coyotes with good public education and pertinent reminders to keep cats and Chihuahuas indoors. But the *response* to all this sharing can be a wild card — stories on the web of urban coyote sightings are followed by comment sections that regularly degenerate into an onslaught of unvetted misinformation that can reach thousands of people. Emotions about urban coyotes run high, fueled more by speculation, false myth, and fear than by an understanding of coyote habits. The dearth of studies on urban coyotes means that the shaping of the public perception is left largely to the media, and even in the supposedly filtered media of television and newspaper, misinformation is rampant. Stories unfold in an intentionally hyped-up, headline-grabbing response to a coyote sighting or complaint, and they are often framed by outworn pre-ecological perceptions that breed fear and hatred rather than by good science or calming common sense. The language used to describe coyotes is loaded and inflammatory: instead of intelligent, they are "cunning"; smaller animals are not hunted by coyotes for food — they are "mauled." One of our top eco-literary journals recently published an essay in which it was said that coyotes frequented a forested area around a New York golf course, a "good habitat in which to den, skulk, and plan." (Why *skulk*, with its overlay of nefarious intent? And *plan*? What are they doing? Laying out little coyote maps, marking the homes of untended cats?) Predator biologist Brian Kertson tells me that in all these ways, the perceived threat from wild predators, relative to the actual risk, becomes tremendously exaggerated in our minds. "Some dad is driving his family around in the SUV at seventy mph while talking on the phone, and he wants to tell me he's worried a coyote is going to bite his kid? I just don't know what to say."

Not that there is no threat. Coyotes do eat cats. They can tussle with dogs and eat small ones. They can (though it is *exceedingly* rare) menace or even bite children. Coyotes rarely threaten an adult in any circumstance. There have been, in the history of North America, two known human deaths from coyote attacks. One, in Northern California in 1981, was a child who lived in a suburban neighborhood where coyotes were regularly fed. The other, in 2009, was the much publicized and heartbreaking death of the beautiful young Canadian folksinger Taylor Mitchell, who was attacked by a pair of eastern coyotes as she rambled a well-traveled trail in a forested Nova Scotia park. Her debut album had just been released, and the maturity of voice and lyrics belied her age. She was nineteen years old. In a media statement following her death, Taylor's mother offered this largehearted response: "We take a calculated risk when spending time in nature's fold — it's wildlife's terrain. When the decision had been made to kill the pack of coyotes, I clearly heard Taylor's voice say, 'Please don't. This is their space.' She wouldn't have wanted their demise, especially as a result of her own." The comment is stunningly magnanimous, but in this case, even the strongest wildlife-rights advocates felt that these coyotes could not remain on a public trail without endangering more people and threatening human tolerance for other wild coyotes.*

All of this information — the positive, negative, accurate, and distorted — leaves us justifiably confused and wondering. How should we respond to the presence of coyotes in the city? Part of us wants to love the presence of the wild that coyotes represent. We think the animals themselves are beautiful, and they are. Part of us fears them. All of us want to make sure that no one gets hurt. Most people don't want urban coyotes eradicated, "But..." we say. *But.*

Some of my contacts in the wildlife biology field are disparaging of the general public. "People are idiots," one state biologist told me. "Every time they see a coyote they call and say, 'Well, don't you want to come out? Aren't you going to *do something?*' And that means, 'Aren't you going to trap it or shoot it?' Lady, get a grip." It's true that coyotes are one of the only urban animals whose presence alone is cause for outright alarm, for which being *seen* is reason enough for wildlife officials to be alerted. But I don't think people are idiots (for the most part). I think we are well intentioned, underinformed, and honestly unsure about what to do. Appreciation of wild nature is alive and well in our art and literature (sometimes). In our school

---

* For context and perspective, while only two people are known to have been killed by coyotes in North America ever, there are dozens of people killed by domestic dogs every single year. And while there were two hundred reported injuries to humans from coyotes in the past thirty years, there are four and a half million dog bites every year in the United States, with about eight hundred thousand of them requiring medical attention. Unlike coyote encounters, most of these domestic dog incidents, including the deaths, are not widely reported. Of course, there are more dogs, and so more dog bites; the point here is that while domestic dogs really do pose a daily threat to us, they are not vilified; the coyotes among us pose far less of an immediate threat than dogs, yet there are fierce and emotional calls for their eradication.

Coyote Pre-European distribution

Coyote current distribution

books (a little). But in our daily education? In our practical knowledge? Our close-to-home world? There is little to none. And now here we are with coyote scat on the sidewalk, and a neighbor with a missing cat. Most adults cannot accurately identify the song of an American robin, probably the most common garden bird, when they hear one singing in the backyard. Why on earth would we know what to think of a coyote?

Coyotes didn't always live in cities, suburbs, or even woodsy rural places. Their historic home range was the western prairie. As humans killed wolves one by one across the country for flock protection, for pelt money, for bounty, or for malice, the coyotes moved easily into the wolves' ecological niche as top canine predator. They spread north and south, into the woods and canyon lands of the west, and eventually over the mountains, across the divide.

It appears that during their migration eastward, they hybridized with the remaining wolves, and today we are just coming to understand that perhaps this widespread hybridization is the reason the eastern coyote is larger and more aggressive and behaves more wolfishly in general (travels more often in packs, attacks larger prey, sometimes hunts in groups). The coyotes that killed Taylor Mitchell belonged to this group. DNA analysis affirms that pure *Canis latrans* is uncommon in the east, and biologists are throwing up their hands in the face of such a confusing genetic muddle; eastern coyotes are often called (to rhyme with the wolf's Latin name, *Canis lupus*) *Canis soupus*. Far from being a remote concern for zoogeneticists alone, this is a problem for all of us who want to understand the coyotes in our midst. Which coyote? Eastern coyotes are different from western, rural coyotes behave differently from urban. For everything we say about coyotes, there can be an exception.

We do know that, like their rural counterparts, urban coyotes are gentle, protective parents. And like humans, generally speaking, coyotes are sort of monogamous. That is, a coyote will stay with the same mate as long as it's working out, perhaps for some years. The outside limits of coyote conjugal commitment are difficult to know, given that individuals in the wild (rural or urban) rarely live more than three or four years. In metropolitan areas, they die because of disease,* predation by domestic dogs and humans, and—more than any of these—cars. The majority of pups do not live through their first year, being subject to all of the above, plus predation by owls, hawks, and sometimes raccoons. Estrus is just two months, and the pups are born furry but blind. Young pups remain in the den with the female, where they nurse, sleep, and grow; the male brings food for his partner and guards the pups from danger (unlike male domestic dogs, male coyotes are active in the raising of the young). When coyotes appear bold, it is often because they are encountered during this time, when most animals, even humming-birds, are aggressive toward anyone who approaches their nest or den. The female is careful, and she will move the pups readily if she feels the safety of her den has been compromised. It is during this period, April through July, when most conflicts between coyotes and larger dogs occur; off-leash dogs stumble across a den, and the adult coyotes defend their pups. Such conflicts came into the public eye this spring, as some off-leash dog proponents in San Francisco worried over coyote-dog interactions in Golden Gate Park, where coyotes have been denning in recent years. One encounter was cap-

---

* Coyotes are particularly susceptible to sarcoptic mange; this is theoretically passable to domestic pets but so far has not been an issue. Rabies in coyotes is limited to a localized population in south Texas.

tured on video—a Rottweiler mix was shown approaching and harassing two coyotes (much smaller than the dog), who made short lunges toward the interloper, trying to drive it away from their den. Observing the video, coyote behavior expert Marc Bekoff commented that the coyotes remained in defensive, submissive postures; the dog was the aggressor, and the dog's human guardian was nowhere to be seen.

At about six weeks, the pups start peeking out, full of more wild, playful energy than any domestic puppy, and their mother begins to take them on short, exuberant outings. I've heard stories of suburban domestic dogs playing with wild coyote pups, running loose in a makeshift peaceable kingdom. I happen to be writing on San Juan Island, at a University of Washington retreat for writers and scholars, and the novelist in the next study tells me that her two big white Samoyeds befriended a coyote puppy on their property in Port Ludlow, a suburban-woodland interface. For a few nights running, Melissa and her husband noticed that the dogs, Silme and her brother Bear, were coming in more winded than usual, wild and excited. They decided to spy one evening, and they discovered that the dogs had a little coyote-pup friend, all three playing and leaping and mock-fighting with abandon. They let this go on awhile, thoroughly entertained, till they began to wonder if the situation could go wrong in some unforeseen way and decided to keep the dogs in for a few nights to break the pattern, which worked. But there is a sweet little aside to this story. One day Melissa's neighbor called to ask if her dogs were missing any toys. Melissa walked over to discover her dogs' orange barbell, their rope toy, and their stuffed hedgehog, all in an out-of-the-way corner. Bear and Silme never ventured into this area because of their invisible fence, but they *did* offer their toys when they wanted to befriend someone—usually just a human visitor. It appears that Silme and Bear brought their toys for the coyote puppy, and the pup carried them off to its own second play area. Coyotes' curiosity toward dogs may be mistaken for aggression. Stan Gehrt tells me that even some adult coyotes love to play with domestic dogs, behavior he's observed in urban parks and cemeteries.

The greatest source of urban coyote-human conflict in the public mind is the threat to small pets. And though coyotes are famous for the spiriting away of outdoor cats, felines are only a tiny fraction of the urban coyote population's diet, just 1 percent, and many of these are likely feral, rather than someone's beloved Fluffy. The bulk of their diet by far is small rodents; coyotes eat rats, mice, squirrels, shrews, voles. They eat rabbits—feral domestics and wild. In the east, where white-tailed deer are common in high-density areas, more than 20 percent of an urban coyote's diet may be fawns. They eat ducks and geese, usually the fat park ones. They eat invertebrates, including many insects, and when chasing a butterfly on the wing, coyotes appear playfully acrobatic, more like a cat than a dog. They eat cat food, dog food, and sometimes birdseed. They eat seeds, nuts, fruit, vegetables, and garbage. Because the coyotes that visit our homes appear to be attracted to garbage cans, and because these are the only coyotes we see and encounter, we overestimate the amount of garbage they actually eat—from studies on scats, researchers know that most coyotes in the urban matrix have less than 2 percent human refuse in their diet. They occasionally eat raccoons but prefer smaller prey. They may fight with domestic dogs, but it is rare for them to kill one that is of medium size or larger. Female coyotes typically weigh twenty to twenty-five pounds, males thirty to thirty-five pounds, which is about as big as a medium-size dog, though they may look a

The Improbability of Coydogs

As we become more aware of coyotes in urban places, there is much speculation about coyotes and domestic dogs hybridizing. I have met two big-eared dogs of dubious parentage in my neighborhood, and the owners of both proudly suspect some coyote mischief. Coyotes and dogs are closely related and can hybridize, but coydogs are less common than we might think. Genetic studies of various urban and rural coyote populations rarely indicate any breeding with domestic dogs, and, while possible, coydogs in urban settings are not likely, in part because coyotes are highly seasonal breeders, while dogs are not. Both male and female coydogs have lower fertility than either coyotes or domestic dogs, and coydog females have a shifted estrus cycle that doesn't coincide with the limited coyote estrus period. There are behavioral differences too, such as the fact that male coyotes are attentive to the young, while domestic dog and coydog males are not. As exciting a prospect as coydogs might be, when we look at our own animals, it is probably more sensible to think *Interesting big ears* rather than *Coyote hybrid!*

little larger because their coats are so full. The closer you get to a coyote, the smaller it seems to be.

Even twenty years ago, ecologists did not suspect that there was a place for a high-level carnivore in the urban landscape. Now many wildlife biologists suggest that as long as humans manage their households to avoid conflict, there can be a positive ecological role for coyotes in the city. Eating and being eaten is how any creature finds its way into ecosystemic processes, and the urban coyote is no exception. That coyotes eat rats is a big fat plus for them as far as humans are concerned (while we rarely see coyotes, we might notice the uptick in rat populations if they were gone). The easy prey coyotes find in Canada geese makes life easier for fish and wildlife departments, which are always looking for publicly palatable ways to manage urban geese. In studies of California canyon lands, areas with a robust coyote population also had far healthier populations of native songbirds, including neotropical migrants, in terms of both species diversity and numbers of individuals. Coyotes do sometimes eat birds and nestlings, but this drawback is far outweighed by the benefit of their control of the feral cat population.* Adult deer are too large for coyotes to hunt, but although coyotes cannot help to reduce the increasingly problematic populations of white-tailed deer outright, they can slow it by preying on fawns.

There is something else coyotes add to the urban landscape. Something intangible, and unquantifiable, and difficult to put into words. They bring something that we modern humans both lack and need, that we both avoid and long for. They bring wildness. Wildness comes naturally to undomesticated animals, but for humans, the concept is more complex. There is something wild and animalish in our shared biology, our ecosystemic connectedness, and our physical vulnerability, to be sure. But wildness can also be a habit of mind, a state of being, of spirit, of imagination that we can choose to access, and to cultivate. This wildness is not chosen *instead* of our uniquely human rationality, our beautiful capacity for pure logic, our rigorous intellectual pursuits, the honed intricacy of our fine arts. It is a way of seeing and being that brightens, feeds, enhances, and stirs up all of these things.

Wild is a slippery concept. Typically, it has been defined in the negative, by what it is not, by a series of *un*-s. Something wild is

---

* *In a modern trickster story, coyotes in Southern California feasted on a colony of feral cats for some time, and after the cats were depleted, the coyotes ate the food local citizens continued to leave for the (now-absent) cats. I am a cat lover, but who could keep from chuckling? This outwitting is so typically Coyote.*

Deer, Humans, and Coyotes

At the beginning of the twentieth century, the overhunted white-tailed deer had been reduced to just twenty thousand individuals on the continent. With careful management, deer populations recovered, then grew abundant, and they now number more than twenty-five million. Like coyotes, white-tailed deer are a versatile species that has adapted quickly to human presence, and they now roam the edges of highways, parks, and suburban yards, creating millions of dollars' worth of damage as they browse foliage, eat fruit and vegetables, collide with cars, and cause general upheaval in the minds of regular folk who always thought they loved deer and now find their households overrun. Hunting has been the traditional way of dealing with cycles of deer overpopulation, but in town, hunting is not normally an acceptable option, both for safety reasons and due to public perception. Nonlethal methods of control—fencing, repellents, noise, and immunocontraception—are used, as are lethal methods in which deer are baited or trapped and then shot out of the public eye. But many cities, especially in the Northeast and the South, where hunting culture runs deep, are now offering short urban-deer-hunting seasons to bow hunters that, with an emphasis on population control, encourage the killing of antlerless deer. Reactions on the ground are mixed. People realize that the deer

are nuisances, but they are also beautiful; people want the deer gone, not dead. And stories of a wounded deer with an arrow in the shoulder trailing blood through a backyard full of horrified children, or hunters who decide to field-dress a deer à la Sarah Palin right there in town and leave the entrails behind someone's fence...well, such incidents may be few, but they grow large in the public imagination. In the end, a healthy coyote population may be the best way to naturally keep deer in balance.

Deer sign is easily recognizable—their heart-shaped tracks and pellet-scats are known to almost everyone, and their dropped antlers are a prize, as they have always been. First-year males grow small points, and a point is added every year up to five. Antlers are often conflated with horns, but they are far more fascinating. Antlers are actual organs, with a complex system of nerves and blood vessels, and while regeneration of limbs is well known in many nonmammal species (sea stars, newts), the regrowth of deer antlers is the single instance of organ regeneration in the entire mammalian class. The antlers have recently been found to contain stem cells and are being studied for a possible place in human health (though many people have not waited for scientific sanction—deer antlers and velvet have long been lauded for their supposed benefit for human vitality. Check the interwebs for the variety of potions available!).

It is a persistent untruth that fawns are odorless, though their scent is fainter than that of most newborn mammals; the mother carefully licks off all afterbirth and consumes the fawn's feces and rune to help prevent detection. She also leaves the fawn completely alone for long hours, visiting only to nurse; she keeps watch and sleeps at a distance so as not to draw attention to her fawn. Fish and wildlife personnel receive thousands of phone calls a year about "orphaned" fawns that are actually being protected in solitude by their careful deer-mothers.

uncivilized, undomesticated, uncultured, unpopulated, unkempt, undisciplined. In his important book *The Abstract Wild,* environmental philosopher Jack Turner warns that the experience of seeing wild animals in nonwilderness places (which for him includes observing an elk in the "mega zoo" of the national parks as much as seeing a coyote in an urban parking lot) presents a danger — a perilous "blurring" in our minds of the urban with the wild, the wild with the tame, the real with the fake and diminished. Turner is right— the urban landscape *is* ecologically diminished; the diversity of species is impoverished. But what, then, of the raccoon, the striped skunk, the sharp-shinned hawk on the branch of my backyard cherry tree? What of the coyote? The one who hollows her den at the city's leafy edge, the one who pads tentatively onto my neighborhood sidewalk in the morning dark? Is she fake? Is she real in a fake place? And what of my own quickening when I glimpse her? My simultaneous stillness, excitement, fear, delight, and recognition? This frisson that makes me want to laugh like a banshee, run like a rabbit, sneak away, celebrate, yelp like Earnhardt the dog?

I am always challenged by the work of Jack Turner, but on this topic, Gary Snyder is more helpful, I think. While wholeheartedly defending wilderness, he speaks to civilization's "permeable" quality. I know from my own life and experience that we can recognize the biological barrenness of an urban place while realizing at the same time that we are connected to wilderness, to the most pristine places left on the earth, by imagination, by activity, and by the wandering presence of the wild creatures that are among us. In a city, these may be few in species number. They may be weedy and scrappy. We may worry, rightly, that if we don't shape up, there will be nothing left other than what we see before us: crows, raccoons, rats, and coyotes.

But we can recognize all of this and still affirm with appropriate wonder the beauty and authenticity of the wildness in our midst, in our nearest co-inhabitants. And if we are fortunate, if we are willing, if we open our eyes and our brains and our hearts, we have the capacity to affirm a sense of wildness in ourselves as well. The coyote, on light feet, traverses our urban-wild boundaries, challenging our preconceived ideas of both. The presence of the coyote reminds us that our connection to wildness, within and without, is worth our daily remembering. And that even if we forget, it's still there.

In mythology and folklore across time and cultures, the coyote has always represented the consummate trickster. He is clever, pugnacious, unscrupulous, playful, plotting, scheming, busy, buffoonish. He is thinking up the most elaborate mischief, which (like Wile E.'s plans to catch the Roadrunner) inevitably backfires. He can have a heart, or not, as suits his whim. This is my telling of one popular myth, believed to be from the California "upriver people," the Karuk:

The human people had arrived, quite new to the earth. Coyote observed them when they arrived in spring, noting their pathetic hairlessness. But the light of the sun kept the people happy and warm, even the ugly pink babies and the skinny old ones. As autumn came on and began to deepen, Coyote once more passed by the human village, and this time he heard the people whining. They were so cold! What would become of them? They wrapped their blankets tighter and closed their teepees up, wishing for a piece of the warm sun to bring inside. *Poor dumb humans,* Coyote thought. In full-on winter, Coyote passed again, and this time he heard wailing. The humans were gathered around a grave, where

they were burying the same babies and elders he had seen thriving in the spring light. He listened to the cries of the women, the singing of how their dear ones had died in the cold. *Serves them right,* Coyote thought, closing his ears and trotting on. But, damn it, he couldn't help himself. Coyote felt sorry for these humans — peltless, stupid, and now also sad and dying. He decided to help them. Being a furry one himself, Coyote had never had a need for fire, and neither had any of the other animal people. But he had heard of the two Fire Spirits — mean, clawed, supernatural beings — who jealously guarded their flaming treasure at the top of the mountain. Coyote crept up and watched them, plotting to steal the fire and bring it to the poor humans. Right away, one of the Fire Spirits heard him. "Who is that? A thief! Brother! A thief after our precious fire!" But then Coyote began to prance among the grasses, where they could see him. "Oh, look, Sister, just an idiot coyote." Coyote watched how carefully the brother and sister

Fire Spirits tended their flame. He watched so long and well that he found the one moment of every day when the fire was left unguarded. Early in the morning, while the earth was still dark, the brother would go into the tent and say, "Hurry out, Sister, it is your turn to guard." And she would roll over, pull the covers over her groggy head, saying, "I am soooo comfortable. Oh, okay, okay, I am going…" It was in that tiny unguarded moment one day that Coyote leaped forth and claimed the flame! Oh! It was so hot, burning into his beautiful pelt, he'd had no idea, but no matter, he took off running. Well, there were many adventures as Coyote was chased by the angry spirits and helped by various animal people, including Frog and Squirrel. But eventually the flame was delivered to the human people, who were grateful and—alas—ignorant. How to keep the fire going? They danced before the fire, they sang to it, they threw things at it and shouted at it while the fire's warmth dwindled to a tiny spark. Finally, Coyote stepped in again and showed them what he had learned on the mountain—how to feed the heat with wood, and cones, and breath. This is how Coyote brought fire—and survival—to the people.

In the Karuk legend, Coyote was a benevolent, if reluctant, hero-trickster, but that is far from always the case in the stories. Trickster Coyote also has a crazy-seductive sex drive; he's a "four-legged Falstaff," as zoo-mythologist Elizabeth Caspari puts it, "a bigger-than-life bad example, ready to take on every available female—human or otherwise." Coyote can bring, and leave, anything: flood, death, pain, evil, heartbreak, yes, but also secrets— urgent, beautiful secrets about birth and life and survival. He is a cloud of contradiction, a disquieting and richly ambiguous figure. "Scourge and savior both," writes Caspari.

After wolves were extirpated from the west, coyotes inherited their reputation and were perceived to be the prime threat to livestock, a reputation that they hold even today, though studies show that mismanagement, disease, and poor breeding habits resulting in weakened stock are the primary threats to livestock health. In the mid-twentieth century, after the wolves were pretty much gone, the western states instituted a coyote-eradication program. Many millions of dollars were spent (about eight million dollars a year in the early seventies alone), many thousands of times the dollar value of livestock loss. Today, about a hundred thousand coyotes are killed each year with government approval and assistance (and funding) and many more without.* Coyotes are shot, trapped, or lured to sheep carcasses laced with cyanide or strychnine. Some government officials involved in the program insist they are seeking "relatively humane" execution methods, but ethologist Marc Bekoff, who has studied the social lives of coyotes for decades, wonders what is "relatively humane about having your head blown off or being maimed." True to trickster style, in spite of all this money, effort, and emotional tension, coyote numbers have only increased across habitats. Ironically, modern grazing practices drive coyote expansion on agricultural land— free range overgrazing creates dusty open spaces with lots of rodents and gopher holes that coyotes love. And, again ironically, studies show that in areas where coyotes are actively trapped, poisoned, and hunted, the females actually bear more pups

---

* Responding to a shift in the public's perception of its activities, the government agency responsible for killing coyotes whitewashed its image and changed its name from Animal Damage Control to Wildlife Services.

than they do in areas where this is not the case, filling the biological carrying capacity of the place and keeping the coyote population nearly constant.

Coyote eradication occurs on a smaller scale in urban settings, where individual or "problem" coyotes are killed because of a threat to public safety, real or perceived. Often such steps are taken quietly, to prevent a public outcry, though at other times it is with full media attention. In the high-end Seattle suburb of Lake Forest Park, a sheep that was being kept for a hobby, on a partially fenced backyard lawn that bordered a greenbelt where coyotes were known to live, was killed by a coyote. When the owners of the sheep insisted that the offending coyote be killed, wildlife officials obliged, but neighbors were in a confused uproar, and many protested the killing of a wild animal that was behaving as any sensible coyote would. The blunder was human—sensible husbandry practices would have protected the sheep. Urban coyotes are removed and euthanized by a nuisance-animal trapper or, like this one, killed by a wildlife-official sharpshooter. Like everything involving coyotes, responses to such steps are far from clear-cut. Some people, usually very few, are outright glad that the menace is gone. Some feel, reluctantly, that it was the necessary course and are relieved and saddened, both. Many mourn the loss of a beautiful wild creature and use the moment to regroup and recommit to learning how people and animals can best coexist in safety and tolerance.

The steps asked of us are plain, and practical. We need to keep our small pets indoors, especially at night and in the morning, and we need to keep from feeding wild animals, intentionally or inadvertently. Inconveniences, perhaps, but such small ones. Wildlife officials encourage people who encounter coyotes to shout at them, maybe even throw a stick. Gehrt admits that this is a difficult paradox for those who love wild animals and want to see them flourish in the city. Aren't we supposed to be kind to animals, to be quiet and peaceful in their presence, to cultivate human-wild harmony? But every human-coyote encounter is what Gehrt calls an "educational moment," an opportunity for both human and coyote to learn how to live alongside each other, and the more that coyotes avoid us, the better the chances that humans will continue to tolerate their presence and cultivate an enduring coexistence. I told Dr. Gehrt that I hardly ever see a coyote, and when I do, I don't want to chase it away — all I want to do is watch it for as long as I possibly can. "Yeah," he said, "me too."

Coyote is bigger than both our perceptions and, as scientists readily assent, our knowledge. Unwittingly, Coyote has become a cipher, a canvas as big as nature onto which we project our wild hopes, desires, beliefs, ignorance, truth, and fears about wildlife. We all write different words on the cipher of Coyote's body. I criticize one author for his use of *skulk* and *plan,* but are these projections so different, really, from my own *prancing?* In *PrairyErth,* William Least Heat-Moon offers his own list of coyote words in a long prose-poem that begins *Now, coyote:*

Yipping, ululating, singing, freely, freely, night-flute coyote,
long leggedness through blackness, (moonless), silent, pausing,
yipping, far responding, quick legs, freely, padded feet, coyote
feet, pausing, silent padding, pissing, running, swinging head,
pausing, back-looking, (tallgrasses frozen, frosted), cold fur

erected, coyote singing, sings-long-dog, coyote, coyote, golden-
eyes-coyote, canine, climbing, singing, sweetness, song dog,
breathing darkness, (hiding darkness), yip-yipping, nose-to-sky-
coyote, singing, sweet-throat-beast, coyote jaw, coyote teeth,
looking-always-coyote, running, singing the darkness, long-song-
dog call, coyote, coyote belly, waiting, watching, wanting, coyote
eyes, eye this, that, scenting, sending, sensing, pausing, pissing,
breathing, smelling, sniffing, snooping, nosing, silent-feet-coyote,
earth-feel-under-foot-coyote.

On and on it goes, this long, lovely, and unusual list. Others
would add *coyote vermin, coyote pest, coyote menace.* I would add
just this: *Coyote glimpsed.* So often this is the view people tell me
they have had of a coyote. They glimpsed it, or caught a glimpse.
(Somehow it seems fitting that *glimpsed* is one of just a handful of
English-language words that has no true rhyme.) The word *glimpse*
is both a noun and a verb, and in this case, I wonder if I can also
stretch it to an adjective. Coyote, perhaps more than any animal in
the urban landscape, is a *glimpsed* animal. Seen only partially. And
when we do see them — how do they do it? — they walk into the
grass or beyond the fence or straight into a tree, it seems, and are
gone. No matter how much we love, hate, tolerate, fear, kill, or even
scientifically study coyotes, we will always see them not in full, but
in part.

In this new nature, this challenging ecological moment where
we seek to find gracious, creative, wise ways of living in a changing
landscape, this glimpse of the coyotes that are with us matters. How
to live alongside Coyote? In a city, of all places? There is no tidy
answer, no pat answer, no *right* answer. Where humans and coyotes

overlap, the coyotes' presence is determined not just by food and habitat availability, as in wilder places, but also by human tolerance for coexisting closely with a large, carnivorous predator. Wolves? Too big, *way* too wild, we decided. Gone. Cougars? Um, no. But coyotes? They might be big, but they are big in a smallish, slender sort of way. They just might slip in on the edge of our tolerance. We allow Coyote in literature, in myth, in art, in imagination. Can we also allow her in body?

As we answer this question, the coyotes are looking to us; in this evolving story, they will follow our lead. Perhaps we will manage to protect and welcome the challenging, wonderful, uneasy presence of Coyote by minding ourselves and our homes. Then we will wait, ears pricked, to see what happens. We will join the two old men in the Navajo myth resting on the porch after their long day's labor. They had finally finished arranging the stars, laying them in neat, orderly rows. As they admired their work, Coyote pranced through, scattering the stars into the night sky, into the wild beautiful disarray we see to this day.

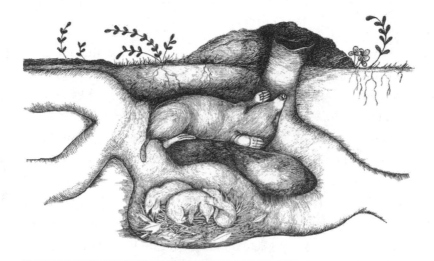

Mole

Squeezing the Earth

One year my dad built the Great Wall of Mole. My parents, Jerry and Irene, then lived in the middle of ten wooded acres and had created a small garden behind their house. The soft, nicely tilled, and freshly planted soil naturally attracted one of the many moles from the surrounding woodlands, and both the grassy areas and the flower beds were soon dotted with unwelcome mole-ish mounds. These were stamped, cursed, and decried by my father. And though Jerry is on the whole tolerantly loving toward wild creatures, eventually he couldn't deal with it anymore; the mole had to go. He tried the usual ineffectual methods, spiraling ever downward through the maze of physical effort and psychological torment familiar to would-be mole eradicators (sunflower-shaped plastic windmills, noisemakers, liquid repellents, tromping, fuming, swearing...), until he found himself deploying a metal-toothed mole-killing trap.

But Jerry felt so saddened by the velvety heaps of mole the trap periodically brought forth (and simultaneously so annoyed that the molehills kept appearing anyway) that he gave up this bloody tack and, in his sleep, where he does most of his thinking, masterminded the Great Wall of Mole. My dad is a mason, and he doesn't mess around. The Great Wall of Mole was a full-on, one-hundred-plus-foot perimeter around the entire backyard made of strong metal hardware cloth buried vertically thirty inches into the ground. It took Jerry and his hod carrier, who was paid union wages for his efforts, three days to complete the digging. Finally, the spade-width trench was filled in, and the grass was replanted. Within a day, the mole tunneled under her very own Great Wall, or walked over it during a crepuscular foray, or maybe she had just stayed inside its perimeter and waited out the whole project. She resumed her tunneling and mounding, and my dad walked around for a week hitting himself in the head and muttering, "Jerry, you stupid sonofabitch."

There is no North American mammal more adapted to a comfortable subterranean existence than the mole. Rats, while excellent burrowers, would have given up before reaching the bottom of the Great Wall of Mole, as would any of the other famous tunnel-underers: raccoons, foxes, weasels. But moles? They are perfectly at home more than nine feet underground, and in nice soft soils like my dad's yard in the moist spring, they can dig at a rate of over fifteen feet per hour. If possessed by a mole-hurry, they can sprint at one foot per minute for several minutes straight.

In general, I oppose technological metaphors for biological things: the mind a computer, the body a machine, the Earth (alas) a spaceship. Metaphor is powerful, and the comparison of living things to machines represents a failing of both truth and imagination. But for moles, I make an exception. How could I not? Comparing a mole to a machine reflects *so well* on the mole. Seattle journalist Lynda Mapes compiled these statistics comparing the Emerald Mole tunnel-boring machine to an actual mole: the Emerald Mole weighs 642 tons to the animal mole's 4 ounces; the Emerald Mole can bore 5 feet an hour compared to the animal mole's 15 feet an hour; the Emerald Mole excavates 0.17 pounds of soil per pound of machine compared to the animal's 57.2 pounds of soil per pound of furry mole. No wonder a group of moles is called a labor. The mole is indeed mightier than the machine.

Human-mole relations are made complex by the fact that humans don't see moles. Or we don't see them *alive*. Moles are occasionally killed by coyotes and dogs that dig them out of their mounds, by owls that find moles during their brief terrestrial excursions for water, or by cats. One morning in her backyard, my sister observed a crow pecking a mole to death. Moles are reputed to taste terrible, possibly because of the increased hemoglobin that allows them to maintain oxygen balance in their subterranean haunts. So when a mole is killed by another animal, it is usually left lying. If you are fortunate enough to find a freshly dead, unmaggoty, nicely intact mole, I would encourage you to embolden yourself in the noble role of urban naturalist and take a close look, as such opportunities are relatively rare. (It's not unsafe — moles are very clean and don't carry diseases that affect humans; just wash your hands after.) There are seven species of mole in North America, and though they vary in size and, somewhat, in habit, they are in general very similar. Many animals display their biological adaptations overtly but few do it as flamboyantly as moles. Running your hand over your dead mole's coat, you will discover that mole fur is not just chinchilla-soft but also reversible — it has no nap, so the hair follicles on a mole are not directional, and the individual hairs can move in every direction. When a mole presses forward or back in its tight earthen tunnel, the fur accommodates; it is literally impossible for a mole to be rubbed the wrong way, something most mammals truly do dislike. The pelt is softer than a bunny's, sweet to touch. In the early 1900s, Queen Alexandra, wife of England's Edward VII, helped control a mole outbreak in Scotland by parading about in a mole-fur coat, thus establishing a trend. (It took several hundred moles to make one rather thin but very soft coat.) Mole hips are narrow and the femoral attachment is flexible, to allow movement around narrow earthen corners. A thin, translucent layer of skin covers each eye, and unlike the third eyelid, or nictitating membrane, that birds have to protect their eyes in flight or underwater, the skin over the mole's eyes is a permanent covering. Moles are not blind, but they are almost blind. We know they can distinguish between light and dark, and we think they can also make out the shapes of medium and large objects at close range. The lack of vision is recouped through a keen sense of touch. Humans are most sensitive in our fingertips, but in the mole, the greatest sensitivity is in the nose. The snout is soft, long, and highly innervated, made for finding insects and grubs by feel. The back paws are underdeveloped, but the front paws are large and spade-shaped, turned out for swimmer-like paddling through the soil, and tipped with substantial claws. Moles are weird-looking little things, to be sure. The opossum, so despised for its pointy ugliness, has nothing over the mole.

Mole traps look like medieval torture devices, and death at their hands is particularly gory in comparison to the snap-trap deaths of other animals we kill with legal and social impunity, such as rats. I am convinced that this is in part because mole trapping takes place out of our sight, so we are not confronted in broad daylight by the ramifications of our actions (one of the most popular traps is actually named the Out O'Sight mole trap). Eventually, we will have to retrieve the trap and its impaled-mole contents, but the messy evidence will be pulled from beneath the earth — an alien, decidedly nonhuman world, where we feel somehow less responsible for what goes on. I believe that we humans are on the whole a compassionate species and that, as a general rule, we do not care to engage in the senseless skewering of small velvety creatures unless we can do it with some level of remove. This is not true for everyone, of course — many are perfectly happy to rejoice outright in their mole-killing. But for most, it is thought of as a necessary evil.

Which invites the question — what, exactly, is necessary about it? Moles *can* cause more than aesthetic damage. Occasionally, mole tunneling becomes so extensive that it makes a plot of land too squishy for safe walking. While moles themselves do not normally eat plants, bulbs, or roots, their tunnels and mounds can uproot plants and seedlings or kill small plants and grasses by burying them in mud. It is said that mole tunnels provide cover and travel opportunities for voles and other small animals who *do* eat roots and bulbs, and although this is true, it is not particularly common. Most eating of plants and plant parts is accomplished by the good

Mole Worlds

Earthworks are the best sign of mole presence. In urban places, moles usually surface in lawns, where their dotted tracks are difficult to spot, and even experienced trackers rarely find mole scats. This is a cross-section of a typical mole's tunnel system. Mole runways can be close to the surface, leaving raised ridges or soft ground, while pocket-gopher tunnels are not visible. The molehill is rounded when viewed from above, and the exit hole is usually indistinct (though you can find it if you dig around with your hand). Pocket-gopher hills are more crescent- or heart-shaped.

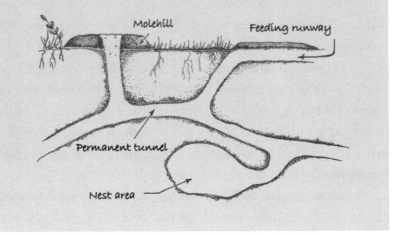

Molehill

Feeding runway

Permanent tunnel

Nest area

old terrestrial rodents—squirrels and rats. (Moles are not rodents; they are related to shrews and bats.)

As with most perceived pests, moles are with us because we create a perfect place for them. The soil around our homes and parks is soft, free of big rocks, and, in the case of gardens, nutrient-rich, with layers of mulch and compost that encourage the insects and grubs that moles love. Overall, a mole in a garden is far more beneficial than harmful. As insectivores, moles eat insects and their larvae; devour slugs, cutworms, and white grubs; and sometimes even prevent harmful insect outbreaks. The molehills and tunnels we see are just the surface of mole activity; beneath our beloved grass and flowers, they work in the depths, turning, tilling, aerating, and fertilizing the soil.

In the great majority of cases, the perceived damage by moles is just visual — molehills in the grass. These are distressing, to be sure. We strive to make something perfect or, if not perfect, then at least *how we want it,* and then a mole comes and digs it up, damaging our lawns and unsettling our psyches. A friend of mine, gardener and writer David Laskin, put it well: "Moles are punishment for the hubris of gardening."

Even so. Our crazed response to the presence of molehills could be perceived as disproportionate. Simple initial efforts to eradicate moles become obsessions, and efforts escalate from traps and poison to propane and sometimes even dynamite. Gardeners lie awake, figuring, plotting. All to kill a small handful of mole. All to make the garden fit into a preconceived sense of the beautiful, to keep it just how we made it. It's only a seven-inch mammal, really, the mole. And the damage? The proverbial *molehill.* But let's give ourselves the benefit of the doubt. Surely something more is going on, more than just molehills — something deep-rooted, maybe, prerational, primordial.

Not long before dying of tuberculosis, Franz Kafka produced a masterful story fragment, "Der Bau," or "The Burrow," in which a molelike creature exists within a maze of tunnels and is menaced by the scratching, unseen presence of another animal. The creature attempts to create a sense of calm safety for himself by tending to his burrow, but he cannot escape his agitation over the unknown presence, and it is in fact this very unknown-ness that causes his anxiety. The mole creature spins downward in a spiral of self-doubt, fear, and a kind of horrified resignation. The whole treatise is one long, growing scream, and when I read it, all I can think is *Oh God, poor Kafka,* as it presents such an undisguised window into the writer's brilliant, manic-depressive mind.

I've had a personal entrée into the horror of "Der Bau." In the summer, and often into the fall, if weather permits, my family and I sleep outside in a tent with a screen ceiling. It is near autumn as I write, and last night at about two in the morning, unable to sleep, I was startled by a scratching, clawing sound coming from beneath my pillow. I had been so cozy — ear upon flannel, sky overhead, nestled in the plaid weight of my big sleeping bag — that I hadn't even minded my insomnia. But this was unsettling. I thought at first it was Tom or Claire snoring, or perhaps I was fidgeting, and the vinyl air mattress was moving a little in response, making frictiony sounds against the tent floor. But no — we were all perfectly still. I recalled that earlier in the week I'd been tidying up in the tent and had stepped on a worrisome lump of something under the fabric floor. Had a squirrel or young opossum ventured beneath the tent and suffocated there? I'd explored further with the underside of my bare foot until I felt safe peeking under the tent to confirm my suspicion — a molehill. Of course. And in the middle of that dark morning, I began to realize — under my pillow, *right* under my ear, a mole was digging. "Tom!" I shook him. "A mole! Listen!" Tom sleeps like a dog, and I could barely wake him, but I dragged his ear over to my pillow. "I 'on't hear nuffin." He rolled back to his own side (and claimed to remember nothing the next morning). I stayed awake, listening with a mixture of happiness and dis-ease to my mole. I mean, on the one hand — what were the chances? It had the entire yard, the entire world, and yet, this mole was exactly beneath my pillow. How wonderful, and how rare. But the mole was unexpectedly loud. And the sound wouldn't stop. Eventually I was sleepy, and pounded on the earth. The mole desisted for about four seconds before carrying on. I was mole-scritched to sleep, and woke with more sympathy than ever for Kafka's harrowed creature.*

I cannot discover that Kafka had anything but metaphorical experience with moles, but "The Burrow" intricately mimics the almost crazed anxiety moles incite in suburban, grass-laying humans. Look, *just look what can happen.* Here is our sweet garden, the garden we created, cultivated, tended, the garden in which we find beauty, refuge, rest. And now a mole has turned up—unwelcome, unpredicted, and uneradicable. It is the hidden, unseen thing. The thing beyond our ken, yet still scratching at the surface. The thing that is coming or not coming. It is the weather, the fault line, the economy, the illness, the mental depression that tosses us into an abyss we didn't even know existed. It lives in the dark, in *our* dark, but can corrupt the light. It is that which we cannot control.

And we can't. When we remove or kill an urban-wild animal, we are often just opening up space for a different one of the same species, and this is especially true of moles. Mole territory is little understood by the typical gardener; it is generally believed that when there are lots of molehills in the yard, there are also lots of moles. But moles are both territorial and solitary. They space them-

---

* *I continued to hear the mole under my sleepy ear for the rest of that backyard tenting season. When we eventually folded up the tent in late October, we discovered a complex, perfectly square maze of mole tunnels excavated in the top layer of sod and soil, exactly matching the tent's footprint—a beautiful mole mandala! We speculate that while the soil in most of the yard had dried up over the summer, the soil beneath the tent remained shaded and moist, and more attractive to our mole.*

selves nicely. During breeding season, males and females will briefly associate, then part quickly after an unromantic copulation. After a forty-two-day gestation, the young are born, and females will stay in small family groups with their three, four, or five tiny mole pups, caring for them for a couple of months before the young disperse to solitary adult lives. But a typical suburban lot is populated, tunneled, and mounded by just one male mole, or perhaps by two females (females are a bit less fussy about slight territory overlap with another of their own sex). When a mole dies, or simply leaves our yard, it is likely that another mole will come. Unless we want to live vigilant, outlaw, mole-killing lives forever, we might as well just keep the mole we have.

Human psychological distress over mole presence has spawned a vast, imaginative, fantastical, and ineffectual mole-control arsenal. We clutter our lawns with feeble plastic windmills. We fumigate mole tunnels with chemical gas cartridges and aluminum phosphide. We bait moles with strychnine and chlorophacinone pellets. We try to frighten moles with electric, magnetic, and vibrational devices. We stuff mole holes and tunnels with razor blades and broken glass. We stand guard over heavy metal bayonet traps, harpoon traps, choker traps, cinch traps, and scissor traps. We broadcast cougar urine or castor-oil repellent over our entire lawn. We hover over mole tunnels with propane torches or pitchforks, ready to strike. Mole biologists caution us: few of these methods are effective, and the official line regarding mole eradication is "generally not practical." But many swear by their personal anti-mole methods (my literary agent deploys an underground torpedo-shaped device that emits a constant high-pitched signal, believed to annoy moles). I would not argue. But here is what the experts say: Moles regularly come and go; they shift territories, or just tunnel in different areas, from week to week or month to month. The lack of mole activity in a place where there were recently fresh mounds allows mole eradicators to rejoice in the illusion that their mole-elimination method has been successful, when in fact there has just been a coincidental confluence of attempted pest control and a mole's moving on, producing a kind of mole-deterrent false correlation. And the methods that truly do seem to work (the medieval traps, for example, really will bring forth dead moles) only create space for another mole to set up mole life. And after that mole? Another mole still.

The one method I know of that works indisputably is a drastic horizontal structural barrier recommended by my father, Jerry, who, in a successful sequel to the Great Wall of Mole episode, restored the small cemetery at St. Placid Priory, the women's Benedictine monastery where I often go to think and to write. (At about the same time my tireless dad moved to a fifty-five-plus community with a tiny yard, I saw a sign posted at the priory saying the sisters needed a volunteer to do grounds maintenance, and I knew it was a match made in heaven—so to speak.) Jerry removed every gravestone, leveled the entire cemetery, covered each grave with several inches of crushed, tamped gravel and a layer of metal hardware cloth, spread just enough soil over the whole thing to anchor sod, then laid the sod and replaced the gravestones. This is a sort of lateral version of the Great Wall of Mole, and it really seems to work. After two years, the sisters' graves are un-moled, though of course the grassy rows between graves, where there is no buried metal fencing, have been discovered by a mole.

But the very best mole control also happens to be the best method for our neighborhoods, for our wild cohabitants, for our psyches:

Pocket Gophers, Real and Imagined

Gopher has become the colloquial catchall name for over a hundred species of ground-dwelling or burrowing rodents and rodentlike creatures, most of which are not actually gophers but ground squirrels, moles, and even prairie dogs. True pocket gophers are small, burrowing rodents with extensive tunnel systems; there are about thirty-five species in North America (give or take—taxonomists argue about the number of species and subspecies). They are named for their stretchy fur-lined cheeks, which they use to carry collected plant foods to their larder hoard. Pocket gophers have yellow incisors that are always visible, even when their mouths are closed; like most fossorial mammals, they have small eyes and poor eyesight. Their tails are short and furless but highly innervated and sensitive, to help the gophers navigate when walking backward through their tunnels. The fur is a shade of brown, somewhere between dirty gray and almost black, usually matching the soil where the gopher lives. Most pocket-gopher species are hand-size, between six and twelve inches long. As with moles, gophers themselves are rarely seen; we see the mounded signs of their presence, the hills of soil created when they press to the surface. Gophers are known for their agricultural damage, but they can do garden damage on an urban/ suburban scale as well, consuming and uprooting cherished plants (moles eat mostly invertebrates, but pocket gophers eat only vegetation). Gopher prevention and elimination is a dubious undertaking. In small-scale urban

gardens, favorite trees and shrubs can be protected by a mesh barrier buried eighteen inches around the plant. Because the gophers' damage is visible and the benefits they provide are not, the good that gophers (like moles) can accomplish is typically given little consideration. A single pocket gopher can move more than a ton of earth to the surface every year, an exchange of wastes and plant material that creates soft, aerated, nutrient-rich soil—gophers basically do our double-digging for us. Amphibians like salamanders and toads, whose populations are plummeting, find refuge in the cool, moist burrows that are abandoned by the gophers.

How about letting the ecological wasteland of urban/suburban lawns die a slow, or even a *quick*, natural death? Across the country, there is a movement to replace lawns with food gardens, native plants, or, in the permaculture movement, a mixture of both. When a molehill appears in a more natural landscape, it is both less noticeable and an indication that the soil is rich, and soft, and all things good—a sign that a wild animal sees fit to grace your yard with its odd, invisible, uncontrollable presence. What if a typical response to fresh mole evidence was not a sinking stomach and a crazed gnashing of teeth? What if it was a beatific Mona Lisa smile that intimated something like *Oh, look what that silly mole did now?* If we don't like where the hills are, we can tamp them down a little, remove the soil, or spread it with a garden rake; new grass will grow with the spring rain. We might delight in our newfound tolerance—moles are singular creatures from a subterranean world that surface unseen in our yards. A punishment for the hubris of gardening? Well, a *reminder,* maybe. That when we move and till and beautify the soil, we must do it by working alongside wild nature, not by overriding it. That any other approach is misguided and might also make us insane.

I happen to be working on this chapter at the priory. It rained yesterday, and along the trails on the monastery grounds, I have found a dozen fresh mole-made heaps of soil. He was busy last night, happy, as far as mole happiness can be determined, with the soil's malleability after a long and rainless month. The mole's dependence on the soil, its life *within* the earth, is absolute. And so, I realize in contemplating these soft earthen mounds, is my own. Gratefully, I do not live a tunneling existence, but I am no less dependent on the health, the flourishing, the life within this soil than the mole. *The Rule of Benedict,* penned in the sixth century and grounding the life in this monastery, emphasizes a sense of positive humility in our everyday lives. The word *humility* is intricate. *Humility,* rooted in the Latin word *humus* — soil, land, the turning Earth itself. Remembering humility, we remember our creatureliness, our lovely dual nature as humans, who live in culture but remain rooted in the soil, indigenous and at home in the lively wildness of biological life. In humility, we enter this essential condition, this earthen grace.

Turning to the mole for guidance on how to live our human lives may seem too far a stretch, but in a Romanian creation myth, even God seeks counsel and assistance from the soil-dwelling creature and its quiet, mole-ish ways. In the story, God has made the heavens and is using a wondrous thread to measure the space that will hold the Earth. Mole offers to help, and God hands him one end of the thread and asks him to let the thread out as needed, as if God were a great kite. God goes about the creation of the Earth, weaving its patterns with the shimmering thread. But as God weaves, Mole is distracted by the beauty of the unfolding Earth and lets out too much thread; the Earth becomes too large for its space. Embarrassed and afraid, Mole hides beneath the soft new soil. God needs to mend the oversize Earth and desires to consult Mole about the best way to go about it. Mole, ashamed and abashed before God, will not come out, so God sends a friendly, unintimidating bee to speak with Mole directly. Still, Mole will not come out. The bee, clever in her own right, pretends to go about her business, gathering pollen from nearby flowers, and as she works, she overhears Mole grumbling to himself. "If I were God, I would *squeeze* the Earth. Mountains and valleys would form, and the Earth would be smaller, just the right size." Bee flies straight to God and reports Mole's musing advice, which God takes immediately. With the help of Mole, the Earth is formed in perfection and beauty.

St. Placid Priory sits on a peaceful, forested property, but over the years, the surrounding area has fallen prey to urban sprawl— lot after lot of architecturally barren chain stores surrounded by endless expanses of asphalt parking lots. I passed one such stretch on a walk this week and noticed that at the edge of the parking-lot asphalt, some pleasant, imaginative people had decided to install a little park. It was a simple thirty-foot-square patch of grass with a bench. The grass, surrounded on all sides by asphalt as far as the eye could see, was decorated by nicely spaced molehills. Because the grass was so fresh and green and new and otherwise perfect, the molehills stood out like crazy and made me laugh. They must have made the grass-park people furious! But I wondered: *How* did that mole get there? How far did she have to tunnel, and for how long, attempting to surface—how many times? —and hitting her soft mole nose against deep hard inches of asphalt? Yes, yes, I know. I'm a Seattle eco-hippie mole-hugger. But still. Humans may cover the Earth with asphalt, but all of us, human and wild, man and mole, are just looking for a place to dwell, to rest, and occasionally to *surface* in the soft green.

Raccoon
Tracking Ourselves

One night some years ago, raccoons climbed our fence and killed our flock of four backyard chickens. Or mostly killed them. I remember looking out the window in my big fleece robe the next morning and seeing Tom standing in the run surrounded by feathers and holding a sledgehammer, his tool of choice for finishing off the not quite dead. Forlorn, we buried our dear hens, shed our tears, and left on the camping trip we'd previously planned. After Claire was tucked into her tent-nest for the night, three raccoons appeared at the edge of our campsite, standing up, balanced on their haunches in that cute raccoon way. Normally, I would have been keen to watch them, maybe waking Claire up to have a look. But this night? I threw rocks.

That same summer, raccoons popped Claire's inflatable swimming pool. I loved that pool, which was small enough to inflate with a bicycle pump but big enough for a whole mom to stretch out. I am sure the raccoons played in the pool before destroying it, as there were muddy tracks everywhere and striped fur in the water puddles left in the heaps of torn plastic. My friend Sheila told me that she saw a huge raccoon floating on its back in her kids' pool. (I love the image — like an overweight, hairy-chested tourist in his condo pool at Waikiki.) After going through two pools in this way, we switched to a slip-and-slide for water play, and we brought it in at night for good measure. The first (and last) time we forgot to take it inside, we came out the next morning to find an expanse of yellow sliced to ribbons, clumps of telltale striped fur clinging to the wet plastic. How did the slip-and-slide get torn from one end to the other if the raccoons hadn't been sliding on it?

Human-wild interactions are often ambiguous, but more than most wild animals, raccoons draw us into a profound, almost willful misunderstanding that seems to be based on entrenched oversimplifications running in opposite directions. For many, the raccoons' primary defining characteristic is their cuteness. Furry, black-nosed, stripe-tailed, inky-eyed, doing the most astonishing things with those busy little paw-hands. Standing up on their hind feet, sometimes right there at the back door, asking for food just like our dogs at the dinner table. Slumping around with that loping walk, mother raccoons turning up in the summer with tiny versions of themselves, little hairs sticking out straight. And *masked*. Masked with vertical black and white stripes down the middle of their foreheads that make them look a wee bit anxious, as if they can't quite think up the next bad thing to do but have to get to it right away.

On top of all its physical cuteness, the raccoon can exhibit behavior that's utterly charming — playful, mischievous, and opportunistically friendly, a cross between a super-smart kitten and a dog, but with a wild edge that makes us feel somehow graced by the animal's attention. Often, raccoon sympathizers have at one point had their emotions solidified by a personal encounter with a raccoon — petting, feeding, or playing with someone's pet, a zoo animal, or a tamed backyard raccoon. It's little wonder so many people are inspired to feed raccoons and encourage their presence.

The great naturalist Rachel Carson was not immune and cooed over her doctor's pet raccoon in letters to friends. She loved the then-popular book about that "mischievous but lovable raccoon" Rascal, and she recommended it widely. My own friend David is convinced (I'm not sure how genuinely) that he was accepted to Harvard because he listed the book *Raccoons Are the Brightest People* alongside *The Odyssey* on the application's "recently read" page, giving him an eccentric edge. But raccoons are not reducible to their cuteness, not by any stretch, and trying to do so diminishes both their intelligence and ours.

Radically opposed to the raccoons-are-cute folk — so radically that sometimes it is difficult to believe that we humans are all one species with the same basic neural pathways at work — are those who hate raccoons with a passion that I can barely fathom. I live in Seattle, a bubble of eco-peace and nature love, and most of the people I know love raccoons, feel neutral about them, never think about them because they never see them, or hate them benignly — that is, they consider them pests but would never actively seek to harm one. So in researching this bestiary, I was a bit surprised to find how common it is to absolutely vilify these common urban animals.

Following are representative comments gleaned from blogs that have brought up the subject of backyard-raccoon nuisances:

Poison them and let them die a painful death.

Solution = The Marlin 981T. Sells for about $175. Add a scope for around 35-40 more and a brick of .22lr.

In response to the fact that hunting is illegal in the city —

Is it still technically hunting if you just shoot them and drop them in the trash?

Raccoons are vile creatures. They haven't a redeeming quality. A 12 or 20 with #2 buck is the weapon of choice.

No redeeming quality. Of all the comments, this is the most remarkable to me. Raccoons have stolen my shoes, killed my chickens, deflated my pool, strewn my garbage, interrupted my sleep, defoliated my pond lily. They have dragged my husband's bike shorts off the clothesline, pulled the padding out of the bum, and spread it about the yard (why?). They have disemboweled my favorite pond fish, dropped cherry pits on my backyard tent while I was trying to sleep, and stolen all of the apples off my newly fruiting columnar apple the day before I was going to pick them. (A common complaint — raccoons have a knack for defruiting trees the night before a human plans to show up with the basket. It seems uncanny, as if they do this just to thwart us, but, like many wild-fruit foragers, raccoons are attuned to weather cues that signal a turn from almost ripe to almost too ripe, and they respond to these cues in their own foraging.)* Even so — even with all this raccoon badness in my own life and yard — it is difficult to imagine a statement such as that one. After all, like them or hate them, you have to admit that raccoons are objectively beautiful animals, with thick, earth-colored fur, and markings that strike observers with their vitality and uniqueness. They are smart. They have a long, rich history alongside humans in the Americas. The females are careful, tender, watchful mothers. Raccoons are industrious, playful, and affectionate, both with one another and often with humans (Sioux children, especially girls, loved to keep raccoons as pets).

It's true: Raccoons can wreak some serious havoc. They remove garbage-can lids and scatter the trash. They come in through the cat door, eat the pet food, and raise a wild rumpus in the kitchen. They remove loose roof shakes and pad into the attic, sometimes giving birth to even more raccoons there. They can undo locks (and remember for years how they did it) and untie knots. They can *tie* knots. When we try to chase them out of the yard, they stare at us like teenagers, as if they couldn't possibly care less, and when they don't leave, they begin to scare us. Occasionally, they have a run-in with a domestic cat that goes badly for the cat. Sometimes they have rabies (though in all of human-raccoon history, only one human is known to have died from a rabid-raccoon bite).

---

* In a Caddo tradition, this ability is explained in a myth: A man has passed to the next life, and is instructed by the Wise One to go straight to the new land, without stopping or looking back. When the fragrance of just-ripe persimmons distracts him on the path, he can't help turning back for one last taste of the sweet fruit. The Wise One forgives this weakness — who could resist ripe persimmon? — but must punish such disobedience. The man will go into the afterlife on four feet, and with a mask. After this, his kindred raccoons walk the earth, plucking the just-right fruit before anyone else can get to it.

Thrown into this fray of wildness, cuteness, human love, human hate, interesting behavior, mischievous behavior, and downright damaging behavior is an enormous corpus of raccoon lore — stories that are oft repeated, widely believed, but largely untrue, rivaling even the Beaver entry in the *Aberdeen Bestiary*. Among them: Raccoons are nocturnal, so those seen during the day are rabid. (While raccoons are mainly nocturnal, they often amble during the day, especially females with young; they forage during the day to avoid their mainly nocturnal predators). Raccoons are rodents. (They are not even closely related to rodents; they are procyonids, with ringtails and coatimundi as their closest relatives and weasels and bears as distant relatives in the same order). Raccoons kill cats. (Well, they usually don't — not unless they are cornered and threatened by the cat, or the cat poses a threat to a raccoon's kits.) Raccoons have no shoulders, and that's why they can fit into tight places like attics. (This is a good one — raccoons are vertebrate mammals, with scapulae and shoulders just like the rest of us vertebrate mammals. They have *narrow* shoulders, and their bodies are smaller than they appear because they are so furry, so they can squeeze through a cat door, but they can't miraculously fit into impossibly small places.)

It is curious that such a common animal is so widely misunderstood — that most urban dwellers make it to adulthood without a basic sense of the natural history of a very common wild neighbor; that this decidedly nonhuman being has been limited to the entirely human categories of pet/friend or vermin/enemy.

This tendency on our part to anthropomorphize raccoons is surely based on their physical characteristics. The front foot, the "hand," has five toes, and the first and last are shorter than the other three. Though not truly an opposable thumb, the first digit can be placed against the center three, making the paw remarkably dexterous. Maybe more than any other wild track, a raccoon track with toes spread looks like a tiny human hand. The back paw is longer, also five-toed, shaped very much like a human foot. The raccoon balances on the back paws by putting pressure toward the outer surfaces as humans and bears do—a plantigrade stance, as the trackers call it—leaving, again, a human-like impression in any receptive substrate. Raccoon paws, though, exceed human hands in their practiced ability to gain information about their surroundings. The soles of the paws are both highly inner-vated and well protected with layers of thick, leathery skin. Like anten-nae on an insect or whiskers on a cat, the sensitive feet of the raccoon allow it to gather information while remaining alert to its surround-ings. Watch raccoons as they eat berries or manipulate and consume other food. They rarely have to look down—it's as if the world is writ-ten in a kind of raccoon Braille. When raccoons appear to be dousing their food or washing their hands in water, they are more likely soften-ing the surface of their front paws to increase sensitivity for the delicate work of eating or foraging.

Names for the raccoon across North American cultures and tribal lines have largely followed this human fascination with tasks raccoons perform with their hand-paws. Our modern English word *raccoon* is adopted from the Algonquian word for the animal, *ah-rah-koon-em*, or "those who rub, scrub, and scratch." There is also the Aztec *mapachitl*, "the ones who take everything in their hands"; the Chippewa *aasebun*, "they pick up things"; Choctaw *shauii*, "the graspers"; Ofo-Sioux *at-cha*, "one who touches the things"; Lenape *nachenum*, "they use hands for tools"; Delaware *wtakalinch*, "one very clever with its fingers"; Kiowa *seip-kuat*, "pulls out crayfish with hands"; and this list goes on and on.

Raccoon Feet

Raccoons have beautiful feet that make distinctive tracks. Observing the delicate toes in a raccoon track, one can easily see how raccoons are able to perform so many complex tasks with such dexterity. Raccoon tracks are easy to identify, with five long toes on both front and hind feet, and nail dots often visible, especially on the front feet. The toes may be spread or close together, depending on the substrate and on the animal's activity at the time the track was left.

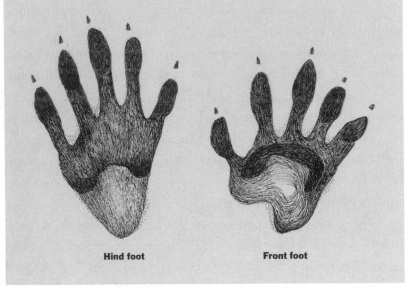

Hind foot   Front foot

The Swedish naturalist Carl Linnaeus was given a pet raccoon named Sjupp as a gift from the crown prince of Sweden, who had traveled to the New World. After his long overseas passage from New Sweden, Delaware, to Linnaeus's garden in Uppsala, Sjupp was himself treated like royalty by Linnaeus, who wrote that although the raccoon would eat almost anything, "what he liked best were eggs, almonds, raisins, sugared cakes, sugar, and fruit of every kind." Sjupp learned to search the naturalist's pockets for treats. Linnaeus loved the raccoon and played with him every day until he climbed over a fence and was killed by a dog. True to form, Linnaeus gathered Sjupp's limp body and plunked it down on his dissecting table, and though his examination was fittingly detailed and scientific, it was sprinkled with affectionate recollections of the raccoon's playfulness and intelligence. Based on his observations of Sjupp, Linnaeus gave the raccoon the Latinized name *Ursus lotor,* "hand-washing bear." The modern term, *Procyon lotor,* drops the misleading *Ursus,* in the name of scientific accuracy, but retains the emphasis on washing paws.

Besides having hands, raccoons wear masks — a potent psycho-mythical symbol, evoking a sense of disguise, duplicity, ambiguity, equivocation, shadow, mystery, and of course thievery. The raccoon mask is so convincing, it is easy to forget that it is not *actually* a mask, just a band of fur that happens to be black for adaptive reasons. Like the rings on the tail, the black band of fur across a raccoon's face provides the animal with a kind of camouflage known as disruptive coloration. Many animals hide from predators by blending into the landscape with their earthen-colored fur and skin, and we can see this in the predominantly earth-toned fur of the raccoon's body. But another evolutionary strategy involves the breaking up of the familiar animal body-head-tail outline with stripes, which keeps a predator that is just glancing at a landscape from recognizing an animal as a complete form. Many animals employ disruptive coloration: think of a killdeer, its two black bands across its chest. The stripes would seem to make the birds more obvious, but when on their ground-scrape nests, they become nearly invisible. The black color also reduces glare, important for an animal like a raccoon that traverses edges, coming out of the dark forest into the bright grasses, sometimes at night, sometimes in daylight. Lots of animals have black masks for the same reason — chickadees, cedar waxwings, peregrine falcons, pandas, professional football players.

In the case of raccoons and other midsize carnivores, newer research suggests that the masks might also be a hands-off signal to larger predators. The related coati, as well as badgers and wolverines — all masked animals of about the same size — share territories with larger carnivores, such as coyotes or cougars, but they are not prey for these animals in the expected numbers. In a real fight, the smaller animal is likely to lose, but because these smaller species possess a ferocity disproportionate to their size, the larger animal is unlikely to come out unscathed. Such aposematic color signals are more common in other taxa — think of insects like ladybugs or amphibians like rough-skinned newts that signal their own toxicity to would-be nibblers with their bright red coloration. In the same way, some researchers suggest, the masks of raccoons and their ilk may signal to predators that the meal might not be worth the trouble.

I am convinced that both the raccoon's humanlike feet and its fur mask, symbols for us of action and power, play a large part in our misascribing a certain *intent* to raccoon activity. It is difficult but meaningful to remember: Raccoons are not actually doing anything *to us.* Their seeming mischievousness is not directed toward us, our world, our interests, our lives. They do not come to vex us, or steal from us, or even entertain us. They come to do the things they need to do as raccoons — find food, play (an evolutionarily complex and essential activity shared by the most intelligent animals), shelter themselves, and feel safe in an increasingly complex and difficult world. Our best response will involve the cultivation of a tolerance for the uncertain, a mature and openhearted vigilance.

Recently, in our online community forum the *West Seattle Blog,* a neighbor wrote about "Urban Super Raccoons versus Pets." In the post, she neatly summed up the essential elements of urban human-raccoon conflict. She told the story of waking to find six raccoons running wild and messy through her kitchen after they'd come in through the cat door. She shooed them out, but in subsequent weeks, one of them attacked her large Maine coon cat and her neighbor's aging dog, and it eventually killed a stray cat she had taken in and named Jasmine. She wrote:

> My neighbor (who is still suffering from the injury she received trying to save her dog) watched in horror from her deck as a raccoon dragged a howling Jasmine by the scruff of the neck over into the Sealth construction project.
>
> What can be done? These are not typical raccoons. They are urban super raccoons who are opportunists. The massive construction projects on all sides of our neighborhood have pushed them into our immediate area. The Sealth construction project is particularly problematic with piles of trash all over the ground. Please advise. These animals have to go!

Of course, *all* raccoons are opportunists, urban or rural. All raccoons adapt quickly to change; they den anywhere, eat anything. But the idea that urban raccoons are somehow an über-variety is partly true. In general, urban raccoons are slightly but measurably larger than rural and wilderness raccoons, probably because of their diet, which includes the junk food of human refuse. And the blog writer is also correct, on the whole, about the cause of increased raccoon presence — habitat encroachment coupled with scattered garbage containing food. The stories of animal attacks are, however, unusual. Raccoons, even human-habituated urban raccoons, *rarely* attack pets or people outright. They stand their ground and make guttural sounds in a way that strikes us as menacing, but in most cases, they avoid physical attack. There are exceptions. Like most wild mammals, raccoons will become physically defensive when cornered. This is particularly true if the raccoon's young are near and is a fact containing a lesson: If you have raccoons in your house or yard, open the doors or gates and scoot them out from behind. Never let them feel trapped. Raccoons will also defend themselves if they are threatened or attacked by another animal. Wildlife-removal expert Sean Met conjectures that domestic animals see their fenced yards as their own territory, but raccoons think of fences as simple obstacles to climb over, which can be an invitation to conflict. Given the raccoon's scrappy wildness, a small dog or cat is not likely to fare well if a raccoon-pet confrontation turns physical (though larger dogs regularly kill raccoons in urban settings, as with Linnaeus's Sjupp). "That's a lot of animal," state wildlife biologist Christ Anderson says of a provoked raccoon.

Across the street from me lives a big fluff of a white cat, and one of our neighborhood raccoons regularly patters up this cat's driveway and along the side fence in an attempt to get to the backyard. The cat languishes broadly in the narrow entrance to the side yard, and whenever the raccoon — a very big raccoon — gets near the cat, he stops and labors back and forth between his front paws, pondering, as raccoons do. Eventually he musters his nerve and moves slowly ahead, giving the cat the widest possible berth, at which point the cat, every time, stretches a long paw and swats the raccoon on his nose.

One of my favorite raccoon stories comes from Sean Met, who told me about a call he'd received from a man who wanted him to come out because he was worried about his cat and a neighborhood raccoon. The problem? Instead of sleeping in her cozy cat bed, the cat was snuggling down to sleep every day with a full-grown raccoon in an old doghouse in the backyard! Shouldn't he get rid of the raccoon? Sean said he didn't see a conflict — the inter-species friendship seemed to be going just fine, and if this raccoon was removed, another would likely move in, and maybe one not as friendly to cats.

Urban-wildlife biologist Russell Link emphasizes the impracticality and potential cruelty of moving raccoons. Although trapping and relocating a raccoon several miles away might seem like a benign method to give a problem animal a second chance, the reality is unpromising. Raccoons typically try to return to their familiar territories, often getting hit by a car or killed by a predator in the process. If raccoons are moved to a place deemed perfect for raccoons, then there are probably already raccoons living there. If the relocated raccoons stay in the new area, they upset the social balance, often fighting (sometimes to the grisly death) with resident raccoons for food or shelter. Significantly, if a raccoon is accustomed to finding shelter and food around human habitations, the animal is likely to seek a similar situation, thus causing the same problems it did before. "People, organizations, or agencies who move raccoons," writes Link, "should be willing to assume liability for any damages caused by these animals." In most cases, relocating raccoons won't solve the problem anyway, because other raccoons are likely waiting in the wings, ready to replace them. Link hopes, and I do too, that lethal control will be viewed as an ethically unpalatable and absolutely last resort.

The blog post quoted above finishes: "Please advise. These animals have to go!" But then it addends words to the effect of: *And don't tell me to keep my cat inside, because I'm not going to do that.* I am a cat lover and have always lived with cats (currently, with our beloved tuxedo-wearing Delilah); I sympathize deeply with the loss of any pet and understand the emotions such a trauma can unleash. But to allow even a marginal wildness in our lives and cities will involve compromise. We will have to store our refuse and secure the lids. We will have to bring the cat food inside and keep an eye on our pets. We will have to do this as a matter of course, with a sense of our constant continuity with the natural world and the kinship between us that includes — and transcends — myth and mask and feet and fact. Ideally, we will manage these things with our creative good humor intact.

A group of raccoons is almost always made up of a mother raccoon and her young, who stay with her for several months. Females rarely tolerate male company, except during their brief estrus, though, curiously, males will often defer to mother raccoons when they find themselves in the same place, say at a communal water source. Young are born in the spring, in litters of up to six but typically of three to five, and we sometimes see these family groups during daylight hours: a mother and her growing kits, the mother foraging for the young, who require frequent feeding (as for all wild animals, survival of the young is uncertain — by midsummer, we often see a female with just one remaining kit, or none at all).

The tremendous majority of indoor raccoon encounters end peacefully, and when both food and avenues of entrance are removed, the raccoons move on. One woman sent me this typical story: After moving to the city, she installed a cat door and kept a big bowl of good-smelling cat food just inside. One morning soon after, she came downstairs to discover a raccoon eating the food as her cat looked on in exaggerated horror, as cats do so well. She scooted the raccoon out and decided she'd have to do something about it. The next morning she woke to a rat that had come in the same way. Rats do not elicit the sympathy that raccoons sometimes do, and so that very day she locked the cat door, forcing her cat to scratch at the door until a human let him in. Another evening she heard a scratch at the door and opened it, expecting her cat but instead finding a big raccoon and a tiny raccoon, clearly a mother and kit. The adult raccoon looked up expectantly, as if to say, *Isn't this how we come in? I saw the cat do it* ... She closed the door, laughing, and the raccoons never returned.

I do not run unless I'm being chased. Not being a runner means that I have managed to avoid the recent trend of running barefoot, which has surfaced every now and then over the course of running history but has been made particularly popular today by the publication of Chris McDougall's bestseller *Born to Run*. Human feet, the argument goes, have been housed their entire pathetic foot lives in the little tanks of shoes. Shoes not only overprotect our feet, and therefore keep them from being as strong or as sensitive to their surroundings as they ought to be, but also force us to walk poorly; people propel themselves heel to toe instead of placing each foot on its outside edge and rolling it toward the center, as is purportedly more natural for human feet and legs and more healthy for bodies (knees and spines, in particular). The latter method of walking and running may also increase endurance. Bears and raccoons, other plantigrade animals that sometimes stand on their hind legs and have palm-like soles like ours, walk this way, as do many elegant four-leggeds (foxes, coyotes, cats).

Trendiness aside, humans *do* walk funny. The upper body leans forward until, at the last second, the foot catches the full force of the body's weight. Exaggerated, the motion becomes a lurch. Long before *Born to Run,* tracker Tom Brown Jr. suggested the fox walk for humans seeking a more nature-tuned gait. We are instructed to stand straight and tall over our feet rather than lean forward, roll our foot out-in at each step, and lift the foot using the front of the thigh instead of propelling from the calf. Exaggerated, this movement becomes more of a prance. Thinking I'd rather prance than lurch, I have practiced both woodland and urban walks this way. I look silly, for sure, but this way of walking *is* lighter and quieter. I can feel that it is easier on my delicate metatarsals and on the slender, brittle tibiae we all share (no shin splints when running or walking like this). Still, I wonder. It doesn't feel natural, and I cannot tell whether this is because I have been walking in the lurch for four decades and am not accustomed to walking properly or because humans are not meant to lift their feet with their thighs. And I miss the nice propelling motion.

I couldn't help thinking of such things as I examined the raccoon tracks in my freshly turned garden bed this morning. Impulsively, I pulled my shoes and socks off and tracked along beside them. Leaning over to inspect the impressions side by side, I felt a frisson of connection. The kinship I sense comes from a kind of shape recognition — *Gosh darn, that little foot sure looks like mine* — more than from any close evolutionary connection (except for the fact that humans and raccoons are both mammalian vertebrates, with the same basic *bauplan,* including the same names for our bones — tibiae, scapulae, radii, ulnae — we are not much related). But the same number of toes can't be the only reason the raccoon makes me think so acutely about my feet, my tracks, the where, why, and how of my own walking.

Master tracker Paul Rezendes writes: "When we experience the natural world, whether it be through tracking, hiking, or just walking in the woods, we are learning about ourselves and our role in nature's process. When we encounter nature, we also encounter ourselves." When I read this, I thought, *How beautiful, this idea that wild tracks lead to human lives — wild lives and human lives so bravely connected.* As I delved further into the tracking literature, I discovered that nearly every accomplished tracker says something of this kind. In tracking and keeping track of the life around us, we are at the same time tracking ourselves. It is a lovely, poetic notion. But in the case of the raccoon, it is true not just in a pretty, provocative, metaphorical sense, but absolutely literally. Where do the tracks lead? The impressions of those little hand-feet? They lead to our garbage cans, our refuse, the stuff of our lives. The multitude of things we were sure we needed and then threw out. They lead to the fluffy dead ring-tailed bodies we saw, or did not see, and ran over. They lead to our rich history of hats and hunts and watchful coexistence. They track through the mud at the corner of the garden to the cat door, the dog food, the chicken coop. They lead straight to the back door.

The Untold Story of Raccoon Scats

Given the raccoons' varied, omnivorous diet, their scats differ tremendously, even from day to day, and though they can form even, blunt-ended tubes, they are often just an amorphous assemblage of seeds and other indigestibles. The examination of scats is a wonderful way to find out what urban animals have been up to, where they've been, and what (or who) they have been eating. But in the case of raccoon scats, extra caution is in order, as they may contain the eggs of *Baylisascaris procyonis*, raccoon roundworm, which are potentially dangerous to humans. If the eggs are ingested, larvae can emerge and migrate to the lungs, brain, or eyes, causing severe and potentially fatal illness (the few reported fatalities occurred in young children who had ingested a substantial number of eggs). Taking a peek at outdoor raccoon poops is harmless, but don't smell them, and do not bring raccoon scats indoors; when removing raccoon waste from an attic or crawl space, wear a face mask, or—better yet—call a professional. Outdoors, raccoons will often use the same sheltered place for their waste over and over—a raccoon latrine. If you have raccoons in your neighborhood, watch for the latrines along the pathways, especially at the base of larger trees where they nap or feed on fruit.

Opossum

The Urban Monster

One recent winter day, an opossum was found under the bench of a subway car in Manhattan. The train was evacuated, and the NYPD in full regalia swooped in to extricate the little animal. When the opossum hissed and bared its teeth, New York's Finest retreated and called the animal-control agents, who removed the opossum and carried him off, in a metal box, into the night. It was a surprise to everyone; other animals have turned up on the subway, of course—chickens, squirrels, raccoons, even a coyote—but this was the first known subway-riding opossum. It's not difficult to imagine how it happened. The nocturnal animal was ambling about in its slow opossum way, perhaps was attracted by the smell of garbage to the subway terminal, became frightened by the noise and bustle, and scampered into what appeared to be a dark, quiet corner. Repeated calls from *New York Times* reporters to the animal-control authorities were never returned, so we can only assume that things ended badly for the opossum. If the police had known just a little more about opossums, or if they had brought along the favored opossum-removal tool (a kitchen broom), the event might have been handled with less fanfare, and no wildlife mortality.

Opossums have a general reputation for viciousness, and though this perception is misguided, it's not difficult to see how it came about. The opossum has a white face that looks ghostly in the night, and lots of teeth — fifty teeth, more than any other North American mammal and about the same number as a *Tyrannosaurus rex* (which is why the snout is so long: it needs to cover all those teeth) — and that many sharp teeth might inspire a general impression of menace. But as far as being vicious or somehow dangerous, opossums are neither. When human and opossum paths cross, it is very often because an opossum has wandered somewhere that a human doesn't want it to be — into the garage, or the kitchen, or onto the back porch where the dog food is kept. My sister found one in her bathroom. So the human tries to get rid of the opossum, who suddenly feels cornered and threatened.

An opossum skull, displaying the animal's impressive number of teeth

An opossum that is confronted by a larger mammal (such as a human) and is afraid will hiss, grunt, bare its fifty teeth, and make all sorts of hideous noises in an attempt to seem as terrifying as possible. It might, if you put your hand way too close, try to bite you (though probably not); it will not outright attack you. The opossum is making all these noises not because it is vicious but because it is *frightened*. It just wants to get away without getting killed (and as a smallish animal, and given its species' track record against predators, it has good reason to doubt its potential success).

I asked wildlife removal expert Sean Met (who specializes in nonlethal removal and has handled hundreds of opossums) about the opossum personality. "Harmless," he told me. "Fraidy cats." Met tells me that this sometimes makes his job difficult. Whereas a raccoon in an attic or crawl space will growl and pace when you enter, an opossum will curl itself tightly into the most out-of-the-way corner, hiding its white face and remaining completely silent, which makes it surprisingly difficult to find, even when you know it is there. In daily life, they are not very social, have little reason to vocalize, and so are essentially quiet. Opossums are the most silent of all urban mammals.

I myself have always been indifferent to opossums. While I could never summon outright hostility over something that seemed so weird and misfit, I couldn't quite muster up affection or even particular interest in an animal that is so pointy and whose eyes always seem so unfocused. But the more I have studied them, the more fascinated I have become, and I realize that my own preconception of the opossum is, like everyone's, mainly superficial — based entirely on a narrow human aesthetic sensibility and the opossum's apparently unforgivable failure to meet it.

People who study them, even those who don't like opossums initially, describe them primarily with the adjectives *placid, gentle,* and

The Broom: How to Remove an Opossum

If an opossum has managed to find its way into your house or outbuilding, the best way to get it out is to quietly open all available exits and then leave for a while. If there is an open food source (dog food, a basket of apples), and the opossum is not too close to it, remove that as well. If the opossum hisses at you, don't worry. Remember that it will not run at you or try to bite you. It will cower away from you while pretending to be ferocious—do not believe it. Just go calmly on your way—the less you worry the opossum, the more free it will feel to move from its corner and out the door. If you feel that the opossum has had time enough and yet does not seem inclined to leave, you can encourage it with that tried-and-true animal-removal device: the broom. Gently place the broom behind the opossum's rear and shove it along. Again, don't be afraid of the hissing. It's just posing. If the opossum freaks out and plays dead, well, then—lucky you. Most people (including me) have never observed this fascinating behavior up close (I'm seriously thinking of trying to badly frighten the next opossum I see, just so I can observe the torpid state). If it does, resist the temptation to lift the opossum onto a shovel. Just leave it until it wakes up and goes.

The broom, while a traditional and popular choice for removing all kinds of animals from the home, is not always appropriate. For animals that can get around quickly (birds, squirrels), it serves only to frighten them, make them flap or run more wildly about, and stress everyone out (them and you). It can actually harm more delicate animals (birds, bats). Always try the leave-the-door-open method first, and then save brooms for slower, robust animals, such as opossums and raccoons.

quiet. Though many people believe the animals to be potentially rabid, rabies and distemper are virtually unheard of in opossums, and there is not a single case on record in North America of rabies being transferred from an opossum to a human or a domestic pet.

Opossum pelage is very soft, and has layers of color. Other than when it is hunting small animals for food, an opossum will never, pretty much *ever* attack anything unless it has been cornered and threatened by that thing or its young are in danger. Cats and opossums generally ignore each other, unless the cat is pestering an opossum's young, and in such cases, frequently the opossum still backs down from the cat. When an opossum takes shelter in your attic or under your house, it usually doesn't stay more than a few days (though if it is very cold or if the opossum has young and there is a reliable food source — like your garbage can or outdoor pet food supply — it may stay longer). And unlike squirrels, raccoons, and rats, opossums do not dig, burrow, chew wood or wires, or wreak any sort of destruction on lawns, yards, or buildings. Opossums sleep up to twenty hours a day, out of which five hours is REM-cycle sleep, implying that opossums dream, even more than humans do. Opossums' favorite foods are things we would like to have eradicated from our homes and yards: mice, rats, cockroaches, other large insects and spiders, slugs, and carrion. Opossums are extremely clean and wash their faces like cats. Their front paws are shaped like small stars.

In spite of the creature's general harmlessness and placidity, the history of human-opossum perceptions is a rocky one. When Europeans began exploring the New World, there were many new and unfamiliar beasts to excite and terrify: alligators, armadillos, rattlesnakes. But none captured the imagination like the opossum. Vicente Yáñez Pinzón, commander of Columbus's ship *Nina*, made the first English-language mention of the beast in 1492 after finding one in Brazil. It was a "Monster," he wrote, something like a fox, but "the hinder a Monkey, the feet were like a Mans, with Ears like an

Opossum Feet and Tracks

An opossum's tracks look something like a raccoon's, but with practice, you will find they are not difficult to tell apart. Both the front and back opossum paws have five fingers, again recalling the human hand, though not quite as fondly as the raccoon's. The front track of the opossum has short, stubby digits, and the softer the substrate, the farther they spread into a star-flower shape. The back track has a truly opposable hallux with no claw. It looks very much like a hand with the thumb sticking way out. This thumb and the prehensile tail that can wrap and hold branches make the possum a capable, though not particularly fast or agile, climber.

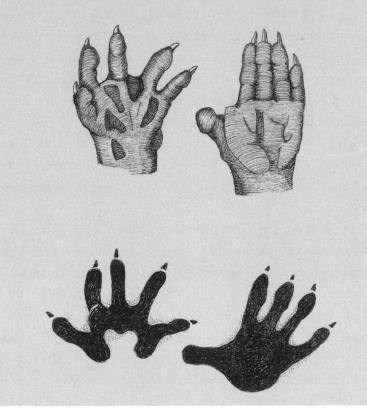

Owl; under whose Belly hung a great Bag, in which it carry'd the Young." He managed to catch one and ship it live to King Ferdinand of Spain. Others were sent back to Europe—live animals, pickled specimens for dissection, drawings and engravings depicting bear-size, misproportioned, fang-toothed beasts—much to the shock, amazement, and perhaps secret delight of the public. All were agreed: the opossum was a glimpse into the menagerie of depraved and loathsome monstrosities that were to be expected on unknown continents, a confirmation of the deep-running suspicion that the New World was a dark wilderness full of mystery and monsters. "Early on," writes Susan Scott Parrish, a scholar of colonial natural history at the University of Michigan, "the opossum was proof of the New World's propensity to produce strange and horrible beasts." Atlantic explorations persisted over the next three hundred years. The opossum continued to fascinate as the fear and ignorance of the Dark Ages and the conjurations of medieval science gave way to comparative anatomy, natural philosophy, and, says Parrish, a sense that all creatures were "part of God's wonderful, providential design." The opossum served as a kind of bridge between medieval and Enlightenment science.

There are more than seventy species of opossum in the Western Hemisphere, but only one in North America—*Didelphis virginiana*, the Virginia opossum, our sole native marsupial. When the original British colonists arrived, opossums were found only in the southeastern part of what would become the United States. Using the new human shelters and food sources as stepping stones, opossums made their way west, and north into Canada. As pioneers migrated farther west, any notion of opossums as monsters was forgotten, and they took the animals along with them. Opossums were kept alive for fresh food, and their pelts were used for clothing. Children tamed young opossums and convinced their parents to spare them from the food larder so they could be kept as pets. Along the way, many opossums escaped, and others were released in hopes that they would take hold as furbearers and stock for wild food. By the end of the nineteenth century, western populations of opossums had become established and were spreading. Even so, not all ecologists agree that the opossum ought to be considered an introduced species in the West, as their range expansion, mirroring their original, postcolonial dispersal, might have occurred even without introduction by humans. They would have padded across the country, slowly but steadily, in their own opossum time.

The Virginia opossum's most shining historical moment dawned in the post–Revolutionary War era, when Thomas Jefferson found a metaphor for his young country in the animal's "heroic" tenacity and maternal devotion. It wasn't until the beginning of the twentieth century that humans began to revert to a Dark Ages mentality regarding opossums, a mind-set that is particularly marked in modern urban dwellers.

More than any other mammal I have ever studied, opossums inspire an abhorrence that is both unapologetic and unqualified. It's not like the raccoon: "I can't stand them, but they are so cute with those masks, and clever." Or rats or crows: "I hate them, but I know they are superintelligent, and I respect that." Or even pigeons: "Pigeons suck, but they don't really hurt anything." Most people feel no impulse whatsoever to soften their revulsion for opossums; the right—almost obligation—to dislike opossums appears to have evolved into an obvious given, an a priori truth of the urban wilderness. Preferred descriptors include *icky, nasty, vicious,* and *pointy.* In response to an opossum post on a popular urban-homesteading blog, one reader wrote, "Nasty, ugly, giant rat-looking critters. Yuck." And another: "I'm an animal lover, but possums give me the creeps. I say, any means necessary with those guys." And another, whose online moniker happens to be Serenity Love: "Hit them with your car. They are nasty vicious creatures. Back up over them to make sure they are dead."* Looking for an opinion that I could be sure came from an informed source, I turned to a friend of mine, an award-winning journalist for a major paper who writes primarily about science and nature and has a regular column on the appreciation of local wildlife. "Opossums?" She wrinkled her nose. "Icky. *Icky-pointy.*"

I knew I could count on my dear writer friend David Laskin to shed some light on this curious problem of opossum perception. He hadn't even gone upstairs to look at my daughter's new gerbils because, well, he was "not that fond of rodents." So I was quite sure he would have some opossum thoughts to share. Opossums, of course, are not rodents, but there persists a curious sensibility, even among those who know better (most people), that it's still appropriate to *think of them* somehow as rodents (maybe it's the ratlike tail). In any case, David did not disappoint. This is what he told me:

"Oh, I *hate* possums! They are worse than rats, and I really hate rats. At least rats are good at being ratty—dirty and sneaky and

---

* *The comments were in response to a post about how local opossums were endangering local chickens (though no chickens had actually been harmed). It is true that an opossum may be attracted to a chicken coop. But an opossum will rarely (I won't say never, but rarely) take on a full-size chicken. That's just too overwhelming for a 'possum. They will be attracted to other things in the coop: smaller young chickens or bantams, eggs, chicken food, and—if you have them (which you do)—rats. In fact, the opossum's favorite food is small mammals, rats and mice, so in this way, its presence is actually a plus for the urban chicken farmer, for whom rats are a much bigger worry than opossums are. If you practice good husbandry and close the coop up at night to keep your birds safe from raccoons (which really will kill them), then opossums will not trouble your hens.*

scary, and you have to respect them for that, sort of like coyotes. But possums are *pure ick.* They seem dumb, they are scary-looking; if you corner one they seem dangerous. I hate their tails. I hate their blobbiness, and they *just freak me out.*"

This was more than I'd hoped for. But David wasn't finished: "I don't like their *size.* Rats are small, and you get the feeling they could just slither away, and raccoons — you know I don't care much for raccoons — are bigger than possums, but at least their fur is sort of beautiful. Possums are just big and gross. There's *too much* of them." And he offered: "The fact that people actually eat them, you know, possum stew? That grosses me out."* David is one of the most eloquent writers I know, so it is gratifying to hear him use phrases like "grosses me out."

After this long, inspired, and probably tiring anti-opossum dia-tribe, David paused. "I guess it's cool that they can hang from their tails," he proffered, thinking perhaps that he'd offended me with all of his possum loathing. I love that the one thing he can find to like about the opossum isn't even true. They do have prehensile tails, and they use them a lot as they climb. An opossum can dangle by its tail for a few moments while it reaches for a branch with one of its feet, which is very handy if you are a mother opossum climbing a tree with a passel of opossum kits on your back. But opossums are too heavy to actually hang for very long by their tails, as they do in

---

* *Here, David echoes British explorer John Lawson, who observed his first opossums in what is now North Carolina and, in 1701, called them "the Wonder of all the Land-Animals" while also noting that "their flesh is very white, and well tasted, but their ugly Tails put me out of Conceit with that Fare." Even so, modern Weight Watchers' charts include the number of points for a serving of opossum. In Seattle, eating opossum would be considered unusual, but as urban sustainability efforts gain ground, so do discussions of eating backyard creatures like opossums and squirrels, which is a move toward ultra-local meat and a version of pest control rolled into one. In the face of such talk, I remain gratefully vegetarian.*

cartoons and in our imaginations. They *can* carry things with their tails, usually leaves and grasses to be used in lining their dens or nests. It's a winsome image, really: the tail coiled around a bunch of leaves, and the opossum scampering (insofar as an opossum can scamper) away with her treasure, then using her icky-pointy nose to tuck the leaves into a rounded nest, either in a protected earthen corner or in a tree. So after this, David made one more kindly effort. "Don't they have a pouch or something?" I was very excited about opossums at the time of our conversation, so I jumped right in with some little factoids, surely more than he wanted to know. "Yes! The marsupium! And the pouch is so extraordinary, it's all soft and fur-lined, and the mother possum can actually swim with her young in the pouch, and it will stay so nicely sealed around them that they won't get wet!" I couldn't have imagined a better response from David: "*Eeew!* They *swim?* Great, something else to be scared of."

What I value most about David's anti-opossum polemic, besides its impressive unrelentingness, is its representativeness. These are the exact things that most people don't like about opossums. And David hit something bang-on with his repeated use of *seem*. Opossums "*seem* dumb," and they "*seem* dangerous." We have to use *seem* with opossums, because we know so little about them. They are nocturnal, we rarely see them, and we don't like them, so we are singularly unmotivated to find out what's really true about them and what is not. Regarding opossum intelligence, I have often wondered over it myself. They certainly don't appear to be terribly clever, so myopic and ponderous, laboring about the street and hedge edges in the dark. (They are not actually myopic, though they are slow; top speed is a few miles per hour, with the tail spinning for balance.) But combing the scientific literature, I discovered that opossums are moderately to highly intelligent, ranking above domestic dogs on task tests. They are believed to be about as intelligent as pigs, and who knows what sort of unexpected, unlooked-for intelligence their nocturnal opossum lives require — unique opossum intelligence we as yet fail to imagine.*

Opossum survival is always a wary prospect. The initial journey of the pea-size embryo from internal uterus to external pouch is a perilous one, and up to a quarter of the miniature opossums will die before weaning. Of those that survive, fewer than 10 percent will live even one year. There is a long-standing myth regarding opossum reproduction that still persists, even on some (not very good, to say the least) natural-history websites: that copulation takes place through the female's nose. The babies are so small when born, and birth usually takes place in the dark, where it is difficult to witness; opossum reproduction remained, in lay circles, little understood until the past century. One day, the uncorroboratable story goes, someone observed a captive opossum female pushing her nose around in her pouch, as they will do when young are present, and she also sneezed a couple of times. Upon examination, the observer

---

* It is not my intention to be an opossum apologist. Like all wild presences, that of the opossum is complicated. With their omnivorous adaptability and the abundance of food available for opossums, they might be a practical menace, but they are not an ecological menace in urban places. However, in rural areas, especially in the West, where they are (possibly) an introduced species, their predation on native birds may be of concern and deserves further study. In New Zealand, where the introduced brushtail opossum has colonized the island's sensitive forests, fragile populations of native and indigenous birds are threatened by opossum depredation. In their North American history, particularly in the East, where they are native, opossums appear to exist in ecological stasis. That is, they do eat birds, but no more than any other bird-eating wild thing, and not out of proportion to their population and range; their numbers are kept in check by predators and cars. But as native habitat is chopped up into ever-smaller "island" relics, the example of New Zealand cannot be ignored. Human impacts bring the relationships among creatures into a sharper, and darker, relief.

found the pouch full of several tiny babies. The fallacy was substantiated by the astonishing fact of the male opossum's penis, which is bifurcated and strongly forked at the end, with two avenues for ejaculation (which of course has led to the animal being considered a prophylactic against impotence, and its member ground and made into a serum in parts of Central and South America). I cannot help but think of Shel Silverstein's lyrics about a young man specially endowed with two *membra virile:*

> *They say that Stacy Brown was born just a little bit deformed*
> *Still his girlfriends they all wake up smilin' every morn...*

And are the female opossums smiling? Well, they do seem to grin with their long snouts, but the females themselves have bifurcated uteruses, adapted precisely for the males' attentions, so perhaps it doesn't seem particularly novel to them. *Didelphis,* the opossum's scientific genus name, means "dual womb." This, coupled with the fact of the bifurcated penis, obviously created by "divine design" to fit into the two nostrils, led to the persistent myth: that opossum insemination occurs through the female nostrils, from whence the young are sneezed out into the pouch.

Being a marsupial, the opossum gives birth to the tiniest of babies—embryos, really, almost completely undeveloped, and each the size of a dried navy bean. These tiny pups make their way into the mother opossum's pouch in their first two minutes outside the womb, crawl into the pouch, and attach themselves to one of the thirteen teats. The nipples expand within the pups' mouths, and they all remain there, attached and growing, until they peek over the fold of the pouch at about thirty days and eventually emerge, very small and—dare I suggest it?—*cute*, at about two months. Surviving young continue to hold fast to the mother's belly or back for some months to come, and she is a protective, attentive mother.*

Adult opossums rarely live more than two years. That's not very long for a mammal of that size, scarcely as long as a field mouse. The size of the opossum actually plays a significant role in adult mortality. It's hard to be a medium-small mammal, especially one that can't run to speak of. An opossum is too big to slither away like a rat. It cannot move fast enough to get across the street when caught in the road by a night-passing car, and especially not when disoriented by the glare of headlights. (*Why did the chicken cross the road? To prove to the opossum it could be done.*) But it is also not big enough

---

* *The young of marsupials such as kangaroos and wallabies are called joeys, and some call opossum babies joeys as well, but it's not officially sanctioned language. There is actually no particular name for opossum young. Kit or kitten is generally acceptable for any small furry thing, but baby opossums are typically called, unimaginatively,* young. *While researching the issue, Indiana State Wildlife Services biologist Judy Loven received some fitting suggestions, including papooses, larvae, and (her personal favorite) grubs.*

to deter predators. A coyote will think twice about eating a raccoon, but an opossum is just the right size. Same goes for the larger hawks, owls, eagles, and dogs, with dogs being the number-one cause of opossum death in urban and suburban places, outranking even automobiles. Tens of thousands of opossums are trapped each year, but their pelts are of little value — worth less than fifty cents each — and in recent decades, the majority of opossum pelts have remained unsold. Those that are sold trim inexpensive clothing or are exported for the manufacture of cheap teddy bears.

I believe that one of the problems with our modern opossum perception lies in the fact of our opposing circadian rhythms. David Laskin mentioned the opossum's nighttime wandering as a source of his own dis-ease with the animal: "I dislike their nocturnalness," he told me. "You only see them when you're really stressed out." I had no idea what this meant, but David explained. "You know, when you are up worrying about an article you have to write, or a review you know someone is writing of your book, or whatever, that's when you see a possum. In the dark, like your fear."

It's true. They are from another kind of world, the night world, the place where in both mythology and psychology our own human anxieties are magnified, where we feel a sense of mystery, a lack of rationality, an inability to know our own footing. The opossum doubtlessly feels the same when it stumbles unwittingly into our world. A quiet, nocturnal animal beneath a bright electric light and a shrieking human or an aggressive dog or a wandering urban coyote or even a mob of crows? Such moments inspire one of the opossum's most singular behaviors.

When it finds itself in the most dire of circumstances, an opossum will fall into a state that mimics, for all the world, sudden death. This zoological strategy is not uncommon in insects, but it is rare in mammals. The goal is to make your adversary believe that you are already dead, and perhaps even beginning to rot, so that it will leave you alone, not kill you and eat you. To this end, the opossum lies perfectly still and seemingly stiff, with its eyes closed; eventually, a musky, death-scented liquid will ooze from its mouth and the glands near the anus. This state will last for some minutes at least, and up to several hours. Though the opossum appears utterly still, and you cannot even see the movement of breath in the breast, the opossum's metabolism does not actually slow. Eventually, the possum will twist its soft black ears all around, listening, and sniff the air. It will lift its funny head ever so slightly and have a peek around. When it deems all is well, it will amble off to perceived safety, no faster than usual.

In cross-cultural opossum symbolism and mythology, playing possum is the predominant theme. When humans take on this behavior, playing dead in response to external stimuli, the psychological term is *dissociation* — to be disconnected, negatively separate. Regarding opossums, it seems, this is exactly what we do ourselves: we play possum, we dissociate by responding to a creature based mainly on the *one* factor that we teach our children is a superficial trait by which to judge a thing — its appearance. It is not my intent to make everyone like opossums; I hope we might simply rethink them. Instead of relegating opossums to the hated thing beneath human notice, why not expansively and intentionally recognize them, allow their presence in the community of beings worthy of awareness and consideration? We don't have to *do* anything differently, except maybe stop calling them names (I agree with Gary Snyder, who argues for maintaining politeness toward wild animals at all times, as they may be listening; we don't know what the consequences could be and should in any case behave ourselves.) The steps to avoiding conflict are small and simple and exactly the same as the things we must do to coexist calmly with most wild neighborhood creatures: bring in the pet food, close up the garbage cans. If we do these things and still manage to see opossums now and then, we can watch with a benevolent curiosity. They are quiet, gentle, strange, pouched, misunderstood beings in our midst. It might seem ecologically insignificant, but I am convinced it would mean something tremendous if we could look at opossums and conclude that yes, they are pointy and decidedly uncute, that their tails are not nicely furred, and that they make us feel a little uncomfortable, but that even so, the presence of actual marsupials co-inhabiting our neighborhoods is an astonishing, wondrous thing—something to watch for, wonder over, learn about. And remembering that they won't hurt us, or our cats, or our dogs, why not have an opossum in the yard? What if we expanded our moral and practical imaginations to include a marsupial with such a pointed nose?

One night, I got out of bed at 2:00 a.m. to pee. Tom was traveling for work in Mozambique, so Claire and I were alone in the house under a full moon. I had insomnia that night and didn't mind getting up—it gave me something to do besides lying awake in bed. While in the bathroom, I lifted the light, faded curtain I'd made from a scarf we brought home from India and looked out to see the moon. There, in the middle of our street, illumined in equal measure by streetlamp and moonlight, ambled an opossum. She appeared to be making her way across the road, but when she reached the middle, she stopped. She sat on her possum rump and lifted her face to the sky, blinking in the moonlight. And there she stayed for several minutes before slowly getting back up on all four feet and walking, with the most absolute lack of hurry I have ever seen, to the far sidewalk.

I paused over the randomness of this vision; if I hadn't thought to peek beneath the curtain, the opossum would still have been there, the moon-watching opossum, unseen, with me on the other side of the curtain, in my near-constant ignorance of the wild life that surrounds me, thinking only of how I might get to sleep. How constant and present and continual, and how strange, the community of beings.

Squirrel (and Rat)

Life in the World Tree

No creature demonstrates the human schizophrenia regarding urban wildlife better than the squirrel. In studies of backyard wildlife, squirrels rank as both the most desirable and attractive animal *and* the most hated nuisance animal. We love squirrels when they are jumping, eating, washing their faces in that adorable catlike way. We love them when they eat the peanuts we put out for them, sitting up on their haunches, so round and fluffy. We love them when they stretch themselves out on a limb and let their legs dangle, napping extravagantly. We love them, sometimes, when they are just running up and down the tree or across the street, carrying bits of chestnut or apple, enlivening the neighborhood and our lives. We hate them when they nest in the attic and wake us at five in the morning with their scratchings and squeakings. We hate them when, after eating from our hands so sweetly for three months, they suddenly one day bite our fingers. We hate them when they nip the blossoms from our cherry trees, unearth our tulip bulbs, and nibble our garden squash. More than anything, we hate them when they eat all the expensive black oil sunflower seeds we put out for *different* wildlife.

Squirrel strife is nothing new. Ratatoskr is a squirrel in Norse mythology, and though the story is ancient, the squirrel is entirely familiar. Ratatoskr spends his days running up and down Yggdrasil, the World Tree, usually depicted as a gorgeous, sweeping ash. This tree isn't just *located* at the center of the world, she *is* the center of the world, and she overlaps the prominent image of the Tree of Life found in religion, mythology, shamanic lore, and even scientific literature across times and cultures. At the end of *The Origin of Species,* Darwin invokes the familiar Tree of Life image as a metaphor for branching evolutionary relationships to ease his theories into a not-quite-ready world. The squirrel Ratatoskr carries messages from an unnamed eagle in the top branches of the World Tree to the dragonlike wyrm Níðhöggr, who lives curled in its roots. Many other creatures dwell in the branches and roots and on the ground beneath the tree, the whole scene evoking a kind of peaceable kingdom, with the squirrel as its lively interworld messenger, running up and down and up again. The story, I read in various commentaries, speaks to the ongoing conversation between heaven and earth, with the squirrel symbolizing our essential connectedness to both these realms.

But delving a bit deeper into Norse cosmology, I discovered a more nuanced portrait. The messages that Ratatoskr bore were mostly insults hurled at the wyrm from the eagle. "Scaly, insipid beast!" And Ratatoskr means "drill-tooth." He is sometimes pictured with a horn growing out of his forehead, a sort of rodent uni-corn, and with this or with his teeth, he bores incessantly into the tree. Some sources picture a wounded Yggdrasil chewed up and down one side by the sharp-toothed Ratatoskr. And the tree itself? It turns out that she spends much of her day grumbling away, annoyed to distraction by the wild denizens that make their home among her roots and branches. A mean-spirited eagle; a sad dragon; a tree-killing, insult-passing squirrel; and, at the center of the uni-verse, a very crabby tree. Some peaceable kingdom.

I have been this world tree. Who has not? Lately, I've found myself grumbling in bed just before dawn while a pair of Ratatoskrs nesting in the attic cornice right behind my sleepy head chew my house to pieces. I've watched them long enough to discover their convoluted route to and through a corner opening in the gutter. We had hired a wildlife expert with a long ladder to cover all such open-ings with steel hardware cloth to prevent the entry of rodents, but this was the one place on our tall and complicated 1920s roofline the ladder could not scale. The squirrels, naturally, get to it easily. They climb the large cypress in front of the house, jump from there to the roof over the entry, and then to the flower box under my second-floor study window. Here they might stop to gorge on the sunflower seeds at my window-suction chickadee feeder, blandly ignoring me as I tap the glass right next to their heads. After this, a run around the roof edge on the west side of the house, and a brave, hard-won (even for a squirrel) leap to the cornice. In early autumn, I wanted to discourage them from choosing this as a winter den, as just a few inches of wood and plaster were separating the Ratatoskr teeth from my bed pillow. So every morning before making coffee and stroll-ing into my study to write about peaceful cohabitation with urban wildlife, I picked up the urban-wild-interface tool of choice, the broom handle, and beat the wall inside the closet (which abutted their attic nest) or hung out the window and reached around to pound loudly on the gutter. This would usually bring them out, but eventually they realized that all I could do with my broom was make noise and that I couldn't hang out the window far enough to actually sweep them without falling to my death. So now the squirrels just stare at me for a moment in that wide-eyed squirrel way and then go back to chewing a bigger hole for their egress.

The squirrels in our attic and neighborhood are eastern gray squirrels, the most common urban, suburban, and city-park squirrel in most of the country. Depending on where you live and how urban-suburban your home is, you might see instead various species of native tree squirrels or ground squirrels (ground-squirrel species are typically striped or lightly spotted), most of which share common squirrelish natural history and habits. From the Mississippi westward, the eastern gray squirrel populations are nonnative, introduced accidentally when pets escaped or intentionally by misguided squirrel lovers, but in many respects, this is a moot point. Wildlife experts agree that there are too many for them to be successfully extirpated, humanely or not. Eastern gray squirrels are a permanent fixture of the urban wild.

Urban/suburban squirrels are somewhat territorial, claiming about half an acre per pair of; if you can find an identifying mark on your squirrel, like the half-missing ear on one of the squirrels that comes to my window feeder, you will discover that you have basically the same squirrels every day.

The supposition that introduced eastern gray squirrels are displacing native squirrels requires some nuance. It's true that these gray squirrels are larger and sometimes more aggressive than other types (though if you've ever crossed a little Douglas squirrel or one of the other red tree species, you know that they are not to be messed with—I have seen plenty of these beautiful little squirrels chase an eastern gray away handily), but in North America, it is the destruction of woodland habitat that reduces populations of native tree squirrels. The edge habitat that results when forested areas are dismantled for the construction of human homes and other buildings (or even grassy parks) is suitable for the gray squirrels, and they move in readily. In the UK, where the habitat of the smaller red tree squirrel overlaps more intensely with that of the introduced gray squirrel, it does appear that the larger gray squirrels are forcing the natives out and threatening their populations. But here in North America, it is human activity, far more than the nature of the squirrel species, that controls squirrel presence and absence.

Urban squirrels are not particularly careful about hiding their nesting places, or dreys, and will construct them throughout the year for different purposes. In the early spring, they find a cozy place safely above the reach of ground-dwelling predators to birth and raise their young. Kits of most squirrel species are nursed and cared for by the mother for three months, a long time for any mammal, let alone a rodent. Male and female squirrels look alike, but in the right season, when females stand on their haunches, we can see the enlarged nipples, signs of new motherhood. We rarely glimpse the young until they are nearly full-size, but they can be distinguished by their relative clumsiness, their caution in navigating trees, and their skimpy tails, not nearly as full and bushy as the adults'. In the winter, squirrels find warm places to den up. Either of these dreys—nursery or winter shelter—might be one of the round balls of leaves we see in trees, easy to spot in winter when the limbs are bare. Crow nests are large, dark presences in the trees too, but they are made almost entirely of sticks, and not covered with a mounded roof, as squirrel dreys are, though squirrels may use old crow nests as bases for their own. There is a small entrance, a hole at the top of the drey.

Leaves are a common drey-building material, but they might also include found mosses, fur, and other soft things. Mysterious bits of shredded newspaper were showing up on our drive one autumn month. The Seattle rain glued the paper scraps to the cement, and we had to scrape them off with our fingernails. Soon enough we discovered a squirrel drey in the neighbor's fir, with *Seattle Times* confetti tucked among the leaves. Squirrels will also nest in woodpecker cavities or in nest boxes put out by humans for larger birds—woodpeckers or owls or wood ducks. The recommended dimensions for a squirrel box and a flicker box are exactly the same (would-be housers of birds need to take this into account).

But why would a squirrel bother with any of this when there are roofline cornices to be had? In urban and suburban neighborhoods, human houses are the favored squirrel shelter. Since there were no electrical wires where the squirrels were nesting in our attic, and since they were unfazed by my broom-wielding, we decided to wait it out. Occasionally, squirrels will take up permanent residence in human homes, but more typically, their presence is seasonal, and if you bide your time, they move out on their own—when the weather is warmer, if they were denning, or after the young have grown, if they were nesting. This is a good time to clean the area out, if you can, and block the entrance route from future rodentia. Lethal control is never permanently effective. There are lots of squirrels (and rats), and if you kill the ones that are present, more will eventually move in. The smell of urine from the previous residents will attract others. The best method is to wait till the squirrels are gone or to live-trap them, and while they are out, effect structural changes to prevent reentry, making sure there are no young left inside. (Not only will they die cruelly of starvation, but dead squirrels in the wall will smell really bad for a couple of months. On this, I speak from sad experience.) Besides the annoyance issue, frayed electrical wires and messed-up insulation are the main concerns with squirrels. Squirrel waste and the squirrels themselves carry bacteria that could theoretically harm humans, but disease transmission, including rabies, between squirrel and human is almost nonexistent.

The squirrels among us are far and away the most ubiquitous observable urban-wild mammals. Rats are present in numbers, but they are secretive and nocturnal. We can observe squirrels almost whenever we want to. Because they are utterly commonplace, accessibly diurnal, and in many places notoriously nonnative, we often consider squirrels as being pretty much beneath our attention. This was my long-standing urban squirrel attitude. While I would go out of my way to observe and study woodland squirrels (both Douglas squirrels and northern flying squirrels can be found in Seattle's forested parks), I knew very little about the squirrels that lived under my nose. But their presence is in many ways a wonder. Here are wild mammals, coming in close, allowing us to watch, to sketch, to learn something through their general behavior about the less-observable squirrel species, to pause and consider at length our shared mammalian biologies, our twined urban ecologies. In its commonness, the squirrel offers an opportunity that is rare.

Here is something I discovered about squirrels while immersing myself in the urban wilds for this project, something I didn't know

Squirrel Tracks and Sign

Urban squirrel sign is subtle. They defecate randomly, so their scats don't accumulate, and you rarely spot them except in a small space where a squirrel has spent a lot of time, like an attic or a toolshed that happens to hold the birdseed supply. And squirrels are too light (and light on their feet) to make tracks on most urban substrates. The exception is a snowy day, when you'll see their bounding trails, back-foot tracks ahead of the front, or their droppings, bright black against the white, sometimes absorbing snow fluid until they burst into circles of red-brown.

But there are other signs that indicate squirrel activity. Look for the debarking of branches, where strips of the outer cambium have been peeled away for food or, possibly, to line the drey, if the tree is a soft-barked cedar. You can actually see marks from the incisors at the edges of the peeled areas. If the scraped patches are close to the bottom of the tree, the creature that made them is likely to have been a vole or a pocket gopher, and wide peeled patches low on the tree may indicate the presence of a porcupine. Squirrels like to de-bark at a height where they can worry less about predators—six or eight feet up, and higher.

Look for clippings. It is astonishing how often we walk past a tree surrounded by tips of its own branches without stopping to consider how this came about. Squirrels and chipmunks can't support themselves on the slenderest outer limbs of a tree, but that is where the freshest buds for feeding and the plumpest cones for winter caching often lie. The squirrel will clip the end of the branch off and let it fall to the ground—sometimes dozens of them—then descend to dine on terra firma, or carry the tips one by one back up the tree to eat on a protected branch near the trunk. Watch also for empty hazelnuts and mast, the squirrel's favorite autumn harvest. Birds like jays and crows will hack nuts open cleanly with their bills; nutshells left by squirrels will have teeth marks. (After larger birds or squirrels open the nuts and eat most of what's inside, chickadees will come and clean up anything left in the shell corners.)

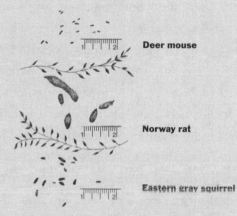

Deer mouse

Norway rat

Eastern gray squirrel

Above is a comparison of deer mouse, Norway rat, and eastern gray squirrel scats, showing their relative size. Other species of mouse, squirrel, and rat scats are similar. Accumulations are found in households where any of these rodents have been attracted by food and shelter that is relatively undisturbed by humans—basements and sheds are perfect. The size of the droppings will let you know who has been visiting. Rat scats are decidedly larger than squirrels', vary more in shape, and show more light-colored fiber. But in spite of anti-rat sentiment, rats—and their leavings—are not "dirtier" than these other rodents.

before: squirrels are beautiful. I always knew that they were bothersome but cute. Classically bright-eyed and bushy-tailed. But it wasn't until I sat on my bum for hours to observe and draw and ill-advisedly tame a few that I noticed their honest animal beauty. Each wide eye is rimmed with golden-brown crescent moons, one above, one below. The fur is ticked, shades of gold, red, gray, black, mingling around a pure white-gray belly. The tail is layered, with soft-edged stripes of these same colors. (Some populations are golden-red with light pumpkin-colored bellies, some are solid black or solid white. Communities build tourist billing around such squirrels, and protect them exuberantly. All are different color morphs of the same species — eastern gray squirrel.) Their feet are softly furred, long and thin, elegant. In more forested parks where they feel less exposed and are calmer, squirrels sometimes become less twitchy in their habits, and their agility starts to seem more graceful than jumpy. I'm not saying squirrels aren't a nuisance and nine kinds of trouble. I'm saying that no matter what else they are, it is possible to step back from our shared squirrel prejudice — whether it reduces them to fluffy cuteness or mere annoyance — and see them from the outside, as wild, graceful, and lovely.

Aesthetically, at least, it is difficult for most people to find anything to appreciate about rats, the urban squirrel's nocturnal counterpart. The rat body is a classic teardrop shape, wider at the back end and narrowing to a point at the snout. There is not much delineation at the neck or the nose. The eyes are black and not large, though not as small and beady as we imagine them. The fur is short, and brown, gray, or almost black, depending on the species and the individual, and the feet are much smaller than a squirrel's. Even a member of the climbing-rat species does not have the long toes and accompanying aerial agility of a tree squirrel. But it is the slender rope of the rat tail (isn't it?) that somehow encompasses all of our psychological distaste for the rat — pale, scaly, hairless, dragging unseen through the gutters of our homes and minds.

The persistent belief that there is one rat per person in urban places is based on a dubious study from rural England undertaken in 1907. And though the statistic is constantly repeated by public-health experts and rat exterminators, for modern cities, it is entirely untrue. How many rats are there really? Well, we don't know; rats are quiet, wary, and nocturnal, and we have no good way to count them. But in the United States, the number is likely to be far fewer than one per person — more like one per family. When I asked a rat-control professional about the one-per-person figure on his website, he copped to knowing it was an exaggeration. "The more rats people think there are, the more freaked out they are, and the more business I get."

Even so, if you live in a city, there are rats living with you, whether you see them or not. And while there are several species of native rat in this country, the human commensals — the two species of city rats — are introduced. The smaller is the roof rat, *Rattus rattus*, a good climber, found mainly in the southern states and California. The most common is the brown rat, *Rattus norvegicus* (also called the Norway rat, subway rat, sewer rat, alley rat, house rat, wharf rat, gray rat, Norwegian rat, or common rat), which, in spite of its scientific name, originated in Manchuria. They spread to Europe by foot and their rat wits, and sailed (along with pigeons) to North America on the ships that brought the colonial settlers in the mid-1700s. It is typical for people who find a fat brown rat in the basement (cornered, frightened, and therefore aggressive) to claim it

Rat Tails

Of all tails possessed by mammalian species on the face of the entire earth, rat tails inspire the most revulsion. "Their icky tails" is often given as a reason that people hate rats themselves. Even people who *want* to like rats—people who respect their intelligence and playfulness and who might consider a rat as a pet for their children—often lament that they just can't get past the ugly tail. What if rats had fluffy tails like squirrels? Would we like them better? In an effort to understand, I carried out an unscientific study, interviewing fifty friends and online contacts to see if I could discern some psychological thread in the complex labyrinth of rat perceptions. While a very few claimed to be unbothered by the tails (no one confessed to an outright fondness for the things), most of the responses to my little study could be grouped into four general trends:

1. We hate rat tails because the tails themselves are ugly. Rat tails are not hairless, but they are quite bare, and the hair that does grow on them is stiff and hard. The tail skin is sometimes dry and flaky, which makes the tails appear scabby and diseased. Rat tails are the sorts of things we are taught from a young age not to touch, for fear of catching a dreaded something. Opossum tails inspire the same reaction.

2. We hate rat tails because they are snakelike. A fearful response to snakes is so universally common that many believe it must be an inborn

SQUIRREL (AND RAT)

evolutionary protection mechanism. Recent work by researchers at Carnegie Mellon, however, suggests that while humans are not born with an innate fear of snakes (or spiders, for that matter), we do have what's called an evolutionary bias that predisposes us to quickly notice things that have posed threats throughout human history (the squiggling thing at the edge of one's peripheral vision) and associate these with fear via cues from the environment—say, your mom shrieking or someone yanking you away. It appears that a rat tail triggers this response, dragged behind the animal, looking as if it has its own unpredictable snaky life.

3. We hate rat tails because, as such things go, they are too big. Hairless mouse tails are attached to tiny little mice. Rat tails cross a kind of psychological threshold. My friend Clare tells me that rats give her the shivers, in part because of the "long, scaly, bony tail that drags along the ground like some forgotten appendage." Mice are different. "Field mice— in fact, all mice—are cute," Clare says. "Tiny bodies, big round ears, even their weenie hairless tails are cute." For Clare and so many others, the tail issue comes down to size. Small = cute. Thick and ropey = *disgusting*.

4. We hate rat tails because they are attached to rats. This is a tricky one, a chicken-egg problem that is difficult to untangle. The bushy-tailed wood rat, or packrat, looks much like an Old World rat except for its tail, which is furry. Not as fluffy as a squirrel's, but far furrier than urban rats' tails. Most of us have not encountered these fluffier-tailed rural rats and so have no opinion about them. There is no good way to tease out revulsion of rats from revulsion of rat tails. One way or another, our conflicted or outright disgusted feelings toward rats are tangled up with their ratty tails.

is evil and "big as a cat." But rats rarely grow to weigh a full pound, and from tip to tail, an average one measures about ten inches. And unless cornered, they are typically gentle and will avoid humans.

Another rat myth—that "after the apocalypse, there will be nothing but cockroaches and rats"—rings truer. Through the decade that the U.S. government was testing atomic bombs in the South Pacific, colonies of roof rats were thriving on Eniwetok Atoll. They created a maze of underground burrows, and though the soil was burned off the islands by atomic blasts, and they were deluged by tidal waves, the rats survived. One tiny island endured eight atomic bombings, and the rats there not only appeared to suffer no negative physical effects from the high radiation levels but continued to flourish.

In spite of the common *dirty rat* moniker, and though they dwell in the muckiest areas of urbania, rats themselves are clean; they spend far more time cleaning and preening than humans do. The diseases that may be passed from rat to human (including salmonella, leptospirosis, and tularemia) are contracted by contact with concentrations of rat feces or urine or by being bitten. In some countries, bubonic plague is still an issue (though not in North America), and it is passed between rats and humans by flea vectors. There has never been a case of a human in North America contracting rabies from a rat. While many would beg to differ, rats are not officially recognized here as a public-health problem.

Still, they cause a lot of trouble. They chew through electrical wires and tunnel into homes and buildings. They reproduce wildly, sometimes within our walls. Rats are among the most omnivorous of omnivores, eating meat, seeds, roots, berries, spiders, beetles, various insects (including cockroaches), eggs, and shellfish and other shoreline invertebrates. Rats will eat any animal smaller than they are: baby birds, small reptiles, fish, baby squirrels and rabbits. They eat our refuse—our trash, pizza crusts, pet food, pretzels. Anything. It is estimated that rats eat nearly one-fifth of the global food harvest. It's a little creepy to learn that the FDA recognized the impossibility of storing quantities of food without the presence of rats and so set a maximum amount of rodent hairs and droppings allowable in processed foods (including peanut butter).

Rats have poor daylight vision and prefer to come out only at night (if there are rats seen regularly during the day, it is a sign of way too many rats in an area and not enough food), and their bodies are covered with fine sensory hairs, which help them navigate through small tunnels and along the base of walls. They don't care to wander out in the open — not because they are furtive, but because they lose the benefit of their sensory hairs and because that's where they can be spotted by cats and owls.

Though we may partake of the common rat revulsion, most of us probably also know that rats are fascinating, intelligent, and make wonderful pets: they learn their names, come when called, bond readily with individual humans, play games like a dog, and snuggle to sleep on laps or in pockets. But rats may possess further depths that we are just beginning to understand. While laughter was long believed by ethologists to be a behavior limited to humans and, perhaps, the higher primates, recent studies show that young rats appear to laugh when they are tickled. They don't emit the high laughter sounds when their backs are tickled, just when their tummies are — like human children. And compelling new research by neuroscientists at the University of Chicago shows that rats may actually exhibit true altruism. When one rat was locked in a small Plexiglas cage within a larger cage, another rat in the big cage often worked tirelessly to release its imprisoned rat colleague, without any reward and whether or not it was acquainted with the confined rat.

When a pile of the rats' favorite treat (milk-chocolate chips!) was also placed in the larger cage, the free rat would not eat all the chips herself but would liberate the caged rat and share the chocolate. The most wonderful part of the study was the behavior of the two rats after the imprisoned rat was released: they would run around the cage together, jumping and chirping, as if rejoicing that the previously caged rat was loose. Then, yes — to the chocolate. (But if you are stuck in a cage, better hope that a female rat finds you — females were far more consistent than males in endeavoring to release a caged friend.)

Wildlife-removal pro Sean Met tells me that the way most exterminators deal with rats is ridiculous. They kill the rats present, then they want to come back regularly to set up traps or a poison perimeter to continuously control the population. Met says that rats reproduce constantly, and they will *always* be around. The only commonsense way to keep them out of living spaces is through prevention. Get rid of any rats that are there, then cover entrances, including gutters and holes in foundation perimeters, with metal hardware cloth (rats can chew through solid wood, cinder blocks, and even lead pipes). Hire someone like Sean who knows rat psychology and habits to help you. Clip tree branches and shrubs that allow rats (or squirrels) easy access to your roof. Tidy food (including birdseed and pet food) storage areas in the basement, garage, or shed, and store all such food in metal containers, like galvanized trash cans with lids, which come in various sizes (rats chew through plastic). To reduce conflict with rats and all other urban mammals, bring pet food in at night. And if you see a rat in the yard, park, or subway now and then? Settle in and watch — rat behavior is endlessly varied and fascinating.

*   *   *

Like rats, squirrels are rodents. And while the two groups share some characteristic rodent-ness (like ever-growing teeth and the subsequent need to gnaw upon the World Tree), and though as smallish mammals they share an ecological niche by dividing it into diurnal and nocturnal halves, squirrels are not, as some like to say, "just rats with bushy tails." The comparison is hard to resist: Aren't they both just useless, pestering, proliferating, omnipresent, nonnative rodents? But the workings of the squirrel's bushy tail actually creates a squirrel social system that separates it from any other rodent. Rats use their tails for support, balance, and thermoregulation, and they may do some other secret rattish things with their tails to which human researchers are not yet privy. But squirrel tails are another matter altogether. For squirrels, their fluffy, swishy tails are more than pretty—they are the very heart of squirrel life, and their function is even more complex than that of the New World monkeys' prehensile tails. Here are some of the ways that a squirrel uses its tail: for balance while running; as a rudder while jumping; as a parachute; to cushion a fall (squirrels sometimes fall from great heights and then shock us by running off uninjured); for warmth (wrapped around itself like a blanket); for shade (held overhead like a parasol—the family name, Sciuridae, means "shade-tail"); as an umbrella; to swaddle young; to confound and scare off intruders; and as a surprisingly complex form of squirrel-to-squirrel communication. There is a whole repertoire of communiqués conveyed in the different twitches and swishes. I love this, that we might learn to speak Elementary Squirrel by carefully watching the quick turn and flash of the ticked fur.

Over and over, I have heard the same gut reaction to the subject of squirrels: "Squirrels are dumb." They might be jumpy, flighty, twitchy, and strange (as any of us would be if we were regular prey to larger birds and mammals that make stealth attacks from behind), but squirrels are not dumb. Colin Tudge wrote, "Arboreal life requires dexterity and hand-eye coordination. Squirrels almost became intellectuals, but not quite." Intellectuals, no. But squirrels are endowed with a strong native intelligence. In addition to tail language, they exhibit complex aural vocalizations. They possess a profound spatial memory, used to recover the nuts they bury as scatter-hoarders (the crows outsmart them here, watching as they busily pat the earth over their buried nuts, waiting till they leave, then swooping in to unbury the nut with their deft crow bills). They discover through tireless trial and error the one slender route into an attic. In spite of our best efforts to keep them from our birdfeeders, not to mention an entire commercial industry devoted to this end, they outwit us constantly, using multistep problem-solving that is beyond the capability of most mammals and probably some humans. In the face of organizations like the Squirrel Defamation Society, which promotes lethal anti-squirrel tactics beneath its banner slogan *All Squirrels Must Die,* squirrel populations continue to flourish. Watching the two squirrels that share my home and garden (whom we call Worthington and Split-Ear), I have discovered that they know things about the place I live that I don't. Secret, practical things. They know exactly which cherry limbs will support the weight of a squirrel and which won't; the quickest, most direct place from whence to leap from the cherry tree to the fence; how to utterly disappear from the fence and into the shrubbery in fewer than two seconds; the best place to hide five baby squirrels. Most wild mammals know such things, useful in the round of their everyday lives. But squirrels know other things too. They know that no matter how many times they eat all the seed in the birdfeeder, we will fill it up again. They know that as much as we wave our arms at them, we can't actually reach through the glass kitchen window. They know that we can't jump high enough to reach them if they don't want us to. And as Richard Mallery writes in *Nuts about Squirrels,* "No, they don't always remember where they buried your nuts, but they do carry little black books with your name in them. They grade you from 1 to 10. If you offered good seed with easy access, you are a 10 and listed under Easy." It is this sort of squirrel knowing that brings grown men to the limits of their sanity.

On the interwebs, you can find tutorials on lethal squirrel control, along with tips for catching the squirrels in your yard and cooking them for dinner. Recipes for squirrel stew, squirrel gumbo, and even a squirrel-melt sandwich abound, as well as recipes for other nonnative garden pests—house sparrow pie, roasted Norway rat. I personally have no interest in eating the urban creatures, but if one is a meat-eater anyway, I suppose the argument could be made that the ultra-local harvesting of nonnative animals is an improvement over meat obtained through the corporate animal-agriculture system.

I don't believe in lethal control of wild animals except as a last resort. But fully apart from my personal feelings about such things is the fact that killing urban wildlife to reduce conflict can be only a short-term solution—as with moles, gophers, and even raccoons, in suitable urban habitat, new squirrels will quickly fill the void left by those that are killed, meeting the biological carrying capacity for squirrel numbers in your yard. So unless you want to continually trap or kill squirrels year after year, remember that lethal control, except for a particular problem animal, really won't work and so is only a rather disturbing way of letting off steam. Though it is some-times difficult to remember, the squirrels are not out to get you per-sonally. They are, like all creatures in the urban landscape, including us, simply gathering food and water, taking shelter, and keeping their young safe. They are surviving — or attempting to. Most squirrels do not live one full year.

For every "I'm gonna kill that damned tree rat" comment I hear about squirrels, I hear another story, of another kind. People tell me of squirrels that they have tamed, or squirrel stories that have been passed from generation to generation. A squirrel raised by a father, or a grandfather, or a mother who kept her pet in a handkerchief-lined box. The stories are often accompanied by beloved photos, black-and-white and worn. A squirrel peeking out from the neck of a child's threadbare flannel shirt. A squirrel cradled in the crook of a freckled boy's elbow, the boy smiling in spite of Depression-era hardships. A squirrel in its basket-bed, carried everywhere by a beloved grandmother who has since passed. The fact of the animal being "wild" adds somehow to the significance of the relationship for these people as they hand down their stories of affection and connection.

Our dear friend Mike raised a wild squirrel from the time it was a naked kitten. He and his mother fed it with an eyedropper until it could eat solid food. They named the squirrel Rascal, and he lived in their house as part of the family. Mike tells about Rascal rolling on his back when they tickled his tummy, and about the squirrel's plate at the dinner table, where he would sit every evening, *on top of the table,* eating cracked corn and other treats from his own little plate while seeming to follow the dinner conversation, looking from person to person, and waiting till everyone else left the table before

If You Can't Beat 'Em...

To control squirrel destruction in the garden, it is best to take a two-pronged approach. First, cover your squirrel-loved crops with netting and your full-grown sunflower heads with translucent drawstring bags. Plant daffodil bulbs, which squirrels don't like, instead of tulips, which they do. At the same time, attempt an "if you can't beat 'em, join 'em" attitude and provide an alternative food source just for squirrels. String peanuts on wires or hang dried corncobs from a branch so they dangle a foot aboveground, just out of reach, so the squirrels have to work to acquire them. This will keep them both fed and busy (and may also keep them away from the birdfeeder), and, contrary to popular belief, it won't attract more squirrels. If there is no alternative "approved" squirrel-beloved food source, they will patiently spend their entire day, and their not inconsiderable problem-solving capacity, figuring out how to get to your birdseed and garden crops. (And they'll win.)

jumping down himself. When Mike's family moved to Oregon, his father told him that Rascal would not be able to survive in the new climate (even though he lived with them in a house), and Mike was just young enough to believe him. When Mike discovered the same species of squirrel common around his new home, he learned the real reason for abandoning Rascal: his dad didn't like the rodent climbing and destroying all the window screens. When you hear Mike tell the story, you realize he has never quite forgiven his father this betrayal.

The official advice, good advice, is to avoid feeding wild animals, and especially mammals. It makes nuisances out of individuals, often resulting in their deaths. But the impulse to feed animals, and to tame them, runs deep. How could it not? We love to get close to creatures, creatures that are wild and yet choosing to draw close to us. We love that sense of hard-won trust, of wild nearness. We can imagine that we have a way with animals, and that this particular squirrel is here for the peanut, yes, but also perhaps because it *likes* us. We find ourselves in a moment of human-animal connection that feels deep, familiar, and true. We can see the huge, liquid black eye, the hundreds of fur colors gathered on one tail, the strangely soft nails, all of it closer, all of it more detailed, more wonderful than we knew. We can gasp, wondering if that darn squirrel is going to run right up our legs.

If we want to be eco-purists, then sure—we shouldn't feed the squirrels. But what if we don't? What if we just want to be people, people who sympathize easily with other creatures and who, though we would never feed a coyote or even a raccoon, just can't convince ourselves that any harm could really come from feeding a squirrel? Well, then, at least be careful. Squirrels are not myopic, but like the eyes of most animals that are attacked from behind by owls or coyotes, their eyes are positioned on the sides of their head, increasing their peripheral vision. This means that while squirrels will not normally bite a human, it is hard for them to tell, at the difficult angle of a nut held in front of the nose viewed by wide-set eyes, exactly where the peanut shell ends and the peanut-shaped human finger begins. Other than trying to grab a squirrel, holding a peanut out to one is the best way to get bitten. If you just can't help feeding squirrels, lay the offering in your palm instead of holding it in your peanut-like fingers. I'm still not advocating the feeding of squirrels, I'm just saying... there is no black-and-white in the World Tree.

My squirrel confession: Even after writing all of this, even after warning against squirrel taming, squirrel feeding, and the whole finger-peanut-squirrel-peripheral-vision business, I have to admit that I tamed the squirrel that visits my study window. I opened the sash just a sliver, and over time I coaxed him into taking peanuts from my hand, beneath the window ledge, while I sat working at my desk. I excused my behavior in the name of research for this manuscript, yes, but also because I had become increasingly fond of my window squirrel, who I'd inexplicably begun to call Worthington. One warm day, I had opened my windows wide for the breeze, and I entered my study to find Worthington sitting on my desk eating peanuts from the bowl I kept there: urban-wild research gone too far.

As we make our daily lives in the World Tree, squirrels throw us a tangled challenge. Of the two of us, squirrel and human, we are the species with the capacity to truly choose how we will behave. How well can we do? How gracious can we be? Surely *gracious* need not mean hosting squirrels in the attic, but it does mean figuring out what to do when they are there. It means finding our way and creating our best place in the community of beings within these confounding, semipermeable boundaries.

This morning, two squirrels ran right over my bare toes. This is our deepest fear about small rodents that we see in or around our homes, isn't it? That they will somehow end up on our toes? I'd gone out to feed the chickens in the early light, and at a crossroads in the garden path, the squirrels flew by in a hot chase that left them oblivious to my presence, and scrambled like lightning over my flip-flopped feet, leaving the tiniest white marks from their nails and shocking all three of us into frozen silence. Instead of running away after recovering from their fright, the squirrels quietly began to explore the garden edges, forgetting the chase altogether. In the

Urban-Wildlife Syndrome

Squirrels are the most accessible and easily observed creature of all mammalian urban wildlife, so they have been studied extensively for their response to urbanization—or synurbanization, the process by which a species becomes adapted to an urban environment. Lafayette Park in our nation's capital may also be the squirrel capital of North America. Hundreds of squirrels are fed daily by federal employees with government lunch hours. It's entertainment for the workers and a kind of restorative connection in a stressful place. Studies of squirrels at Lafayette and other city parks form the foundation of what some wildlife biologists have begun referring to as urban-wildlife syndrome, a complex of behaviors exhibited by a population of wild animals in response to urban living and characterized by three interrelated elements:

Increased density. The population density, or the number of individuals of a specific species in a given place, is normally determined by the usual ecological factors: suitable habitat, which includes food, shelter, and water. In urban squirrels, population density is not closely related to the amount of suitable natural habitat available. Given the loss of trees in urban landscapes, there should be far fewer squirrels than there actually are, but instead, squirrel density in the urbs and suburbs is higher than in most rural/wild places. This is possible because the natural food sources are supplemented so heavily by humans—we toss peanuts, provide birdfeeders, and generally leave squirrel-food refuse about while providing warm, sheltered nest areas in the shape of street trees and attics.

Decreased wariness. Animals in urban habitats are more accustomed to, and less wary of, the presence of humans and some other mammals, such as cats and dogs. One of the reasons is obvious—there are lots of humans among the squirrels as they go about their squirrel days, and so they simply become used to us. The other reason has to do with the social complexity of squirrels and some other urban animals. When there are so many squirrels in one place, there are more individuals to act as sentinels, sending up the familiar squirrel chatter when something, such as an unsettling human presence, is noticed. The squirrels go about their lives feeling more at ease, since they know that if something is amiss, they'll hear of it.

More intraspecific aggression. Urban squirrels fight more. While the role of chasing in squirrel society is not fully understood, one of the functions is exactly what it appears to be—the routing of an unwanted squirrel in a place/tree/general territory that another squirrel considers to be its own. With more density, this appears to be unavoidable, and while some aspects of the urban-wildlife syndrome may make urban living more comfortable, the proximity of so many other creatures can also be stressful and detrimental. Young animals, in particular, are subject to chasing and aggression from older animals that have claimed certain places as their own.

Urban-wildlife syndrome appears to exist across taxa, and animals as diverse as mice, blackbirds, raccoons, and coyotes all seem to simultaneously benefit and suffer from its effects. We are called to reevaluate our own role in this system—does human presence restore or deplete, benefit or harm? As with all questions regarding urban wildlife, there is no one clear answer. When we add food into the system, we create an uncertain tangle of benefits and conflict. And while we might have known about the conflicts between humans and animals that feeding can bring, we now have to think as well about how it interrupts the relationships between the animals themselves.

coop, the chickens were pecking at the new hen we introduced into the flock. There was a partially white starling in the front yard (rare!), and the neighborhood crows, who do not tolerate aberrance even in another species, were dive-bombing it mercilessly. Down by the green space at the edge of the neighborhood, folks have been seeing and hearing coyotes, and the electrical poles are nearly covered with missing-cat posters. Out in the garden, there are tiny tooth marks in the two measly pumpkins I managed to grow this rainy summer. I look again at my white-scritched toes and remember: This is it. This *is* the connection I seek, the movement, the creation, the re-creation. This is the peaceable kingdom — gorgeous, complicated, wild. This is the World Tree, the only one there is. And sometimes in my own human confusion, I envy the squirrel her running up and down again, her easy, intimate conversation with this knotted, messy, perfect tree.

Black Bear and Cougar
The Big Wild

Let's see who won the Friday sweepstakes," *Brian calls as he leashes* Timber, a bouncing young yellow Lab. I had driven ninety minutes north of Seattle to meet predator biologist Brian Kertson at his home in a new subdivision on the edge of the Cascade Mountains. Before heading off in his pickup to search for signals from radio-collared cougars, we have to take his dog for a walk. "Friday sweepstakes?" "Yeah. It's garbage day — that means everyone took their bins out last night. I like to walk around on Friday and see how many of them were pushed over by bears. Those are the winners." Brian grins.*

Garbage rummaging is one of the chief complaints about black

---

* *Kertson likes to point out that, unlike a real sweepstakes, the winners here are not random — they are drawn entirely from people who, even though they know bears are around, drag their trash to the curb at night instead of waiting for morning.*

bears that Brian fields in his state fish and wildlife office. His advice shoots straight: If you move to bear country, there will be bears. If you don't want them to raid your birdfeeder, then take it down. If you don't want them to get into the garbage, then chain it up. Brian gets frequent callbacks:

"I did what you said, I put a bungee cord on the can, and bears still got into it."

"Bungee cord? You need a chain with a lock. It's a bear."

"But I —"

"It's a *bear.*"

An hour later, we're zigzagging the off-roads in Brian's Ford F-150. Just as I'm getting ready to confess my carsickness and ask him to pull over, the radio monitor picks up a weak signal. We turn onto a narrow dirt road. Behind us is a long drive leading to a freshly built mansion on acreage. Ahead is a wide grassy field edged by conifers and laced with flowering chicory. George Emerson might plunge through these grasses in *A Room with a View* and take young Lucy Honeychurch in his arms; I can see why someone would want to build a house here. Brian lifts his receiver overhead, and the beeping signal gains in strength. "This is a young male," Brian tells me. "He strayed into town once, and so I trapped and collared him; I'm keeping my eye on him. I'm hoping he stays out of trouble." Brian conjectures that the cougar is within six hundred yards. We turn to contemplate the idyllic setting behind us, a little wine-ready bistro table set up at the edge of the huge lawn overlooking the field. In the pasture behind the house is a paddock. "Those are thirty-thousand-dollar horses," Brian says, speculating on the thoroughbreds. "Recipe for disaster. People move in here, loose their horses, and freak out when they find out there are cougars." That suburban castle?

"Dude," says Brian, "it's in big wildlife habitat." He suggests that every real estate listing in the area should include this disclosure: *Stunning view. Granite countertops. Situated in picturesque bear-and-cougar country.*

In a way, it's squirrels and coyotes all over again, but with higher stakes on all sides. These are animals that typically avoid us but, when it comes down to a close encounter, could kill us. And if, because of human feeding or habitat loss, they become emboldened or confused enough to wander among us? Well, this is the line, isn't it? No matter how much we love these animals, we can't share a sidewalk with them. A human-habituated squirrel is just an annoying rodent. But a human-habituated bear? It's not for nothing that the wildlife officials tell us "a fed bear is a dead bear." Two years ago, a city councilman was visiting his cabin in the Cascade foothills and was mauled by a bear, an adult female that was accustomed to being fed by humans. The councilman was critically injured, but he lived, and the bear was shot, a story that is repeated across the country year after year. No matter how much it belies common sense, black bears in campgrounds and around summer cabins are often fed by hand. It's come to the point that while people are instructed to face a cougar by standing up tall and yelling, "Bad cougar, go away," they are told to chase bears away without actually saying *bear*, a word the animals might have learned to associate with food, as in "Here, bear, here, bear, have this sandwich."

Bears will eat sandwiches. But most of the black bear's diet consists of berries, nuts, roots, fruits, and flowers. They love insects and will raid anthills and beehives (like Winnie-the-Pooh, they can sniff out honey, but unlike Pooh, they prefer the larvae within). Black bears are much smaller than grizzlies, with a typical adult female weighing about 160 pounds, a male about 250, and both standing up to six feet tall. Though we think of them as hibernators, black bears fall into more of an extended torpor than a true hibernation. They den up and take a "long winter's nap" for five or six months, starting in the late fall, and while they won't eat, drink, urinate, or defecate during this time (keeping the den free of odors that might attract predators — like a cougar), they *are* wake-able, and they will lift their heads for a drowsy look-about several times over the course of the winter, or even defend the den if needed. My friend Bill found a denning female in a fallen stump while out for a snowy walk at the edge of his sugaring field in Wisconsin. When the bear woke up and lifted her head to look at him, his heart stopped with that common mingling of joy and fear that we feel in the face of the wildest things. She blinked, then dropped her heavy head and went back to sleep.

Black-bear dens can be as small as garbage cans — they regularly use hollowed stumps, areas beneath fallen logs, or spaces beneath rural outbuildings. Though the bears mate in the summer, the delayed-implantation reproductive strategy allows the tiny embryo to go dormant for some months, free-floating about the uterus. When the female curls into her den and settles for the winter, the embryo will implant, after which the fetus develops rapidly, and the cub will be born in the den. One or two cubs will emerge with their mother in the spring, everyone hungry and ready to grub for food. The next winter, they'll den with her as yearlings before finding their own way in the world the following spring; females give birth every two years.

Lack of exposure to and knowledge of the wild might be one reason we do stupid things like try to feed bears, but it can't be the whole story; our reactions to other potentially dangerous wild animals — cougars, snakes, alligators — are rarely so misguided. It may have something to do with the bears' round furriness, their rolling gait, their gentle-looking faces. It may be something about their plantigrade stance, so unusual among the four-leggeds, so human-seeming, that invites us to try to reach across the divide of wildness and danger to create semirealistic stuffed bears (one of the most often stuffed animals in North America, even before Teddy Roosevelt), seeking (even longing) for a connection that is safe, and intimate, and maybe a little magical — lacking all common sense, perhaps, but alive with psychic meaning. We tuck our children in with their bears as we read them stories from *Winnie-the-Pooh*.

No one sleeps with a stuffed cougar. Who knows what might happen? Unlike berry browsing bears, these are full-on-carnivore predators. In cougars, humans across mythological time have found a fierce protector of the cosmos; we have carried fetishes in hopes that we will be imbued with the cat's hunting prowess. When the first Europeans reached the Americas in the fourteenth century, recognition of the cougar's power took a perverse turn. Many of the early explorers came from countries that were heavily settled, the large predators nearly extirpated. The European view of native cultures and wilderness influenced the pattern of settlement and the relationship to the wild, where it was considered a moral duty to civilize the "savages" as well as the land. Cougar biologist and historian Kevin Hansen suggests that a dearth of factual information led to a knowledge vacuum in which "the outrageous was accepted as true." Tales of a supernatural creature evolved, depicting the cougar as cowardly, gluttonous, devious, and brutish. "By imposing human

Bear Tracks and Lost Humans

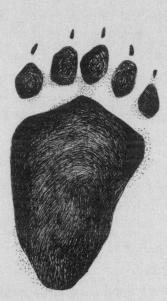

The hind-foot track of a black bear is between six and eight inches long, and it will usually register all five toes (though the last toe impression might be shallow or missing), short nail marks, and a large heel pad. For an experienced tracker, black bears are relatively easy to follow—they break twigs as they go, leaving deep tracks and great heaps of berry-filled bear scats. But a human lost in the wilderness, trackers tell me, will leave as clear a trail as a bear. Panicked, lost hikers walk fast, heavy, and cut a wide swath. Bearish.

ethics upon wild predators," writes Hansen, "it was easy to make the step from viewing them as competitors to viewing them as enemies." Cougars were eradicated with religious zeal—an attitude from which we have not fully recovered.

But for many, cougars and bears evoke the wildest kind of beauty. Along with wolves, these animals embody for us the deepest nature, the most primal earth, the hidden and elemental places. Much of our human wandering in bear-and-cougar land is psychic. Remembering these wildest beings, knowing they are present and real in the wilderness beyond the sightlines of our daily lives, we gather vitality, and sustenance, and a sense of our own inner wildness. We dream of these places, the bear-and-cougar places, and when we can, we load our packs and wander their paths for a day or a week, walking with care and practical caution, with awe and love. But we know that we ultimately *return from* bear-and-cougar habitat. Home again, where there are opossums and raccoons and maybe even coyotes aplenty but where, unless something has gone terribly wrong, we're not about to spot a black bear or a cougar, or even see a sign of their presence. And for those of us in larger towns and cities, this sense of home is essentially true. But as sufficiently expansive tracts of wild habitat become less common, the big wild — beautiful, loved, desired, feared — is becoming increasingly confounded.

Bears require large home ranges, about fifteen thousand acres. Cougars require *enormous* home ranges, about two hundred thousand acres, or a hundred square miles for a male. Tracts that big are getting scarce, and those that do exist are bisected by roads, sometimes even highways. Only rarely do cougars and bears wander into dense urban places, and then it is usually by accident. But as suburbs cut into remaining wild lands, humans in these semiwooded places begin to encounter the big wild more regularly. Bears are opportunistic, and a little lazy. If there's a fish or fruit pie in a trash bin with an ill-fitting lid? That's a no-brainer. Black bears also possess a singular inquisitiveness that sometimes entices them into our paths. Wildlife researcher Ellis Bacon suggests that we need to take this into account in wild-bear management, to remember that actions perceived as aggressive in black bears by humans might just be the bears' high native curiosity. With our focus on visual learning, humans forget that other species may emphasize different senses; bears explore novel objects by turning them over and over in their paws (much like parrot-family birds, as well as baby humans) and by mouthing them. Exploratory pawing and mouthing by something as big and strong and toothed as a bear can be destructive without being hostile. When bears maul a mailbox or peek into car windows, they might not be acting aggressively; they might just be curious about what's going on inside.

Cougars, though, are different. They have always avoided humans. Brian Kertson tells me that there is no way cougars will turn into the "next coyote," adapting to a denser urban environment and eating neighborhood cats. "People keep saying that cougars are losing their fear of humans, and pretty soon they'll start preying on us," he tells me. "That's bullshit. Cougars have never been afraid of humans. But they *avoid* humans. They make a living off of not being seen." He's picked up signals from collared cougars within about 550 yards of human homes thousands of times, but Brian believes that none of these cats have been spotted by the homeowners. Different from bears, the cats are timid, elusive, present in far fewer numbers, rare in every sense. They are seldom seen. This has always added to their sense of mystique and to the irrational fear they sometimes inspire. "We don't understand what we don't see and imagine cougars are hiding behind trees, waiting to pounce on our kids," Kertson says. "Trust me, if cougars wanted to eat people, there would be a lot more dead people."

What *is* happening? Young cougars, especially young males like the one Brian and I were tracking, are seeking enough space for their own home territory after they are chased off their natal turf by established males. As contiguous cougar habitat becomes scarce, these young cats find nowhere to settle, and they wander into the "human matrix," the semirural/suburban neighborhoods that are on the edge of viable habitat. Cougars prefer venison, Kertson tells me, but they are not above opportunism. You won't find them nosing in a trash can, but fresh fenced goat or sheep? "For a cougar, that's like McDonald's. Wild is better, but sometimes you just want the calories."

We know that cougars do attack and kill people, but it is exceedingly rare, which, as Kertson points out, is not because they don't have the opportunity. Some researchers speculate that cougars do not normally recognize us as prey; their "search image" for prey is a four-legged animal, typically an ungulate. The most common cougar attacks on humans involve runners or children. It is possible that in addition to provoking a chase response, the running posture, more hunched than walking, better matches the cougar's search image, as do children, being smaller and closer to the ground. The worst thing a runner can do in cougar country, if this theory is correct, is bend down and tie her shoe.

In the wild, cougars have few predators. Some are killed by other cougars (established territorial males are a threat to younger males who are seeking territory). Females have sole care of the young and protect the kits from aggressive males, though some of

Cougars Tracking the Country

Cougar tracks are large and soft, and evoke the vivid presence of an animal most of us will never see. The historic range of the cougar is huge—from southern Canada to the tip of South America and across all of the United States. Roaming across cultural and linguistic borders, this one species, *Puma concolor*, is also called mountain lion, puma, panther, and catamount. (Black panther is not a species but a colloquial name for any individual big cat that happens to be all black, the result of an uncommon mutation where extra melanin produces darker fur.) Habitat loss, subsequent reduction in ungulate prey, and, especially, "predator control" led to the extirpation of cougars in the East by the turn of the twentieth century; remaining animals found refuge in the western wilds. But in recent decades, cougars have been finding a slender foothold in the prairie states, the Dakotas, the Midwest, and even the Northeast. There have been thousands of sightings, most of which are erroneous. (Reports of cougars usually turn out to be dogs, house cats, deer, bobcats, or some other wild animal—this is actually just as true in the West, where there really are cougars. We make up far more cougars than we see.) Researchers require tangible evidence to accept an east-of-the-Rockies cougar sighting as valid, such as DNA-tested scat or fur, a clear photograph, or the body of the animal itself. Small breeding populations are established in the Badlands of North Dakota and Nebraska, and there are confirmed sightings across the map. In June 2011, a cougar was killed on a Connecticut highway, just seventy miles from New York City! Now that the white-tailed deer conservation has led to an overabundance of the cougar's historical East Coast prey, it will be a matter of human tolerance, habitat conservation, and a measure of luck in combination that will determine whether cougars can return in healthy populations to their historical range.

the young are still killed, either by these male cougars or by dogs. Humans and human activities are the main source of cougar mortality. When Kertson and his colleagues radio-collar a cougar, the collar is joined by a leather spacer that will, in time, wear off. But in Brian's studies, nearly all of the cougars die before that happens. They may be hunted by humans (legally or not); be killed by fish and wildlife officials in response to human cougar conflict; may contract feline leukemia by consuming infected feral domestic cats; or may get hit by cars. One cougar researcher calls highways "the most efficient wildlife slaughtering mechanisms ever devised."

Bears, too, have few nonhuman predators. Grizzlies and black bears sometimes come into conflict with each other, and cougars, bobcats, and coyotes will sometimes attack bear cubs if they get the chance. About fifty thousand black bears are killed yearly in the United States by hunters. A recent study by the Wildlife Conservation Society shows that urban black bears living at the edge of suburbs and gathering much of their food there by gleaning human garbage have a higher mortality rate and shorter lives than bears that stay in the hills. Lead author Jon Beckmann calls urban areas the ultimate bear trap. "Because of an abundant food source — namely garbage — bears are being drawn in from the backcountry into urbanized landscapes where they meet their demise." (Note that the word *urban* is used here in the ecological sense and indicates any place populated by humans. Confused young bears occasionally wander into dense urban centers, but this study refers to the suburban and exurban places where bears are becoming more common.) In this study, twelve female bears living in urban areas around Lake Tahoe were tracked for ten years, as were ten female bears that lived in sparsely populated outlying areas. Certain results were predictable, but their extent was surprising: urban bears, who feasted on garbage, weighed 30 percent more than their human-avoiding counterparts. The increased weight brought on earlier sexual maturity, and urban bears gave birth when they were just four or five years old, rather than the typical seven or eight. A couple of the bears were only two or three when they reproduced. The urban bears also died younger. Every urban bear in the study was dead before she was ten years old, all of them hit by cars. The study terminated with the death of the last urban bear, at which time six of the wilder bears were still alive. Extrapolating beyond the study site, the researchers suggest a seventeen-fold increase in bear deaths due to auto collisions in the past twenty years. Urban places are functioning as ecological sinks for black bears — "drawing in bears from outlying wild areas, where they ultimately die."

What are we to do? Kertson tells me that the only sure way for humans to avoid being harmed by bears or cougars that live nearby is to kill them. But, he asks, "Is this who we want to be?" The challenges of today's new nature are different and more difficult than ever before, but they are not impossible to navigate. We have entered a time when the continued presence of the big wild, something that ought to be a given, is instead a human choice, and one that will demand of us some uneasiness, uncertainty, and even risk. But it is possible to wield our overarching presence lightly, humbly, and with gratitude for the continued existence of the big wild. In his refreshingly straightforward way, Brian says, "It's not cold fusion. Humans have been living alongside these animals forever." In the places we already live, the steps are simple and practical — manage our food wastes, practice good husbandry to protect our pets and farm animals, and, for God's sake, don't feed the bears. If we choose to live in bear-and-cougar country, then we have to be prepared to witness these animals, to act from knowledge instead of hype and fear, to help our neighbors do the same. And in the future? "We have to think about how we distribute humans," says Brian, provocatively applying the language of wildlife management to our own species. Humans clustering in well-planned towns and cities allows the wildest creatures their space. The peaceable kingdom of the urban bestiary has nothing to do with lions lying down with lambs. It is about all of us lying down right where we are supposed to be.

Close Encounters

Unless a black bear is human-habituated and associates humans with food handouts, it will avoid people. And while black bears tend to be shy and gentle, they are still big, strong creatures that can be dangerous if not treated respectfully. If you see a bear in your yard, stay inside. If you see a black bear while out wandering, pause and gauge the situation. If the bear is some distance away or appears to be unaware of you, then just leave quietly. Keep an eye on the bear as you leave. If the bear seems interested in you or begins to walk toward you, then identify yourself as human by standing tall, waving your hands over your head, and talking to it in a low voice. Try not to use the word *bear*, which it may associate with food. If the bear continues to approach you, try to scare it away by clapping your hands, yelling, or banging things together. The more persistent the bear, the more aggressive you have to be. Never run from a bear, unless you are sure you can reach safety very quickly—they can run thirty-five miles an hour.

If you somehow end up face to face with a cougar, you have likely come upon the cat unawares; your goal is to help the cougar do what it wants to do—get away from you. Cougars have a strong chase instinct, so don't run. Pick up children, face the animal, and try to make yourself seem bigger than the cougar by raising your arms or getting up on a rock or stump. If you can, back away slowly while speaking in a low, firm voice. An aggressive cougar will lay its ears back, bare its teeth, twitch its tail, and rock on its hind feet as if readying to jump. In such cases, you want the cougar to understand that you are not prey. Be bolder—yell, wave your arms, throw anything you have. Do not crouch or hide. Never corner a cougar, and leave it every possible escape route. If you glimpse a cougar from a safe distance, count your blessings—even experienced outdoors people who regularly explore areas populated by cougars go a lifetime without seeing one (I'm still hoping...).

PART III

The Feathered

Bird

The Enlivened City

At the beginning of time, the bird spirits Ara and Irik floated upon a world made only of water, and through these birds, into the sea, there came forth two eggs. Ara crushed one egg with her slender foot to release the sky. Irik crushed the other to unfurl the earth. Just as the birds we see today are busy about their nests, Ara and Irik fussed over this new earth, picking at it with their delicate bills, shaping bits of twig and soil into the first people. The people were beautiful but arid and inert until the birds roused them to life with their cries.

Like the first people in this lovely myth from the Ibans of Borneo, we are called into life by the birds among us. In the eighth century, the bishop of Lyon proclaimed that animals could not go to heaven because they did not contribute to the Catholic Church's coffers. Poet-novelist Jim Harrison declares this attitude "ghastly" as he points out that "at the same time they all decided that hell was a place without birds." Birds form a thread through our daily lives, almost without our knowing it. Recently I resolved to take one full day and pay attention to the presence of birds in the round of my activities. I have been a student of birdlife for decades, and I always notice birds, but on this day I wanted to pay special attention — to notice my noticing. There was the expected: Crows awakened me, robins and starlings argued over the ripening cherries in our back-yard tree, a black-capped chickadee fed at the tiny window feeder just inches from my face as I worked on this chapter, and spotted baby robins bathed at the edge of our garden pond. There was the unexpected: an Anna's hummingbird flew straight through an open window and into my kitchen, hovered there like a faerie apparition about six inches beyond the frame, then, thank goodness, flew back out again. There was the bizarre: Checking on what I thought was a house sparrow's nest tucked into our gas stove's vent, I stood on my tiptoes, stretched my arms up to feel for the baby birds, and instead felt a cold lump of feathers. Not good. I called Tom to come and reach it for me, and he pulled out a dead, fully grown Bewick's wren, desiccated and perfect — a mystery I'm still pondering (meanwhile, I set the bird up on the kitchen windowsill, where its blank little eyes watch me make dinner). I would normally see and pay attention to each of these small avian visitations, both the living and the dead, but making it a point to watch them throughout one day reminded me that awareness of birds offers a constant source of connection to the ever-present wild. There is a trail of birdlife among us, a story told in feather, nest, egg, song, and flight. Birds are liaisons from earth to sky, from the distractions of a technologically mediated life to the immediacy of nature. From the separation of these worlds to the realization that we can walk well in both.

This chapter is an anomaly in *The Urban Bestiary;* whereas most chapters consider a particular species, this one focuses on birds generally. Birds are by far the most common vertebrate wildlife we see in the places we live, whether we are urban, suburban, or rural dwellers. There are nearly a thousand bird species in North America, and of these, hundreds are possible in towns and cities. (Recall the Bestiary's Bestiary at the start of this book; while writing, I observed only one wild terrestrial mammal but forty-eight species of bird.) I am able to treat just a few individual species at length in the scope of this book, but there remains much to consider regarding the birdlife among us as a whole — their language, identification, life habits. Birds are not just the most numerous wild things among us, but also the most lively and most easily observable. It is thrilling and essential to think about the unseen coyotes in our midst, but it is birds that we see every day, that call us into enlivened participation with everyday nature.

Most people today can't identify many birds, not even the most common backyard species. But our easy attentiveness to birds, no matter how unnurtured that attention is, is a natural one. The flash of feather, the shadow overhead, and we turn, however briefly, however unknowingly, to the winged one who passed over. The reasons for this are many, and intertwined.

Birds are like us. Warm-blooded, bipedal, color-visioned vertebrates. We find this wonderful.

Birds are not like us. Feathered, flying, scale-footed dinosaurs. We also find this wonderful.

Birds are beautiful. They are shining, colorful, graciously proportioned beings that daily perform an act that lies beyond every human body but inheres in every human imagination—flight. It is natural that we turn toward them with wonder, joy, gratitude, and a touch of envy. (A very few birds are difficult to call beautiful. While visiting Kenya, I tried, and failed, to find aesthetic pleasure in the Marabou stork, though it is graceful in flight. Surely the flaw is in my own perception.)

Most compellingly of all, **we are biologically and evolutionarily attuned to the presence of birds.** We are wired, in our innate, primal selves, to be attentive to birds' language, to enter and engage in their discourse. Birds are vigilant to our presence and movements. While we might watch birds for recreation, aesthetic delight, or scientific study, they watch us for the same reasons they watch all animals with such bright awareness—to avoid danger, and to survive. Human societies that relied on hunting had to be attuned to the haunts and ways of birds. An agitated bird will fly out of a hunter's reach or alert other quarry—another bird, or a mammal—to the hunter's presence. We humans had to know how to search out birds and how to walk among them without causing alarm. I believe we still feel and respond to this ancestral knowing in our own lazy modern bones.

Attuning to urban birds reframes the bird-watching endeavor. We think of birding as something that requires a bit of planning, effort, and knowledge—carrying binoculars to some pretty, leafy, sun-dappled place with warblers hiding in the leaves, or waterbirds resting on the peace of a secret pond. But urban birding asks something different of us. It asks us to find the wild thing, the peaceful presence, the animal awareness, in the ordinary moments of our daily lives and places. It asks us to bridge any disconnection between home and wild nature, to accept the constant continuity with the more-than-human world that is an essential part of human life, no matter where that life is lived. There is certainly not as much avian biodiversity in urban places — the majority of bird species are habitat-sensitive and cannot live in a city at all. But among the species that can thrive in cities, individual numbers of birds are often very high; these birds are accustomed to human presence and can be more approachable than those in untrammeled environs. Here, we can invite the birds into our yards and onto our window boxes with food that we buy at the grocery store. We can draw near, watch for hours. Humans have never lived in closer proximity to birds than we do now, in cities.

It is odd that this is so. The anxieties of living in the city, one might think, would make birds even more wary. The strains of urban bird life are real — stress from noise, humans, habitat degradation, cars, light pollution, and as many predators in the form of cats, dogs, raccoons, and crows as in any supposed wilder place.* How can they handle it?

Studies comparing various urban and rural bird populations teach us that, in general, urban birds exhibit a syndrome of interrelated characteristics. Individuals are often slightly larger than individuals of the same species in rural places; they sing for more hours of the day (because of artificial lighting) and sing louder and at a

---

* *Curiously, an increase of predators such as raccoons and coyotes in urban environments has not resulted in a simultaneous increase in predation upon bird nests, as might be expected. Research out of Ohio suggests that this is because anthropogenic food sources provide ready sustenance for at least part of these predators' diets and decouples the long-standing connection between predator presence and nest attacks. The urban forest is a strange place in which the essential relationships are both present and active but also messed with and tangled, in ways that we are just beginning to understand.*

higher pitch (to compete with human noise); they are less afraid of approaching humans (having become habituated to their presence); and they are less stressable overall.

Wondering about the role of stress in urban animal populations, researchers at Max Planck Institute for Ornithology in Germany studied the common Eurasian blackbird (actually a thrush in the genus *Turdus,* similar to our American robin) and published their results in the journal *Ecology.* They took nestlings from urban nests and forest nests when they were just hatched and reared them in identical circumstances. At five months, eight months, and eleven months, the chicks were all subjected to the same traumatic capture and handling, and the researchers discovered that in these stressful situations, the young urban birds released less of the glucocorticoid steroid hormones associated with acute stress than the forest birds did. The implication is remarkable — it means not only that individual birds adapt to urban living but that natural selection actually creates populations adapted to stressful environments; like humans, birds exhibit classic country-mouse/city-mouse manners that are observable. The authors of the study are cautious, noting that there are other contingencies at play, but it seems that this general conclusion has merit, and it makes sense that the results might be similar for other avian species, and perhaps even mammals — including humans. Walking around the University of Washington with my friend Andrew, who lives in rural Skamokawa, Washington, I was struck when he said, rather wide-eyed and warily, "Gosh, there sure are a lot of people here." I looked around at the students coming and going and didn't see a lot of people at all. To me, though I don't think of myself as being particularly well adapted to urban life, it seemed like just a sunny day on the leafy campus. The upshot of this research for us as observers is that we can often watch birds more easily in places where they are accustomed to us, because they don't stress out and hide as quickly, or ever. This is ideal for certain aspects of study — observing avian physiology, habits throughout the day, dietary preferences, nesting, rearing of young; sketching in a field diary; doing simple experiments; making a detailed study of a particular species or even an individual bird over time.

One thing that strikes me in the typical human observation of birds is a general failure to recognize the connection of bird actions to the seasons. Most of the questions I receive about birds have to do with the seemingly insane, hormone-activated behaviors of birds in the spring: woodpeckers, especially the common urban Northern flickers, that seem to be banging the house down (actually, they're drumming, in lieu of song, in order to establish territory and connect with mates); crows dive-bombing (protecting vulnerable nests, eggs, and young from humans, dogs, and raptors); robins throwing themselves at windows (presumably mistaking the reflection for another male robin and defending its territory by fighting it off); hummingbirds flying straight up into the sky, then nose-diving at breakneck speed back down (the breeding display of the male for impressing and attracting a female mate — the species can be identified by the pattern of this display). Though the round of birdlife will vary somewhat depending on species and location, most urban birds will follow this general pattern:

Late winter and early spring will bring mating displays between the sexes and copulation. Throughout spring we'll hear the males' songs, and birds will become increasingly aggressive, industrious, and also secretive as they secure breeding territories and nest sites and begin building nests.

Birds and Lights

Birds can't see glass. Where we see a window, they see a safe, transparent passage or a habitat that looks inviting; outdoor trees and plants reflected in a window, or houseplants on the other side of a window, can look to a bird like something it might like to fly *toward*. Nighttime lighting confounds birds further, especially in cities with tall buildings, where the many surfaces reflect one another and create a maze of bewilderment. All of this confusion is heightened during migration, when birds are attempting to navigate unfamiliar terrain in huge numbers. If they don't hit windows outright, they may circle lighted buildings in confusion until they collapse from exhaustion. Audubon estimates that every year, ninety thousand birds fatally collide with buildings in New York City, and the numbers may be much higher (counts are difficult—early-morning street sweepers clear the streets of migratory-bird bodies before the rest of the city wakes up).

Both residential- and commercial-building dwellers can help provide safe passage for birds. For new construction, low-reflective glass or pattern-imprinted glass is available. For existing windows, a pattern laid across the pane is most effective—strips of paper, polka-dot decals, painted zigzag stripes, whatever you like. The key is an overall pattern that is easy for birds to quickly perceive and avoid. Those popular hawk silhouettes are not effective on their own (they don't really scare birds), but a bunch of them arranged in a pattern across the glass will help. Many businesses are joining in the national Lights Out campaign, keeping building lights off from dusk to dawn, especially during migration times. Apartment dwellers can encourage the same throughout their buildings.

As the young are born in late spring and early summer, birds become highly protective—small birds like warblers hide out in silence; larger birds like robins, jays, and crows vigorously defend their nests against other birds and perceived threats.

The young emerge into a period of tremendous frailty; many will die from exposure, starvation, parasites, cars, and cats. Those that grow and fledge will be begging boisterously throughout the summer, following the adults and also finding their own wings, their own lives. It is a beautiful time for observation in the bird year.

Come fall and winter, the family groups will break down and open up. Birds might form communal foraging groups, and many species will start gathering into the flocks that provide both communication and protection during the winter months.

As I write this day in July, the neighborhood young of the year are out of the nest, grown to full or nearly full size but still begging from the adults. They are naive and quiet, unafraid. I can hardly keep my eyes on my written words as a young chickadee quakes in the begging posture. But then, why would I? Stopping, I pick up the binoculars and watch. This is all that is asked of us, isn't it? Just to stop and see sometimes. We go back to our work enlivened, enlightened, and more deeply embodied in our own wild lives.

Without knowing the name of a single bird, we can enter this enlivened bird city. We think of bird language in terms of their vocalizations. We know that each species has a particular song that is sung mainly by the male during the territorial breeding season, and we know that although a few people are very good at identifying birdsong, the vast majority of humans, visual-knowers that we are, are not. When birding by ear is taught, it usually involves memorizing song after song, a dubious process, to be sure. But the good news is that we do not really have to identify a birdsong to species in order to enter the discourse of birds, and in fact, by loosening the focus on identifying individual songs, we can learn a great deal

Spring Woodpecker Drumming

The wonderful desert-nature writer Ellen Meloy wrote, shortly before her death, about a flicker that had been incessantly drumming her house. She had named him Stalin, and one morning she found him trapped in her screened porch. "I feel wicked," she wrote. "Stalin, you ignorant slut. You are trapped. This bird batters the nest of our resident phoebes. He drills the house as if it were a giant sugar cube. He could peck away until only a roof on sticks remained. Or I could let him die here." I love it when nature writers show malice toward wildlife—it makes them seem more human.

Every spring I hear from friends who want to know what they can do about their own nemesis—the woodpecker that is maniacally drumming the house at all hours, almost always the Northern flicker, the most common urban-suburban woodpecker. They are beautiful fawn-colored birds with black spots, longish bills, and pretty, dolphin-like faces. Unlike many birds, woodpeckers don't sing—instead, they drum to attract a mate in spring and to proclaim a territory. They rap their bills repeatedly and rhythmically on whatever surface provides the loudest noise—they love metal drainpipes, electrical transformers, and the most resonant parts of our houses. They drive many people completely nuts.

Remember that the flickers' goal is not to destroy your house; they just have a hormone-driven need to make noise this time of year. To deter them, you can tack a simple length of cloth over the flickers' favored drumming places. Birds don't like things that move randomly, so a wind sock or a trash bag cut into streamers and hung near the flickers' favorite spot will help discourage them. My own tactic: I run outside waving a broom and yelling, "Bad woodpecker! Go away!"

You can also try a gentle attitude shift. Woodpecker drumming usually doesn't hurt anything (besides one's nerves—oh, and of course, there's the small matter of the 1995 space-shuttle mission that was delayed when flickers tapped six little holes in the *Discovery*'s external fuel tank). If flickers really are drilling holes into your house, they may be seeking food rather than noise, or they may have discovered soft wood in which to excavate a nest hole. In such matters, they rarely err—check for termites, carpenter ants, or wood rot.

But overall, these woodpecker rhythms are heralding the season of light and fertility, and the noise is temporary (once they get into nesting, they stop drumming). We can try to relax and celebrate the role that our households play in the cycles of nature. Think of the unseen cavity nest full of fluffy little woodpecker babies that will be helped into existence by the resonant capacities of our very own dwellings.

more about what birds are saying and how their language responds to our presence.

Most of the bird conversations we hear daily are the songs, calls, and chatter of the passerines, colloquially called the perching birds or, even more colloquially, the songbirds. This is the large order of birds that evolved for life in the trees, and it encompasses everything from crows to bushtits, including the swallows, thrushes, blackbirds, chickadees, kinglets, wrens, warblers, and many others. In spite of the great variety of passerine species, all of them share basic physical adaptations. Three toes point forward and one back, and the toe-nails are long and pointed for perching and grasping tree limbs. There is an automatic clutching mechanism in the feet that keeps them wrapped securely around branches, even during sleep. Most passerines are good flyers with nine or ten primary feathers, and many, like the warblers that live in Central and South America but breed here in North America, migrate long distances. There are a few passerines that do not sing, among them the corvids — the crows, jays, and ravens. These birds have a highly complex vocal repertoire that they deploy year-round, but they do not have a sea-sonal song. And though there are other sorts of birds populating the urban landscape — gulls, woodpeckers, pigeons, hawks, ducks — the songbirds are the ones we most often see and hear in the trees on our walks; these are the birds that most often alert us to what other birds and animals are doing, the little bird that tells us the secret news. Entering into avian discourse through attention to the passer-ines is a lovely occupation, accessible to all of us, every day. Bird lan-guage is complicated, but as Wilderness Awareness School founder Jon Young explains in his book *What the Robin Knows,* there are basics of vocalizations that, with practice, are relatively easy to tease out:

1. **The seasonal song.** This is an often complex and sometimes very beautiful song, normally sung by the male during the mating/ breeding season to attract a mate, defend a territory, and continue to

claim territory during the nesting/rearing of young. Some think that birds also sing when they are happy, or because they just like to sing. These songs are unique to species, and a practiced ear can tell what bird is singing, even if it is hidden in a leafy spring forest.

2. **Contact calls,** or what I like to call chatter. This is the moment-to-moment communication we hear among birds, both male and female, in flight, while feeding, and in the other activities of the bird day. We pass through all this chatter daily, and if we listen, we will hear that it sometimes changes because of our presence.

3. **Juvenile begging.** If you have ever lived near crows in the summer, you have heard this vocalization. It is a long-drawn-out somewhat annoying sound, often accompanied by a hunched, wing-shivering posture. Some people have a very maternal response to this sound, even when it comes from crows. It is part of the background sound of summer birdlife.

4. **Alarm calls.** These are vocally charged calls in response to a perceived danger. Their pitch and intensity carries beyond the normal baseline bird talk. Alarm calls often signify the presence of a raptor or other predator, and following them can lead to all manner of urban-wild encounters.

Aggression between birds can also be physical, with a little chest-fluffing and posturing, and is almost always symbolic. It's in everyone's best interest to avoid a fight.

This may all seem like common sense, but until it is laid out in this way, most of us just lump bird vocalizations into a kind of ambient sound, or something pretty and cheering to hear. With just a little attention to nuance, we enter a whole new way of knowing. We find that we are walking not just through movement and sound but through an unfolding story, and we begin to inhabit this story ourselves — to hold one end of this thread that weaves between the birds' lives and our own.

Along with these vocal clues, birds employ a physical language understood among themselves and other animals. A single bird's response to disturbance can resonate far beyond the location of the bird itself, creating a ripple of alarm among nearby creatures. When a person (or a fox or a cat or a raccoon) steps oblivious into a natural area, walking heedlessly, perhaps chatting with a friend, he unwittingly creates what Jon Young aptly calls a bird plow: the birds in his path will fly up and away and lapse into hushed silence; their flight will signal other birds and animals to get out of the area as well. This avian response to human presence seems so normal, and happens so often, that we've come to believe it's just what birds *do*. We hardly attribute their flying away to our own bungling selves.

But Young and I discussed the curious reversal of the bird blow in urban places. The birds that are resident in cities are so used to people moving quickly and noisily and fiddling with their phones that they hardly take note of us. If you want to freak out an urban bird, try silently stalking around the sidewalk! I see this in my own backyard, where the resident birds are accustomed to my family's habits, and to those of our cat. If Delilah is lying about or wandering around the lawn sniffing into the sun, as cats do, the birds take note but keep on with their lives; if she starts crouching and sneaking, the birds sense it right away and fly to a higher perch. (For the protection of birds, Delilah is officially an indoor cat, but she is allowed to sit in the backyard when someone is there to watch her.) If I amble out to sit beneath the wax myrtle with a book of poetry and a glass of lemonade, the chickadees go about their business. If I tiptoe out, they go silent. The goal for an urban birdwatcher is to be calmly natural, not furtive. Some sensitive species always worry over human presence, but if we walk peacefully, mindfully, and in a manner appropriate to the place, then our path—whether it leads through a forest of native trees or the disturbed wilds of an urban neighborhood—will remain alive with birds living in fullness and activity, alert but unafraid.

While we don't *need* to know the names of bird species, it is gratifying to know those of the birds that live near to us, to know, with Hamlet, a "hawk from a handsaw." Thoreau wrote, "When I know the name of a creature, I find it difficult to see." This is a pretty, poetic notion—that we can see more, discover more, when our experience of a creature is unmediated by the intellectual dimension of the human mind. But I have never found it to be true (and it is a touch disingenuous coming from Thoreau, who knew well the name of every bird and obsessively learned the scientific name of every organism in his wood). Certainly I've been annoyed on birding trips where every participant's goal seemed to be to name faster than anyone else anything that moved. But when I see a glimpse of yellow-edged fawn-brown tail feathers, and *cedar waxwing* comes involuntarily to my lips, I feel a peaceful intimacy. I believe it is an act of neighborliness, of politeness, of basic goodwill, of intellectual hospitality to learn about the birds around us, beginning with their names. This bird before me becomes not just *a* bird, but a particular bird—a yellow warbler, a hermit thrush, a rufous hummingbird—and its presence (or absence) on the electrical wire above my sidewalk speaks to many things:

Identifying Birds

It takes practice to identify birds, but it gets easier as you go. With vision as the dominant human sense, we tend to focus on a bird's color, which is not always the best place to start. People always wonder if crows are related to blackbirds, the sole connection being that they are both black. But look at the two birds' beaks: the blackbird's is long and lovely, with sharp, curving sides characteristic of its family, the icterids, which includes the orioles. One day, a woman I'd never met contacted me about a bird she'd seen. It was a Blackburnian warbler, she told me with an infectious enthusiasm, and she knew it would be of interest since she could see in the field guide that it was an East Coast bird, and here we were in Seattle. I asked her a few questions and guided her to the black-headed grosbeak farther back in the passerine section of her book, a bird that, besides having the same bright orange and black coloring, bears little resemblance to the Blackburnian. Yes, she admitted with good humor, this was the bird. Color is one thing to take into account, but if you are not sure what a bird is, paging through the entire field guide looking for a color match can be rough going. Instead, look at the size of your bird (compare it to a robin), the structure of the bill, the shape of the body, their proportions to one another. See if you can discover what sort of bird it is generally—finch, warbler, woodpecker, duck—and start there in the field guide. If there is a bird in front of you, try not to reach for the field guide too quickly. A mycologist has the luxury of holding a book up and keying out his fungal quarry for hours at a time, and my geologist friend likes to remind me that he can spend thousands of years studying a formation without its changing much, but birds can fly. Seize the moment to take in everything you can about the bird's physical shape and the uniqueness of its topography: Are there wingbars, eye rings? Is the tail long? Is the bill heavy or slender? Have you seen everything, and is the bird still there? Then make a simple sketch, either in your notebook or in your head. Still there? Well, then you can choose between enjoying it further or finally turning to the guide. Eventually, you will know the birds, not through the

effort of identifying each one, but in the sweetest way, by *just knowing*—
seeing a bird from afar and knowing it like you know the shape and way
and walk of a friend in the distance before you can see her face. There is a
singular comfort in this knowing, a sense of shared belonging.

evolution, habitat, communication, migration. As an *it,* this is just a
bird; as a dark-eyed junco, it is a whole world.

Birders, from attentive backyard birders to regional experts,
know pretty much every bird they are likely to see around the places
that they live. For everyone else, learning even the common birds
can seem overwhelming, even impossible. But it's not. First, arm
yourself with a good field guide (and, if possible, a knowledgeable
friend), and take some time to learn the five most common birds
around your home. I cannot tell you what these are, as they will
vary geographically, but in urban places, they are likely to include

To Feed or Not to Feed

Birdfeeders encourage study and observation that has precious value, but the decision to feed or not to feed is more complex than it seems on the surface. Some things to consider before setting up a birdfeeding station:

1. Birdfeeders need to be kept scrupulously clean, or the birds that visit them can get very sick. It is not uncommon to see finches with growths on their eyelids (a kind of avian conjunctivitis that leads to blindness and possibly death); sociable birds such as finches and siskins that gather readily at feeders are particularly susceptible to communicable diseases spread at feeders through feces.

2. The pesticides used on commercial birdseed may be harmful to birds. Since the sunflower and millet used in birdseed is not a human food crop, the regulation of pesticide use is lax.

3. Feeding birds attracts alleged vermin. The inexpensive seed we buy at the hardware store is full of filler in the form of millet that most birds toss away as they try to get to the good stuff—the larger sunflower and other seeds or nuts in the feed. The throwaway seed on the ground (as well as the seed in the feeders) draws rats, mice, squirrels, raccoons, starlings, house sparrows, and pigeons.

4. Birdfeeders attract predators who want to eat little birds. Cats and sharp-shinned hawks make them regular hangouts.

5. Birdseed is expensive. The typical birdfeeding household spends over $100 a year on seed. Birds are just as happy with natural birdfeeders in the form of garden sunflowers, fennel gone to seed, and especially native plants and trees that provide flowers, fruits, and seeds evolutionarily suited to local birdlife.

Taking all this into account, I have struck a compromise by keeping just three small feeders attached to my study window by suction cups: a hummingbird feeder, a sunflower seed feeder, and a recently added suet feeder (which draws several species that weren't attracted by the seed feeder, including bushtits, woodpeckers, and various warblers). I can fill the feeders easily just by reaching out the open window, and extra seed drops into the planter box beneath the window, so I can clean it up easily. These feeders are small enough to discourage large birds, and placed high enough on the windows that rodents, including the nimble squirrels that race up and down the nearby cypress, can't reach them easily (and cats can't reach them at all). The opportunity such feeders bring for detailed study is unparalleled, and having so many native neighborhood birds visit me continually (and just inches from my nose) as I sit working at my desk is a source of constant delight.

house sparrows, robins, crows, house finches, starlings, and perhaps chickadees. Take some time to learn these birds inside out. Know the subtle female house sparrow, making sure she is not a female house finch. Know the brown plumage and dark bills of juvenile starlings (and if this is difficult, know you are in good company — Darwin often thought young birds, in their more subtle plumages, were separate species), as well as the adults, and know that while they are black birds, they are not blackbirds. Know the robin tip to tail, and if you learn one single bird's song, learn this one. If you do this, you will be more familiar with birds than 98 percent of Americans.

After learning the first five birds, make an effort to learn twenty more—the next twenty most common birds seen around your home and neighborhood. Even if you live in downtown LA, there will be twenty. (For perspective, I have seen nearly ninety species just from our urban yard, and I see about twenty of these regularly without lifting my bum from the chair in which I now sit.) Twenty is a perfectly reasonable number of birds, not large, yet potentially life-changing. Again, I cannot tell you what they will be. They will likely include flickers, some species of hummingbirds, perhaps a variety of duck, goose, or gull. I have Steller's jays and chestnut-backed chickadees; you may have birds that are common near you but that I will never see in Seattle—blue jay, tufted titmouse, cardinal. It is good to know the first five birds, but in the next twenty species lie the secrets of the urban wilds.

On my desk is a calendar open to a page for the day. On that page, I list, alongside appointments, reminders, and to-dos, the birds that I see every day through my study window while I sit there, thinking and writing. Rather than distracting me, this little list engages me, daily, with life beyond my window, beyond myself. It heightens my attentiveness. It keeps me happy while I work, and it keeps me aware of the presence and seasonality of birds. The warblers that arrive in April, the cedar waxwings in autumn, the young chickadees begging as they shake their wings today, in mid-July. I add their names to my page in green ink. And it makes me realize just how present, changing, and wild my home field can be. Once we can identify some of them, keeping track of the bird species seen in a given place or over a certain amount of time is a simple way of engaging with the birdlife around us.* Lists are a lovely way to cultivate an attunement to a place—a seasoned sense of what to look

---

* For something that seems so innocuous, the listing of birds is a strangely controversial habit in naturalist circles. Listing birds, the argument goes, reduces individuals and species to twitches on a list; it doesn't involve any real observations of birds seen, any edification for the watcher. It's true that listing for the sake of listing can grow into more of an egoistic competition (even if the competition is just with oneself) than a naturalist pursuit. But it is also true that the majority of listers I know also happen to be the most amazing avian naturalists I know, full of love for their subject.

for, and when, and where; to be expectant, and sometimes surprised. It is in this light that I also keep a list of all the bird species seen in our yard. All of the usual birds have long since been spotted, so any new bird is a small celebration and a reminder that even in the diminished urban wild, anything can happen.

Birders are criticized, mimicked, and belittled for their monomaniacal focus. But surely there is far more useless knowledge to be had. There is much to be said for knowing a bird, its name, something of its life, at a glance. I am not arguing that we should all become expert birders, just that we might begin to know the birds, a little, and in the way that makes sense within the round of our individual lives and homes. I like to think that such knowing is a kind of gracious hosting, one that enriches not only our own lives, but also the lives of birds. What is it that we know? The mingled spiral of our lives—human and nonhuman, flesh and feather. How wonderful that something like everyday birdwatching, an activity that stands so far outside of the consumer-economic model of value, has meaning still. My little daydream is that we will all live in urban communities where a person saying, "I saw a hermit thrush this morning, the first one I've ever seen at our house," will be met with more than a blank stare. The kind of community where the hearer, though she's not a birder, just a neighbor, might still know this bird and what it means, and will perhaps share a bird visitation of her own.

Starling, House Sparrow, Pigeon
Duality, Humanity, and the Nonnative Triumvirate

Last summer, we had a new roof put on our house. Our roofline is complicated, and the job took nearly a week to complete. One day while the roofers were there and I was out working at a café to escape the noise, two voice messages were left on my mobile phone. They were from the owner of the roofing company, and the first said, "Hi, Lyanda, we found a nest full of baby birds in the cornice and wonder what we should do." Then the second: "Well, we made a house for the little birds so they wouldn't die in the sun and put it on your house, close to where the nest was. It's not a very good house because we didn't have proper materials, so I'm sorry about that." I listened to the messages, smiled at the thoughtfulness of the roofers, and wondered just how horrible this ramshackle birdhouse was going to be. But when I got home, I found the cutest nest box, neatly made, with a leather hinge to open the box and a perch for the parent birds. The roofers happily showed me photos they'd taken of the process — muscly, large-handed men delicately lifting the tiny birds and their mess of nest stuffs into the new box. How good of them to take time out of the hot day and their busy job to take care of these birds.

The nestlings are, of course, house sparrows, sometimes called English sparrows, an introduced species, an urban invasive, and one of the most ecologically despised of all North American birds. Bluebird advocates in particular hate the sparrows for attacking bluebirds and evicting them from their nests, and they recommend lethal control for the sparrows. One intrepid elder in the movement catches them in a live trap, then cuts their heads off with her kitchen scissors.

House sparrows join European starlings and rock pigeons to form a triumvirate of ubiquitous and disdained nonnative urban birds. These species are complex and confusing in their duality. They are, of course, far outside their places of origin and so in the ecological sense *all wrong*. And yet they are birds. As individual birds, they are — well, they are just birds, with no moral rightness or wrongness inherent. They are both ecologically disastrous and biologically perfect. And in light of their presence, our human responsibility is likewise complicated. We have two tasks, seemingly at odds, but I think intimately related:

1. We are obligated, I believe, to learn from them. A house sparrow might not be valuable or desirable as an ecological member of the local avifauna, but as an Old World sparrow, it is a nifty little bird, offering a window into the well-kept secrets of birdlife.

2. We are obligated to do all we can to limit their populations and keep them from taking over the earth.

I use the word *obligated,* which sounds stern, and uninspiring, and little fun. But I think of this obligation as a creative one, rooted in the Latin *obligare,* "to bind." We are bound, twined, wrapped together, obligated in a rich mutuality to the natural community. And when something goes awry, as in the proliferation of the sparrow? Then we are bound in the context we find ourselves to mine it for its value, to correct it as we are able. Each of the birds in this chapter of the bestiary — pigeon, starling, and house sparrow — brings something of value to the observer. It may be a sidelong, dark-clouded sort of value, and yet we begin where we are, with what is in front of us.

The presence of all three of these species in North America is interwoven with European settlement. Every urban pigeon in this country is considered a feral bird, descended from domestic stock brought over by settlers for food as early as 1600. The historical relationship between humans and pigeons is profound. We know from Egyptian hieroglyphics and Mesopotamian cuneiform tablets that pigeons have been domesticated for more than five thousand years — along with poultry, this is the longest known cohabitation between humans and birds. Because their history is so twined with our own, it is not possible to know with certainty the rock pigeon's native wild range, though it is believed in general to be North Africa and parts of Eurasia. Perhaps because of pigeons' connection with human sustenance and their long history in North America, pigeon presence is taken as a given, an inevitability. People may dislike urban pigeons, but they don't spend a lot of time condemning previous generations of immigrants for bringing them here. The introduction of starlings and house sparrows is far more contentious.

Regarding the starling, some blame Shakespeare. It could not have been intentional on the part of the Bard, but one small hint of a

bird in *Henry IV* appears to be the basis for one of the most successful and devastating avian introductions in North American history.
It is a pivotal scene: King Henry demands that the headstrong sol-
dier Hotspur release his prisoners, but Hotspur refuses to do so until
the king agrees to pay the ransom that will free Hotspur's
brother-in-law Mortimer from the enemy. The king flies into a rage,
forbidding Hotspur to mention Mortimer's name. After the king's
exit, Hotspur speaks a quiet rant:

> *He said he would not ransom Mortimer;*
> *Forbad my tongue to speak of Mortimer;*
> *But I will find him when he lies asleep,*
> *And in his ear I'll holloa, "Mortimer!"*
> *Nay,*
> *I'll have a starling shall be taught to speak*
> *Nothing but "Mortimer," and give it him*
> *To keep his anger still in motion.*

These lines appear in James Edmund Harting's 1871 labor of love
The Ornithology of Shakespeare, in which every bird mentioned in the
whole of the Shakespearean canon is listed, along with the quotation
in which it appears and the citation for the play or poem. The Bard
had an ear for birdlife; there are larks and nightingales and chaffinches aplenty, winging and singing their way through the sonnets,
the comedies, the tragedies. But there is just this one slender starling.

In the mid-1800s, various naturalist and avian-acclimatization
societies began to form in the eastern states with the goal of establishing European species in the New World. In 1871, the American
Acclimatization Society incorporated in New York, its mission pro-

claimed in its bylaws: "the introduction and acclimatization of such foreign varieties of the animal and vegetable kingdom as may be useful or interesting." *Useful or interesting* was interpreted broadly. Most of the literature tells us that English sparrows were brought over to eat insect pests, but the broader hope at the time was that they, along with the thousands of other individuals of nearly twenty different species that were released, would comfort human settlers from England with their cheerful presence, a reminder of the birds from home. There were literary aspirations as well, and when the zealous Eugene Schieffelin joined the group, he found an organization that matched his love of Shakespeare and that supported his glowing wish to bring every bird mentioned in the Shakespeare canon to the pale New World, with its substandard, unliterary avifauna. Schieffelin was an eccentric (some conservation biologists say lunatic) who raised a king's ransom to purchase eighty starlings from England in 1890. He met their ship at the dock. It was a cold, snowy day in March when Schieffelin, along with the servants he'd enlisted to help, carried the cages full of starlings into Central Park. Attempts to acclimatize larks, nightingales, and chaffinches had all failed, and two earlier starling releases were unsuccessful; perhaps Schieffelin whispered something like a prayer in his quirky heart for the starlings' well-being before letting them go. The starlings were likely still stressed from their journey; this release could not have been the romantic bursting into flight that Schieffelin had surely imagined. The birds would have walked uncertainly about in the unwelcoming snow before finally flying, as quiet as starlings can be, into the maple branches. Today there are an estimated two hundred million European starlings in North America, and modern DNA testing confirms that they are all related to those snowy Central Park birds.

I love this story. Starlings are an ecological disaster, to be sure, a cautionary tale about what can happen when humans meddle with the ways of nature, the distribution of creatures. But the combination of love, fetishism, birds, literature, and tragically misguided intent is so richly human. We can all find ourselves, our lives, our human condition in this flawed man, these unwanted birds.

In the fall and winter, we see their great flocks. The young have grown, and the breeding territories have broken down. The birds gather to feed, and then to roost, in murmurations (the rather poetic name for starling flocks, a reference to the thrumming of wing and voice accompanying their movements) that typically include hundreds of birds but may grow to include tens or even hundreds of thousands of starlings. As with other birds that flock, starlings gather for communication, foraging, and protection from predators.

Historical range expansion of the starling

Current starling distribution in North America

The movements of starling clouds are precise, quick, fluid, and mes-
merizing; they remain a mystery to ornithologists.

The spread of starlings and house sparrows was swift, and
complete. Both species were happy to live as human commensals,
already accustomed to human habitation in their native Europe; they
quickly colonized places that other birds avoided, those around human
homes and towns, urban and rural. Starlings and house sparrows meet
every criterion for successful invasion: they reproduce prolifically (with
two or more clutches per season, and five or more birds per clutch);
they fledge quickly and achieve sexual maturity before they are nine
months old; they are not picky about where they nest and will fiercely
defend their chosen site; their food sources are readily available and
widespread; they are inquisitive and will eagerly explore and colonize
new places. House sparrows fly down New York subway stairs for
potato chips and stay to nest on the ledges. They nest in Death Valley
at 280 feet below sea level, and in the Rockies at altitudes of over 10,000
feet. (In Yorkshire, they reportedly lived in a mine shaft 2,100 feet
belowground, where the miners fed and befriended them.)

House sparrows were once the most hated of introduced birds.
Now that starlings are just as common in urban places, most people
focus their wrath upon these larger, more conspicuous, and supposedly more aggressive birds (or on the calmer-but-poopier pigeons).
In fact, though the house sparrow is one of the most ubiquitous
birds in the country and on the earth, and though they are loud and
stocky and busy from morning until night and in all seasons, in
modern urbania, most of us pay little attention to these birds, or
even consciously recognize their presence. I made a bet with myself,
which I won, that if I polled my sweet but slightly overeducated
friends, almost none of them would know exactly which little city

bird is a house sparrow (more stringent studies by others bear out my findings on a wider scale). Both sexes are stocky and feathered in drab gray-brown, with plain, unmarked breasts (female house sparrows and house finches are often confused; the latter have heavily brown-streaked breasts). Females have a buffy stripe across the eye, and males have a gray cap, black throat, gray-white cheek, and a rich rufous nape.

House sparrow taxonomy is fraught with misinformation. All of the native sparrows in North America are New World sparrows, and because of the word *sparrow* in the house sparrow's official common name, and because the birds are sparrow-size and their feathers are shades of sparrow-brown, they are generally considered to be in the New World sparrow group. For years, informed birders have known that this was erroneous, and they believed them to be, as had been long taught, a species of Old World finch related to the weavers. Images of the handily knit weaver nests were displayed in books and museums alongside the tangled nests of house sparrows, apparent evidence of the connection. But more recent DNA and hybridization studies demonstrate that house sparrows are Old World sparrows of the family Passeridae. There is one more in North America—the much less common Eurasian tree sparrow, introduced at about the same time as the house sparrow, and for the same reasons.

Starlings are easier to identify than house sparrows, but there is still plenty of confusion—I'm often asked whether they are blackbirds, or even baby crows. They are actually members of the Old World Sturnidae family, a group of gregarious, terrestrial songbirds that globally includes many other starling species and the mynas. Our European starlings are a shimmering, iridescent purple-black, and in the breeding season, their plumage is edged in gold. While most birds molt into a nonbreeding plumage, the starling's is acquired by wear—the more delicate gold tips wear off over the course of the summer, leaving the starlings a drabber but still pretty black in fall and winter. The bill is bright golden, and though the males and females are alike, you can actually tell them apart by a patch of blue or pink at the base of the bill—blue for boys, pink for girls. The testosterone-imbued males also strut a bit more and have longer spiky feathers under their necks that fluff when they sing to attract a mate.

If you call it singing. The irony was not lost on anyone: among the many species the societies attempted to introduce so that, as the Cincinnati Acclimatization Society put it, "the ennobling influence of the song of birds will be felt by the inhabitants," the only two whose introductions were actually successful were the two that, though they vocalize loudly, do not produce any kind of melodious song. Why the settlers could not have simply come to enjoy the native birds is an obvious question, but solace in the familiar is a potent psychological force.

House sparrows have several vocalizations, the most common being a loud *cheep*. It is difficult to think of this as a song, but since house sparrows have no multinote phrase or warble, and since they do use this loud, persistent, repetitive, sometimes annoying *cheep* to accomplish the usual tasks of birdsong — the claiming and defense of territory or nesting place, and the advertising for a mate — most ornithologists do call this the house sparrow song. But while most songs are proclaimed only by the male bird, female house sparrows also cheep, though not as loudly or as often. Both sexes prefer not to cheep at all in the cold or the rain. Simple calls, chirps, gurgles, and chips are heard year-round, and groups of females in particular will gather and chatter, as if knitting together at a stitch-'n'-bitch.

Starling vocalizations may not seem melodious, but they are varied, complex, and speak to the species' intelligence. Starlings are capable mimics and passably imitate other birds (killdeer are a special favorite), cell phones, jackhammers, creaking doors, orchestral instruments, and human speech. It was the murmuring of a caged starling at a market in Salzburg that prompted Mozart to buy it and take it home, where they mutually inspired each other — the starling mimicked Mozart's piano concertos (though his G was always a bit sharp), and the starling's warbles were a kind of muse for the maestro. When the starling died, Mozart composed a poem for her and organized a more elaborate funeral than he did for his father. I have raised several starlings, including one right out of the egg. I named her Delphinium, and though she was eaten by a cat before I could teach her to sing a Mozart concerto, as I'd hoped to do, I lived with her long enough to learn that starlings are delightful, playful, interactive pets and will follow you around the house as loyally as any puppy. I remember attempting to create a rare moment of starling-free solitude by locking Delphinium out when I used the bathroom, but she called piteously from the other side of the door, then rejoiced when I finally opened it, jumping up and down on her stout pink legs.

For house sparrows and starlings, the historical fall from public grace was as swift as their geographic dispersal. As early as 1883, just a decade after house sparrows were successfully introduced, the Pennsylvania *Messenger* proclaimed: "The little sparrow has been declared an outlaw by legislative enactment and they can be killed at any time. They were imported into this country from Europe some years ago as a destroyer of insects, but it has been found they are not insectivorous. Besides they drive away all our native songbirds and give no equivalent. Let them all be killed."

William Leon Dawson is my favorite historical ornithological writer, beloved by myself and many others for his winsome combination of avian knowledge, dry wit, and over-the-top florid prose. "The increase of this bird in the United States," Dawson wrote of house sparrows in 1908, "is, to the lover of birds, simply frightful." But he is just warming to his subject:

> What a piece of mischief is the Sparrow! how depraved in instinct!
> in presence how unwelcome! in habit how unclean! in voice how
> repulsive! in combat how moblike and despicable! in courtship
> how wanton and contemptible! in increase how limitless and
> menacing! the pest of the farmer! the plague of the city! the bane
> of the bird-world! the despair of the philanthropist! the thrifty and
> insolent beneficiary of misguided sentiment! the lawless and
> defiant object of impotent hostility too late aroused! Out upon
> thee, thou shapeless, senseless, heartless, misbegotten tyrant! Thou
> tedious and infinite alien! thou myriad cuckoo, who dost by thy
> consuming presence bereave us daily of a million dearer children!
> Out upon thee, and woe the day!

The list of house sparrow and starling ills is much the same today as it was at the turn of the nineteenth century: they damage crops; eat flower buds and pull up seedlings; deface buildings with their droppings; stuff their bedraggled, stringy nests into every nook and cranny of our houses, shops, ledges, gutters (where they can cause water backup), vents, cinder blocks, and the visors that surround stoplights (here they seem to prefer the top light, and they have caused accidents by blocking the flash of red); and wake us early with their incessant, repetitive, unmelodious chirring that drowns out even the crows. All of these are relatively minor inconveniences for humans. But there is one more, the unforgivable thing: they compete aggressively with beloved native birds, especially cavity nesters (those that lay their eggs in hollows rather than constructed nests), for nest sites. House sparrows and starlings do not excavate their own nesting cavities but are happy to take over those excavated by others, even if the creator of the nest happens to still be inhabiting it. Eggs will be tossed out; resident nesters fought, evicted, and sometimes killed.

The Pennsylvania *Messenger's* plea was one of the first eradication efforts, the "important hostility too late aroused" that Dawson spoke of. In the latter nineteenth century, many states instituted a bounty, just a couple cents each, for the birds. Children killed them with slingshots and used the money for hard candy. In just a three-month span in 1892, the county treasurers of Illinois reported paying out eight thousand dollars in house sparrow bounty on a total of four hundred and fifty thousand birds. There was no noticeable impact on the bird's population.

All avian conservation groups recommend population-control efforts for house sparrows and starlings, but it is the bluebird societies that are the most zealous advocates of lethal measures. Some common methods of house sparrow euthanasia proposed in their literature are capturing the birds in traps, then compressing their chests or tracheae; putting them in a plastic bag and filling it with car exhaust; snapping their heads between thumb and forefinger; and holding them against a big rock and smashing their heads with a hammer. Because starlings are audacious omnivores, sometimes descending en masse to ravage agricultural crops, with subsequent heavy economic tolls, farmers and government agencies join conservation groups in working to eliminate the birds. They have deployed traps; explosives; Roman candles; plastic owls; amplified starling distress calls; chemical sprays; poisons; and a special concoction that is sprayed on the birds' plumage and doesn't dry until the birds freeze to death. None of these have worked in the long term.

The ornithologist Margaret Morse Nice, one of my personal heroines, asked Konrad Lorenz how he managed the house sparrows that showed up on his porch to nibble the scratch he put out for pet birds. "I never kill birds," said the revered scientist, who confessed a respect for the ubiquitous sparrow. "To a certain extent I am a friend of successful species. This goes so far that I even like weeds." I personally am not in favor of killing birds, and there are more effective things we can do to limit house sparrow and starling reproduction around our homes (see box, page 191). The reality, as the ecological concept of carrying capacity teaches, is that creatures in a given place will always reproduce and grow in numbers to fill the space, food, and habitat available to them. If we want fewer house sparrows and starlings, we do not need to kill them, we need to create an urban landscape in which a richer variety of species can thrive.

What is the true impact on native birds? Tina Phillips of the Cornell Lab of Ornithology says that regarding house sparrows, we just don't know. "There are no long-term studies showing the effect of competition between house sparrows and our native cavity nesters." She heads up a citizen science nest-box monitoring project that she hopes will give us some numbers. But anecdotal evidence abounds, and anyone who pays attention is likely to observe house sparrow aggression. Bluebirds may be the species most affected by house sparrows, but even living in a bluebirdless city, we can watch how house sparrows operate. They will first try to chase unwanted birds away, cheeping and flying at them. If that doesn't work, they might corner adult birds in their nest boxes, evicting them physically or sometimes even killing them, hacking at their skulls with those pointed, conical beaks until the birds die. Sometimes the brain is sucked out and eaten, a sparrow version of *Babette's Feast.* A friend told me about house sparrows building nests right on top of the bodies of tree swallows they'd killed in the nest boxes around his home. Chicks of native cavity nesters are killed or just pushed out of the nest, and eggs are destroyed by the sparrows' poking big holes in their shells. (House wrens destroy eggs of other songbirds as well, piercing the eggs with their tiny, needle-tipped bills — house sparrow destruction is easy to differentiate.) Starlings are bigger than house sparrows and take over more nests from larger species than the sparrows do, including those of woodpeckers, wood ducks, buffleheads, and even small owls.

As is true for house sparrows, the ecological impacts of starlings are little understood. Almost everyone who lives alongside starlings has seen them behaving badly to "nicer" little birds. In a DIY study published in *The Condor,* Norman Weitzel surveyed the birds on his land in the foothills of Reno every day for a decade and documented the nesting habits of native birds there. Before 1978, there were no starlings (in a charming detail, this is corroborated by Mrs. George Minor, who was born on the land in 1900 and lived there until Mr. Weitzel purchased it from her). In 1979, five pairs of starlings nested in Weitzel's two big cottonwoods, and over the next eight years, that number grew. During this time, Weitzel watched as the starlings aggressively displaced mourning doves, house finches, kill-deers, Lewis's woodpeckers, spotted towhees, and western bluebirds who used to nest in the area around the cottonwoods until finally no natives at all nested in or around the trees. Just starlings. Turning out to be something of an avian vigilante, Weitzel took matters into his own hands in 1984 when he "began a systematic extermination of the starling population on my property by shooting individuals with a 20 gauge shotgun." By 1987, he'd killed forty-seven starlings, and there were, once again, seventeen pairs of nesting native birds.

With all of this observed aggression, it was long taken as an ornithological given that starlings wreak havoc on native populations, but it wasn't until recently that researchers at Berkeley did extensive years-long surveys to precisely determine the impact of starlings on native birds, and they were surprised that for most species, they were unable to find quantifiable harm. The population records from historical times to the present were examined for the twenty-seven species believed to be most at risk from starlings, and of these, five species' populations increased rather than decreased after starling colonization, including the red-bellied woodpecker, which regularly suffers nest usurpation by starlings. Five species showed insignificant population declines, and the losses could not be directly linked to starlings. Study author Walter Koenig some-what reluctantly concluded that his data could not support the long-held belief that starlings had severely affected cavity-nesting birds. He did say that the exoneration of the starling was "provisional," as the story of starlings continues to unfold. In urban places, starling impact is likely insignificant, given that human disturbance already prevents more sensitive species from nesting.

Studying the nonnative triumvirate for *The Urban Bestiary,* I have temporarily done things I previously purposely avoided: I have scattered millet for sparrows and cracked corn for pigeons; put out a birdhouse with a large, sparrow-size hole that would intimidate a native chickadee; carefully watched the progress of sparrow and starling nests rather than removing them. It was easy enough to enjoy starling research, for though I do wish they'd never darkened our shores, and though the shotgun-wielding Weitzel would surely disagree, this is a species with charm to spare. Starlings are intelli-gent and highly watchable little birds, and their abundance, toler-ance, and accessibility make them a natural for urban-wildlife study. They are diverting to watch as they feed on our lawns, with widespread legs that give them a waddling gait. Starling mandibles are hinged with uniquely powerful abductor muscles that allow them to poke their bills in the soil and then open them, gaping for hidden invertebrates. A sign of starling presence is the pattern of round holes they leave in the grass. Their nests may seem like a mess of nothing special, but they are worth a second look — sometimes the male will decorate with bits of colorful paper, shiny ribbon, or foil, presumably to impress his mate, as bower birds do. This was once thought to be the reason male starlings often thread their nest entrances with greens and flowers, but now we suspect that these may be a deterrent against the ectoparasites that plague starling chicks. One of the most common plants they use is yarrow, a natural insecticide. In addition to being jesters and mimics, starlings are also, apparently, practical botanists.

In the beginning, house sparrow research took a lot of psychological effort for me. Having spent years dutifully disliking house sparrows, ignoring and discouraging them as best I could, here I am, turning the tables on myself. Now I am learning all I can through close observation of these round, despised avian presences. As the neotropical migrants began to show up this season, I found myself giving just a passing glance to the glowing yellow arrival of the Wilson's warbler who had just flown all the way from Mexico to my cherry tree and, instead, scanning the bushes for a stupid house sparrow. Attention breeds, if not love in this case, then at least a reluctant and complicated affection. House sparrows are fun to watch.

Rural house sparrows eat corn, waste grain from the fields, and their favorite — the partially digested grain found in horse dung. City sparrows eat just what you'd think they would — birdseed. They are partial to the millet from commercial mixes that is tossed aside by other, more discerning birds in search of sunflower seeds. They forage on the ground, in groups, and get around by hopping. Very rarely will you see house sparrows walk, foot by foot. Like most songbirds (but unlike the highly terrestrial starling), house sparrows have legs that are designed to grasp branches, and walking is difficult or impossible. Older sparrows sometimes walk, their grasping muscles presumably in decline (and a hint at our shared biological frailty — humans hop less as we age too). Their foraging habits merge with their social nature and general tameness when

Doing Our Part to Keep House Sparrows and Starlings from Taking Over the Earth

1. If you feed birds, use only good-quality seed—black oil sunflower for general feeding, or Niger thistle for goldfinches. Avoid cheap mixes with the millet favored by house sparrows. Use feeders with tiny perches and refrain from scattering food on the ground.

2. House sparrows and starlings begin nesting early. If you put up nest boxes, put them up as late as possible. Watch resident chickadees for signs of nesting readiness (exploring cavities in trees or electrical poles, carrying nest materials in their bills as they fly overhead) or watch for the arrival of migratory swallows or other target species before putting your boxes out.

3. Use nest boxes with holes that are the appropriate size for the species you want to attract, and keep them as small as possible—an inch is good for most small birds—as house sparrows and starlings prefer larger entrances. Do not use perches—starlings and house sparrows like them; other small birds don't need them.

4. Cover all vents and tubes around your house with metal hardware cloth or commercially available vent covers. Also try to cover gutter corners and any other bird-nest-friendly openings. If you see starlings or house sparrows investigating a spot, cover it. Remove nests as they are built. If there are eggs, remove those too. Then cover the entrance!

5. If you are up to it, addling eggs (rendering them infertile), then returning them to the nest may be more effective than nest removal—it makes the birds think the eggs are still developing, so they won't attempt another clutch, and it is humane if accomplished soon after the eggs are laid (not when the chicks are about to hatch). The best method is refrigeration: Pop the eggs into the fridge for twenty-four hours. Let them return to room temperature before replacing them or the birds may reject them. Another good method is oiling: Cover the eggs completely with food-grade oil, then

let them dry. This blocks the airholes required for the chicks to develop. Wipe the eggs gently, then return them to the nest.

6. Cultivate native trees, shrubs, and plants to encourage a diversity of native birds.

7. Share this information with neighbors (maybe at a nice community-building party with homemade cookies).

we see them at sidewalk cafés hopping among the crumbs at our feet. There is something satisfying in this, dropping crumbs from your chair and watching a wild little being scuttle in to eat them. Most people don't know enough about house sparrows to dislike them and so can enjoy the moment with purity — the sense of graced closeness when an animal that could at any moment fly chooses to stay near instead. Yes, this is what Dawson referred to as "imbecile sentimentality," the indiscriminate gushing over "dear little birdies," but it is something else as well, something important and beautiful: the honest thrill of connection, and the native delight in communing across species.

House sparrows are incredibly sociable — they nest close together, and in spite of the occasional intraspecies male arguments, they are not particularly territorial among themselves, and outside of the breeding season they are constantly in the company of their kind. Some activities, like dust-bathing — flapping about in dry dirt to dust their skin, which stimulates the production of beneficial oils and discourages ectoparasites — are nearly always undertaken alongside other sparrows. They dust-bathe enthusiastically, dirt flinging wildly, and leave empty, sparrow-shaped holes behind. Even during the breeding season, males will gather nest stuffs side by side with other males, with minimal antagony. Activity about the nest is ceaseless. The male is constantly present, watching, guarding, carrying food, peering in.

I had a chance to observe how devoted a parent the male house sparrow can be when our beloved domestic predator Delilah the cat — who is supposed to stay indoors — sneaked out and killed a mother house sparrow, the one who had raised her brood to near-fledging in the roofers' birdhouse. If it were a different kind of bird, the chicks might have starved, as the males of many songbird species do not tend the young. But the male house sparrow, though he seemed a bit agitated and confused after observing the demise of his mate, quickly manned up and started feeding his motherless young. The next day, the first fledgling emerged, and he followed her everywhere while watching and feeding the young that remained in the nest.

I have been studying the sparrows today, all day. Two males have been hopping furtively about the chicken run, skulking like baby chicks right beneath the bellies of the hens, who oddly don't seem to mind their presence (they will chase crows and squirrels). To enter the coop, the sparrows didn't fly through the big door on the front but followed the hens through the little chicken door on the side, hopping behind them. Funny. But once inside the coop, they didn't eat the cracked corn and poultry mash, which I assumed was their reason for being there in the first place; instead, they looked for something, heads turned to the side, eyes cast down, persistent. Finally I realized they were searching for feathers and were finicky in the extreme about the ones they chose. Individual feathers were picked up, examined, discarded. Of course — it's early spring, and the sparrows are looking to literally feather the nest. I'd seen nests near my house featuring the feathers of my own chickens, but I'd never actually watched the gathering, and I'd assumed the feathers used were random ones that had blown into the yard. Who knew the sparrows were actually choosing the exact feathers they wanted? Esmeralda, the fat and beautiful barred rock hen, had been molting, so in addition to the usual small downy bits, there were large wing and tail feathers. Finally, one male house sparrow selected the very biggest and longest—a primary wing feather. Such a prize! The feather was larger than he was but weighed nothing; he picked it up horizontally in his bill and attempted to make off with it, flying straight into the hogwire fence. Hogwire is characterized by vertical wire rectangles, two by four inches each, a good sparrow-size opening but not a sparrow-with-long-feather-size opening. I was stunned to observe what happened next: the sparrow dropped to the ground, put his feather down, walked through the fence, then reached his head in, grabbed the tip of the feather, and pulled it through. This was problem-solving, the sort of thing we expect from primates and maybe the higher avian orders, such as corvids and parrots. Certainly not from a plain, hated little sparrow. Yet here it is—the unexpected grandeur of the commonplace.

It is one of the curious twists of the urban bestiary that sparrows and starlings give us an opportunity to learn even more of certain ornithological secrets than we can from native birds in wilder places. Being approachable, accessible, and legally unprotected, they offer scope for careful home study. Nests of native birds should always be left undisturbed—not only is it illegal to mess with them, but it makes the adult birds fussy, and might call the attention of predators—jays, crows, coons, cats—to the presence of the nest. For scrappy house sparrows and starlings, such things are of little concern, and all kinds of possibilities emerge for the amateur naturalist, or family science project. Peer into the nest every few days as the nestlings grow, and observe the feather tracts and order of feather growth. Let your child carefully hold one of the hot, fat-bellied, transparently skinned little babies (and try it yourself). This will change a child's sense forever of what it means to see a bird on the nest (adult birds will *not* "smell human" on their chick and abandon it).

Professional scientists make use of the house sparrows' abundance and the public's lack of concern for the species in their research as well. The literature is immense, with nearly five thousand academic papers gathered in a scientific bibliography of the genus, and it overflows with studies of avian metabolism, thermoregulation, evolutionary mechanisms, and the role of birds in pest control. Even so, some simple things about the daily habits and natural history of the bird are astonishingly little-known. We have gained a great knowledge of avian circadian rhythms from house sparrows in the lab, but there is still more to learn about the most common bird on earth as she goes about her day in the world. Daily time expenditures—how much eating, sleeping, nesting, and preening occurs in a normal sparrow's twenty-four-hour period—is not well studied. We know very little about the complex house sparrow social structure; intraspecies communication, both vocal and physical; and how these shape their days and lives. Any amateur watcher can contribute to the understanding of the species by watchful note-taking from an apartment lanai. And there will always be more to learn from this species about ourselves—how our presence creates and encourages the presence of house sparrows and the absence of other birds. How our habits and the wild are incontrovertibly mingled.

While starlings and house sparrows are reviled for their ecological impact, the ecological ramifications of pigeon presence appears to be negligible. In the wild, rock pigeons nest on cliffs. In cities, they substitute steep building eaves and ledges. The nest is simple — just a bit of straw, grasses, small sticks — and they're located in places that few native urban birds would find acceptable. Pigeons even provide an unexpected ecological benefit as the perfect food source for once-endangered peregrine falcons that have moved into urban places. (In Trafalgar Square, where pigeons are prolific and pooping on the statuary, it was proposed that falconers release their birds to cull the populations. Animal-rights activists went mad in pigeon defense. When I visited London a few years back, my shoulder bag was stuffed with Save the Pigeon flyers I was handed in my wanderings. U.S. animal activists can't hold a candle to the zeal of Londoners.)

Even so, as a nonnative bird of presumably small brain at home in the murkiest corners of the inner city, the pigeon is singularly disrespected. In Seattle a few years ago, several downtown pigeons were shot in the head with needles. The needles were each about four inches long, and it was surmised they had been launched through a peashooter sort of apparatus. It didn't kill the pigeons, so they'd walk around with the needles sticking out — very creepy. This just wouldn't happen to any other bird.

The official common name of the pigeon was recently changed from rock dove to rock pigeon, in order to bring the colloquial English in line with international trends. Taxonomically, there is no difference between a pigeon and a dove. Pigeons and doves are in the Columbidae family, and they are all closely related. There is a colloquial separation in their common names, based mainly on size, with the larger birds being called pigeons, the smaller being called doves, and no objective dividing line between the two.

I preferred the term *rock dove,* which served as a reminder — and a surprise to some — that pigeons really are doves. People tend to separate them in their thoughts and attitudes. Doves are seen as clean in feather and heart, gentle, peaceful, calming, even holy somehow, and they have the prettiest blue eyelids. Pigeons are viewed as grimy, poopy, pestilential, and they suffer the indignity of being utterly commonplace in human habitations. But the columbids we call doves are certainly no cleaner than the ones we call pigeons — even the deepest urban pigeon is scrupulously well-groomed, iridescent, and tidy of feather. Tar on her coral-red feet, perhaps, but no dirtier than a woodland-wandering mourning dove.

Though Darwin's finches have all the fame, Darwin wrote far more about pigeons than he ever wrote about the Galapagos finches or all of the island birds put together. The entire first chapter of the *Origin of Species* is devoted to pigeons, as are nearly one hundred pages of his *Variation of Animals and Plants Under Domestication.* It is common knowledge that pigeons were important to Darwin but less commonly known that pigeons were also *beloved* by Darwin. His studies led him down the road of personal obsession, where he kept a private dovecote and hobnobbed below his class with the pigeon fanciers of London, learning their secrets. For Darwin, pigeons offered the perfect domestic analogy for the way natural selection functions through variety within lineage in wild nature.

Darwin never questioned the consciousness of animals, and given that he spent so much time interacting with his beloved Almond Tumblers, I doubt that he would have been surprised by the

Urban Pigeon Project

Darwin would have been intrigued by the question that prompted the Cornell Lab of Ornithology's Urban Pigeon Project. The fact that individual pigeons are uniquely colored is a scientific mystery. The natural color of the rock pigeon is that nice blue-gray we see so often, with iridescent purple trim. But in urban places, while the natural color is the most common, we see all sorts of other pigeon colors as well—whites, browns, golds, pied black-and-whites. It makes no sense—according to the laws of natural selection, anomalies should be either weeded out (meaning that the errant colors would show up only occasionally) or, if they lead to reproductive success for the birds in some way, propagated (meaning the pigeons should all be multicolored). Cornell's ornithological labs have organized a citizen science effort to research the various pigeon colors, and anyone can take part.

recent study published in the journal *Science* demonstrating math competence in pigeons. They can not only discriminate quantities but also learn abstract mathematical concepts. Researchers in the Department of Psychology at the University of Otago in New Zealand began by teaching pigeons to order the numbers 1, 2, and 3. Images would appear on a touch screen, each with one, two, or three objects, and the pigeons learned to peck the images in ascending numerical order. When they did so correctly, they were given a wheat snack. Next, they were tested with a more abstract rule. Presented with pairs of images containing anywhere between one and nine objects, the pigeons again had to determine ascending order—if they were shown a group of four things and a group of seven, for example, they were supposed to peck the group of four first.

"Remarkably," said lead author Damian Scarf, "the pigeons were able to respond to these novel pairs correctly." And even more remarkable to primate-biased humans? "Their performance was indistinguishable from that of two rhesus monkeys that had been previously trained on this task." We might be less surprised if the birds were among those we already consider to be intelligent (Alex the African gray parrot understood the concept of zero, an abstraction that humans don't normally comprehend until they are three or four and that we have long considered beyond any animal, let alone a bird). But pigeons can navigate by the stars. Why should we be flummoxed when we learn they can count to nine?

New research by ornithologists at Uppsala University in Sweden shows that a disproportionate number of urban birds have big brains. That is, the size of the brain in relation to the body is larger in urban birds than in similar birds who do not take up in urban places — presumably, the larger brain size allows for the adaptability, innovation, and plasticity of behavior required of city birds. No one wants to say yet that this correlates with higher intelligence, but the implication is there, and the surprising capacities of house sparrows and starlings and, now, pigeons appear to bear this out. Scientists who live-trap house sparrows report that they quickly learn to obtain the tasty bait without tripping the trap (and once caught, they are funny; rather than flapping about restlessly like most birds, they seem calm, sitting or walking around as if studying their novel situation). In New Zealand, a flock of the birds has become notorious for entering a city bus station through the sliding glass door — they've learned to fly in front of the sensor that activates the doors, nibble on the treats left by untidy travelers, then leave the way they came. We have finally come to understand just how intelligent corvids and parrots may be.

Now we have problem-solving sparrows, musical starlings, and mathematician pigeons! The entire creaturely world, it seems, is busy tossing our presumptions back in our faces.

Most of the birds in the urban landscape are songbirds (as are starlings and house sparrows) or park waterfowl, perhaps with a few gulls, hummingbirds, and flickers thrown in. Pigeons are something altogether different—a ubiquitous but unique presence among us, affording us the opportunity to study avian adaptations and diversity across different taxonomic groups. We see pigeons bursting into flight with the suddenness that ground-dwelling birds require. Rather than perching like songbirds do, pigeons roost— more of a sitting on top of something than a strong grasping. Their feet are fatter and shorter, and their toenails are less curved, more dull. On the same substrate, a crow will make a complete track, a full outline of the crow foot and toenails, while the pigeon will make just a suggestion of a pigeon foot. Just as humans have handedness, pigeons have footedness. Watch pigeons land, and you will see that one foot touches the ground and stabilizes the bird before the other foot, and for an individual bird, it is always the same foot. As in humans, the right is typically dominant, with a small percentage of birds being left-footed (about the same percentage as humans who are left-handed), and an even smaller percentage change feet, or land on both feet at the same time—ambipedalous pigeons.

Pigeons are the only birds on earth that drink by submersing the entire bill into a pond or puddle and sucking water up, rather like a horse. Other birds dip their bills, then tip their heads up, allowing water to trickle down their throats. Related is the pigeon's need for an impressive volume of water—5 percent of its own body weight daily.

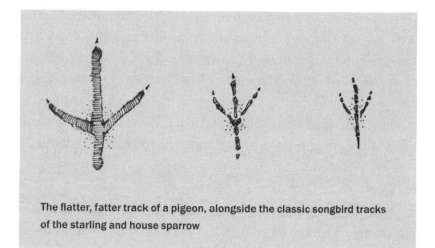

The flatter, fatter track of a pigeon, alongside the classic songbird tracks of the starling and house sparrow

Pigeons are not the easiest birds to raise from tiny hatchlings. Once they are a couple weeks old, they can eat a nutritious seed mash, but very small squabs get crop milk from their parents—a thick, soupy mixture produced in the crop of both male and female pigeons. It's not actual milk, which is unique to mammals, but it is chemically similar. To drink it, the young stick their heads way into the adult's throat and suck the crop milk up. It makes them fat and happy, and by the time they leave the nest, at about four weeks old, they will weigh nearly as much as their parents. I've raised a few mourning doves and pigeons, and I tried to re-create the experience of drinking crop milk for the babies. I mixed meat baby food with a thick canned liquid baby formula, Similac, added crushed vitamins, and put the whole thing in a baby bottle. I cut a slit in the tip of the bottle's nipple, held the bird in my lap, and pressed its little bill into the opening. Without exception, every chick eagerly sucked up my DIY crop milk and grew healthy. You have to do something like this if you try to feed baby pigeons, because, unlike songbirds, they don't open their bills wide, gaping for food that the adults drop in. The only problem with my method was that it made an absolute mess, with sticky fake crop milk dribbling down the chicks' breasts. I put little bibs on them but still had to administer tiny dove baths to keep a Similac crust from forming over the feathers. Real pigeon parents don't seem to have this problem. Hand-raised pigeons are delightfully tame, cuddly, gentle, and have the endearing habit of settling all warm and feathery under the hair at the base of your neck.

Pigeons are highly confrontational with one another when mining communal food sources or competing for mates, sometimes attacking other birds (though usually the "attack" is symbolic male posturing). Parental care does not extend long beyond fledging, so the young of the year, unused to the pigeon-eat-pigeon way of things, fare worst among the foraging flocks; they are the butt of most attacks, and when autumn arrives, the most underfed birds in the flock.

Even so, the pigeons' mythical reputation for peace and gentleness is mostly well earned. Pigeons are in general not aggressive with non-pigeons. Their soft breasts and sweet cooing have made them symbolic of wise femininity, and they perch on the shoulders of the most beautiful goddesses across cultures, including Astarte, Isis, and Athena. Though in ancient Japan, pigeons were considered messengers of war, in the modern world, we are more commonly inspired by their mythic sense of calm gentility — carriers of the olive branch, bearers of peace and love. In this spirit, we send them forth at weddings and at funerals. My favorite mythological image of the pigeon comes from the Festival of the Circumcision of Christ, where a pigeon holds, instead of an olive branch, the divine prepuce in its bill.

Ever since the 1800s, pigeons have been used in wartime. During both World Wars, the U.S. Army Pigeon Service was an official unit (there was a similar unit in Europe) maintaining dovecotes for birds that could fly with secret messages beneath radio interception. In World War II, more than three thousand soldiers maintained fifty-four thousand pigeons, and 90 percent of the messages sent by pigeon were received. The Maidenform Bra company designed a pigeon bra (though the preferred name for the thing was pigeon vest) that would hold pigeons close to a paratrooper's chest as he jumped from a plane. Pigeons have literally saved thousands of human lives. In 1943, the UK animal-welfare pioneer Maria Dickin instituted the awarding of the Dickin Medal, a bronze circlet stamped with a laurel wreath and bearing the words *For Gallantry* and *We Also Serve,* to honor animals that have shown particular valor during military service. Of the sixty-five medals awarded thus far, thirty-two were draped around the feathered necks of pigeons; the others went to horses and dogs. Hero pigeons include Winkie, who was released with a message out of desperation by a World War II British aircrew forced to ditch in the North Sea. They'd given themselves up for dead when they remembered Winkie, and attached an SOS to her leg, doubtlessly whispered a prayer over her blue head, and let her go. She flew home, where her owner found her exhausted, read the note, and alerted the Royal Air Force, who swiftly mounted a successful rescue. (The crew later held a dinner where Winkie was toasted as the guest of honor.) The pigeon Mary of Exeter was awarded the Dickin Medal for carrying messages back and forth across the English Channel during her five-year service, in spite of being injured three times and having her loft bombed. The most famous decorated American pigeon is the World

War II bird G.I. Joe. The village of Calvi Vecchia, Italy, was scheduled to be bombed by the Allied forces, and at the last minute, G.I. Joe delivered the message that the village was occupied by the British, and the bombing was abandoned, saving not only the British occupiers but also the civilian inhabitants of the village.

It may be ironic that this bird, a symbol of peace, has been so widely utilized in war. But there is another side of the story that captures my imagination, one I haven't seen in print but that perhaps exists in a letter, or a diary, or the personal remembrances of an aging trooper. I am convinced that one of the reasons pigeons are little liked is that so few people have spent much time with them. Pigeons may not be the smartest (by human measure) or the most loved bird in the city, but as individuals, they are sweet-tempered and easy to tame (most wild birds need to be raised from chicks to become tame, but even adult wild pigeons will come to enjoy the presence of a favorite human). Once accustomed to you, pigeons love to walk up your arm and burrow into the crook of your elbow or against your neck. They coo. They are both calm and calming. When I first learned some years ago about the pigeon corps, I immediately wondered about these men — so terribly young, homesick, and frightened — who cared for the pigeons, some responsible for a single bird, holding her close for hours a day and even into the night. What a comfort this must have been, this secret, warm being whom you could whisper to and nestle with and who would whisper and nestle back.

Can we do both of these things? Can we hold both mind-sets? Can we decry the presence of these birds, work creatively and mindfully to decrease them, and at the same time be reminded that there is a shared source of presence? That humans brought them here and continue to create the conditions under which they flourish? That we can seek their eradication or reduction and still, on a daily basis, appreciate their birdness, their feathers, flight, ingenuity, and varied intelligences?

We often talk as if the elimination of house sparrows or starlings would mean a neighborhood full of varied and glorious woodland birds, as if such a magical substitution were a possibility. I wish it were. But these birds aren't here because they have chased away everything else; they are here because *we* have chased away everything else, because there are so few other species capable of living on little besides concrete and car exhaust and bread crumbs. And so here is a bird at my feet at the bus stop. While most of the birds here this morning look fat and handsome, this little pigeon hen is rumpled and lean. Her feet, though, are bright coral red, her eyes light and alert. She walks, and picks, and makes her way. I feel sympathy, *empathy* really, us two girls here on the damp sidewalk. And if I look at her from a certain angle, I see her, simply, as she is — a lovely bird, sacred in the round of life we share.

Chickadee

Tiny Truth

Many times I have witnessed birds eating other animals, both in the remote wilderness and the urban wilderness—everything from ravens on the body of a wild elk in the high Olympic mountains to a crow with a bloody rat in the backyard. Generally, we modern humans summon the expansiveness to accept such moments as part of an essential circle of life, even when they do involve rats. I've observed only one instance of an avian predator and its prey that made me actually squeamish. One day when I was a graduate student in Colorado, I went for a solitary hike in the foothills of the Rockies, passing birds I rarely see in my Seattle life (Clark's nutcrackers, Townsend's solitaires, indigo buntings). Turning a corner on the switchback, I startled a Cooper's hawk on the trailside clutching a mostly dead Townsend's solitaire beneath its yellow feet. This was a juvenile Cooper's, and making it through the first year of life with enough to eat is never a given for this scrappy species. I love solitaires and took a moment to honor this one's good life but quietly whispered to the hawk, "Good for you." The Cooper's would normally have flown at such an intrusive human presence. But hungry and young, this bird held its ground, and I walked quietly onward, bothering it as little as I could. This was not the squeamish moment — that came around the next bend in the trail where I met, on a low branch just at eye level and only a few feet from my face, a black-capped chickadee with the largest, most fat and fleshy caterpillar I have ever seen. It was a luna moth larva, as big as the chickadee and surely outweighing her by at least ten times. The larva, though its belly had been torn open by the chickadee's tiny but very pointed bill, was still alive and squirming. Its insides, a nondescript yellow, were oozing out. And the chickadee's delicate bill was covered with what I can only think to call caterpillar goo.

The sight of the tiny chickadee disemboweling the enormous luna moth larva turned my stomach. I emitted an involuntary *eeew* sound and turned away, then forced myself to regroup and look again. I learned something about chickadee foraging behavior that day, to be sure, but the larger question for me became: Why do I find this so gruesome? I have seen an owl with bloody rodent entrails hanging over its bill and the disemboweled animal under its feathered feet, and my only thought was *What a gorgeous bird!* Was my problem here that the larva was just too unnervingly fleshy for a creature with no skeleton? (It was.) But being honest with myself, I had to admit that there was something about the larva eater being a chickadee that was equally unsettling. Might it have something to do with black-capped chickadees being so darn cute? And if a bird is cute, do I also want to suppose it to be transcendently benevolent?

Or at least nice? We see chickadees at our feeders eating sunflower seeds. Isn't that what they ought to be doing, not murderously patrolling the forests seeking to disembowel their fellow creatures?

The chickadee is the representative garden songbird in this *Urban Bestiary*. A common denizen of kitchen calendars and greeting cards, the chickadee is perhaps the best-known, most popular, well-loved backyard bird in the country;* it is also among the most oversimplified. The problem for the chickadee is that its perceived cuteness is largely unmediated. There is no overlay of human vilification as there is with, say, the raccoon (just as appealingly masked, but with a marauding reputation) to temper our perceptions. There is no gray area in which our human compassion leads us into conflict, such as when we see a sharp-shinned hawk take a favorite small backyard bird (a chickadee, perhaps). The hawk is elegant and bold, its actions thrilling and essential, but, we might think in our less scientific moments, not particularly *nice*. And we all know that if we had to label them, chickadees *would* be nice. Chickadee cuteness is a given, almost a scientifically objective truth. But the chickadee remains tenaciously wild and irreducible; seeing the bird beyond its seemingly undemanding cuteness is as necessary as it is difficult.

And it *is* difficult. Chickadees have fat, round bodies, charming masks, bright round eyes, and they appear to exist in a constant state of busy good cheer. We see them in the morning, and our spirits lift: there are chickadees among us, and the day is a good one. Early

---

* *I am referring here to the black-capped chickadee, the most common species of chickadee in North American urban, suburban, and park settings. There are seven other species of chickadee, some of which are also common in such places. While there are a few differences in behavior among chickadee species, most of what is true for the black-capped is pretty much true for the others.*

The Enormousness of Hummingbirds

Hummingbirds were made from the pile of feathers and fluff left over after all the other birds were created. The Mayan Great God gathered the bits together and fashioned them into a tiny bird—there wasn't enough to make anything more. The little bird flitted and hummed joyfully about the Great God's head, and he was so overcome with delight that he made a present for the hummingbird—a female hummingbird. Preparations for the wedding were merry, as all the creatures loved the hummingbirds. Only one thing dampened the happy mood—the hummingbirds were wonderful, but being made of leftovers, they were drab. Depressingly gray. In the wedding spirit, the beings came together to make the day more festive. Spiders spread their iridescent webs on the ground to create a bridal path, and flowers dropped their petals in a circle where the small couple would exchange vows. Butterflies surrounded them in a wall of glowing wings. All the beings searched for tiny colored feathers, which they pressed onto the birds' heads. Most wonderful of all, the sun sent special rays of red and green to fill the butterfly-room. When the male turned toward these rays, everyone gasped. His throat glowed.

The play of natural selection upon the organisms of earth is always an experiment. A wild testing of limits. What can the *bauplan* of a bird accomplish? Evolution is expansive, seeking, reaching into possibility but limited by physics. How big can you get and still fly? Mute swan. How small can you get and still metabolize energy quickly enough to be a bird? Hummingbird.

Hummingbirds weigh, almost literally, nothing—between 0.1 and 0.3 ounces. Their tininess appears absolute—shimmering small face, almost invisible feet. Jewels, we call them. Hummingbirds are Western Hemisphere birds, so they are absent in both the field guides and the mythologies of Europe (where their place is taken by faeries) and Africa. The modern urban hummingbird suffers a fate similar to the chickadee's— it is its surface, its diminutive beauty, that is most eagerly admired. But in North and South America, they are woven brightly into the cross-cultural mythology, where the hummingbird's size is measured by the strength of its spirit. In Mojave stories, the hummingbird is sent to the upper limits of the sky to seek sunlight for the people who live in an underground darkness. For the Hopi and Zuni, the hummingbird flies heavenward and intervenes for the humans, convincing the gods to send rain. Just last week, I saw a hummingbird dive-bombing a Cooper's hawk in flight. I have seen them vocally scold raccoons. We have a rufous hummingbird in our freezer, and when we look at his tiny feet under the microscope? They look like they belong to a dinosaur.

naturalists, no matter how learned, heaped unembarrassed, sentimental prose upon the bird. In her still indispensable *Handbook of Nature Study,* Anna Botsford Comstock wrote of the chickadee in 1911: It is "the most fascinating little ball of feathers ever created, constantly overflowing with cheerful song…that happy song 'chick-a-dee-dee-dee' finds its way to the dullest consciousness and the most callous heart." And my beloved William Leon Dawson, a respected businessman, woodsman, ornithologist, and hunter, rhapsodized ad nauseam about these common birds and their antics. He was especially charmed by their arboreal acrobatics, which are enhanced by specialized leg muscles that make chickadees fearless in the trees: "Chickadee refuses to look down for long upon the world; or, indeed, to look at any one thing from any one direction for more than two consecutive twelfths of a second. 'Any old side up without care,' is the label he bears; and so with anything he meets, be it a pine-cone, an alder catkin, or a bug-bearing branchlet; topside, bottomside, inside, outside, all is right side to the nimble Chickadee."

But all close observers, no matter how charmed, eventually recognize the dogged tenacity I witnessed in the chickadee with her luna larva. In 1902, American naturalist Ernest Ingersoll wrote of the chickadee, "He is the hero of the woods," possessing the "Spartan virtue of an eagle" and "an added pertness and ingenuity all his own. His curiosity is immense, his audacity equal to it." Though they prefer nest cavities that occur naturally or that have been created by small woodpeckers, chickadees are capable of using their tiny beaks to excavate their own nest holes. I observed the process from start to finish once, and after the first couple of hours I felt a terrible pain in my neck. I realized it was not from sitting still, but from visceral sympathy for the birds and their astonishing exertions, seemingly out of all musculoskeletal proportion. (The next part of the process is daintier — the nest will be filled with all manner of soft things, mosses, and rabbit hair, and bits of lichen and spiderweb. The female will cover the eggs with blankets of this fluff whenever she must leave them, then she'll return and sit on top of it all, an avian Princess and the Pea.)

Caterpillars are a favorite food in season, even some of the hairy ones, such as gypsy moths in their early instars. Chickadees eat a miscellany of insects and spiders (as well as their eggs and pupae), small slugs and snails, centipedes, soft fruits, and berries. There are many field reports of chickadees eating the eggs of other small birds and also nibbling the fat from the bones of dead vertebrates, including deer, skunk, and fish. This is a varied diet for a small bird, and it calls for persistent physical rigor.

Chickadees are well known for their vocalizations, and even nonbirders recognize their onomatopoetic-namesake call, *chickadee-dee-dee,* a buzzy vocalization made in all manner of circumstances and throughout the year. The male's breeding-season song may be the most familiar of all spring songs to nonbirders — the two-note, high-low *dee-dee.* I'll never forget the day my own namesake, Grandma Lyanda, called to tell me that a bird was crying outside her window. She needed to find it and help it. It was lost, lonely, or hurt. My grandmother is prone to crabbiness, and when I told her after listening to her good imitation that I was sure the bird was a chickadee singing, she indignantly put me in my place. "Lyanda, this bird is *cryyyyyin'!*"

Most of us know these two chickadee vocalizations, as well as the almost constant *seet-seet-seet* contact call they make as they go about their day foraging for food, feeder-hopping, hanging upside down and every which way in the tree limbs. But human researchers have recognized at least sixteen different vocalizations that chickadees use in both intra- and interspecific communication. These include a squealing distress call, an antagonistic snarl, rare confrontational twitters and growls used only when bickering with other chickadees, and a loud hiss coupled with a snapping of wings to create a "snake display" that frightens adversaries. In addition to all these calls and others described by ornithologists, chickadee language continues on an aural plane beyond human perception.

The Essential Art of Pishing

The buzzy *chickadee-dee* call imitated even passably can convoke a whole passel of chickadees for close observation. William Leon Dawson calls it "the quickest summons in the bird-world," the "open sesame to all woodland secrets." Try it if you find yourself in the company of chickadees—a little *dee-dee*-ing, or some pishing. Pishing is a singular technique in the birder's arsenal—the art of making a certain kind of noise to attract birds. To become a pisher, try making a raspy, whispery sort of *pish-pish-pish* sound. Your lips will move, and the air will pass through your teeth. The pishing should not be overloud—you are basically saying to the bird, as you would say to a person, *Psst...over here!* There is no one right way to do this—the pisher's art is unique to the individual. Practice, and see what works for you. Another method is to make a moist squeaking sound by kissing the back of your hand while producing a soft *smack,* as a child might when kissing you on the cheek. (Kissing another person works too.)

Some think pishing is effective because it imitates the sound of a bird in distress, and the other birds want to see what's going on. Some think the birds want to know why there is a human standing under their tree making odd sounds. I believe that for most species, it is a general curiosity. Not all birds respond to pishing, and in fact it will inspire some species to withdraw into an unmoving silence. But chickadees are mad for pishing, as are kinglets, white-crowned and white-throated sparrows, hummingbirds, and many others. It's worth experimenting with your technique and with various birds in differing habitats. When it works, pishing is miraculous—a seemingly barren tree with birds out of sight in the highest branches can suddenly be filled with curious fluttering. Chickadees are likely to gather just overhead, and when they do, the feeling of communion—to speak the language of birds!—brings a sense of rare magic and easy joy.

Their signaling repertoire is one of the most sophisticated known, not just among birds, but in all the animal world. All this complexity in a bird that we see and hear near daily. A bird that, if you held it in your hand, would seem to weigh nothing at all.

During breeding season, chickadees are paired off on territories, but for much of the rest of the year, they join in groups, forming the nucleus of mixed-species foraging flocks. In these flocks, chickadees appear to be the leaders — when they fly off to a new foraging area, the other birds in the group, usually kinglets, nuthatches, small woodpeckers, sometimes sparrows and finches, follow along. Benefits for the chickadee followers include the chickadee's bold response to predators. It gives a loud call — a version of the *seet* or the *chickadee-dee-dee* call that alerts other birds to the presence of the threat. If the perceived threat is a perched bird — a small hawk or owl — the chickadees may also lead a mob on the bird. Other species will join in the physical mobbing or maybe just sit nearby scolding in their own voices. On the surface, it might seem foolish for such vulnerable birds to throw themselves at a dangerous raptor, but it makes good evolutionary sense: a mobbed predator becomes confused, loses the advantage of surprise in its attack, and might be pestered into flying away (though sometimes it just hunches there on its branch, looking beleaguered). Recent research has revealed an astonishing depth to the chickadee's alarm calls, which use a recombinant note system to encode specific information about the predator, including the kind of animal that it is, its size and location, and the perceived level of peril. For overhead predators, such as a hawk in flight, a series of *seet* alarm calls are given. For a perched predator, say an owl on a low branch, a wide-spectrum version of the

Chickadee Tracks and Sign

Chickadee tracks are left in the lightest of substrates—dust, soft mud, snow. They are classic small-bird tracks, difficult to distinguish from those of other birds. For a challenge, notice that the two inside toes form a unique straight line. The toes of finches, swallows, and warblers tend to splay farther apart, and finch tracks generally curve slightly inward.

Other signs of chickadee presence include cocoons that have been pecked and torn and small pecked holes in insect galls. Many bird species feed from cocoons and galls, but chickadees and their relatives the titmice have such small bills that the openings they make, instead of being clean round holes, are messier series of pecks and jabs. Chickadees are tenacious in this, as in all things.

chickadee-dee-dee call is sounded, with many more *dee*s added at the end—five, ten, sometimes more than twenty, depending on the immediacy of the threat. Size of the predator is a major factor in the chickadee's threat perception. A huge great horned owl might seem an ominous presence to us, but to a chickadee, the small pygmy owl is the larger menace, being agile enough to catch a nimble chickadee in flight, which bigger birds usually are not. But the chickadee perceptive capacity has to do with more than size. Other than giving a quick glance, it will not react at all to the presence of, for example, a bobwhite quail—a pygmy owl–size bird that eats seeds rather than chickadees—which means that chickadees can actually identify some birds to species, or at least general kind. Other small birds listen to the information encoded in the chickadee alert and respond accordingly, suggesting that the language of chickadees is understood by other avian species. Birds will gather and often join in mobbing and scolding an owl after a perched-small-owl alert but not for a large-owl-overhead report. This recognition of chickadee language is very recent in human ornithological understanding. In trans-species research, we are hindered by our sense of how communication should and does take place—it should be rather like our own, we think. In scientific research and in everyday watching, there is room for expansion of both whimsy and wisdom.

Inside those pretty little feathered heads resides a highly developed hippocampus, the part of the brain that deals with spatial relations. Chickadees are one of many birds that cache food. When a chickadee comes to a feeder, it takes a moment to choose a seed, then flies away with it, rarely staying to eat it in place. The same is true when chickadees find seed-bearing plants. If you have a sunflower with a heap of shells beneath it, they were likely dropped there by a goldfinch, or squirrel, or other seed-loving creature—chickadees take their seeds away with them. Watch as the bird tilts its head to eye the seed pile. That pause at the moment of choosing is not random; studies reveal that a chickadee will select the nicest, biggest seed it can see in the heap. It takes the seed to a nearby branch and eats it, undisturbed by other birds, or it caches it for later eating. Chickadees have been observed relocating a cache without difficulty after twenty-eight days, and the temporal limit of their spatial memory beyond that is not known. They hide seeds, berries, and even insects under bark or dead leaves, among lichens, beneath clusters of conifer needles, and within other natural safekeeping crevices. We think they relocate their caches using visual cues from the landscape, memory, and orientation by sun-compass.

While we hand out Hallmark cards picturing chickadees alongside flowers, bunnies, and unfortunate examples of iambic pentameter, the chickadees themselves are hissing like snakes, mobbing owls a thousand times their weight, navigating by the sun, engaging in a whole language beyond our hearing. Scientific knowledge of the chickadee's behavioral range is relatively recent, but many humans have long understood that the chickadee is filled with tiny depths and expansive truths. The Spearfinger legend from the Cherokee tradition is good and creepy, and full of insight into chickadee ways. Here is my telling of the myth:

> Utlunta was an ogress who lived in the high hills. She loved the cloudy crests, where the edges of earthly truth were blurred and clouded. Her body was covered with a stony crust, and on her right hand there grew a terrible finger—long, pointed, hard as

obsidian, and sharp as a blade. Her name, Utlunta, is translated in English as Spearfinger. Utlunta loved two things: she loved dancing on the rocks in the hills, hearing them crunch beneath her heavy feet, and she loved to hunt and eat her one and only food — the livers of children. "Liver, I eat it! Su' sa' sai'!" she would sing as she danced, brandishing her deadly finger.

Utlunta was a shape-shifter, and her favorite form to take was that of an old woman, a village crone that a child would easily mistake for a beloved auntie or grandmama. Her happiest days were those in autumn, when the Cherokee villagers would burn leaves of the lowland trees, forcing the chestnuts to the ground. The smoke aided Utlunta's deception, and she would skip gaily down the mountain, anticipating her meal, and waving her deadly finger with glee. "Liver, I eat it! Su' sa' sai'!"

As she approached the village, she might pass an old woman and assume her face, her shape. Her dance would change to a hobble as she made her way undetected among the children gathering hot chestnuts in baskets. "Oh, my dear boy," she would croon, as she slumped decrepitly onto a boulder, "can you spare a chestnut for a tired old granny? Come, child, sit on granny's lap." As the other children wandered among the smoke, happily filling their baskets, Utlunta, fast as a striking snake, would plunge her spearfinger into the child's back, give it a horrible twist, and pull the fresh liver out. In this way, she would gather a whole bagful of livers to carry home and feast upon as the sun set. So quick was she in this operation that death by her hand was said to be painless. Sometimes a child would wander back to his home feeling a strange listlessness but not knowing that his life was draining away, and days later, Utlunta would hear the keening and wailing of the child's parents rising to the mountain crest. At this, she would smile. Oh, these villagers are so stupid! So easy to fool!

Utlunta had a secret, and this too made her smile. She would gaze down at her fat wrist, bulging beneath her palm, and watch it pulse with life. Her heart! Utlunta's heart was not in her breast, but in her wrist. This made her all but invincible to those stupid Cherokee warriors, always aiming their spears at an enemy's chest. All the villagers finally resolved that their fear was too strong and their sorrow too deep, that too many children had been lost and they had to find a way to fight back. The warriors gathered with their spears and plotted how they might kill the ogress. The medicine people warned of her shape-shifting ways and told of her penchant for the form of an old woman. Together the villagers dug a deep pit, lined it with green wood branches carved into sharp spears, lit a fire to attract the deceptive Utlunta, and waited. As predicted, Utlunta was drawn by the smoke, and when the form of a humped, wrinkled auntie hobbled through the bushes, the warriors laughed. "You want us to kill a little old crone?" But when Utlunta walked fearlessly into the pit and was unharmed by the hundreds of spears, the warriors' laughter changed to silent fright. They shot her repeatedly with their sharpest weapons, and Utlunta stood there, crushed spears that had broken when they hit her stony chest all around, and mocked them. The soldiers were alarmed — they were almost out of spears, and what would happen then? Utlunta could wander the village at will, killing them all. It was then that out of the highest skies a small bird appeared, a chickadee, with a tiny bill, a happy call, and a shining black cap. The chickadee flitted, as chickadees do, down into the pit, and it landed on Utlunta's wrist. There it sat, looking at the warriors with its bright black eyes and at all the villagers, calling *seet-seet-seet*. The villagers wondered, but the warriors understood the chickadee's message. *Here! Seet-seet! Strike here!* And so the village was saved by the message of the chickadee. The Cherokee people, who had always loved the chickadee, now revered her, and they gave her a new name: Truth-Teller. This chickadee from the highest heavens stayed with the humans until, after many generations, they behaved too cruelly to the earth for her presence. She flew skyward, and her shadow image remains in the chickadees we see every day.

What is the truth-telling of the chickadee? It resides in her knowing the location of the misplaced, the displaced heart, and in her willingness to tell us where this heart is kept. Certainly I fail the chickadee's truth-telling, almost constantly. I fail this truth-telling by neglecting to bring my best intelligence to the observation of a common creature, preferring instead the distant, the showy, the seldom-seen. I fail this truth-telling by proclaiming that I long for wildness and yet refuse to see it daily, where it flits in front of my face. And when I do stop to watch the chickadee, I fail her truth-telling again by wanting to keep my wild nature just as this bird appears on the surface (pretty, simple, charming, and at a pleasant distance), rather than as she is in her depths (tangled, tenacious, audacious, startling, sacred, difficult, frail, intimate with death). With chickadee, we turn again to the common creatures, the wild community of home; we open to unflinching intimacy and relocate our own misplaced hearts.

Crow

A Storied Intelligence

We do not need scientific research to tell us that crows are smart — our own good, natural commonsense intelligence tells us that. We know crows are smart when we see them drop a nut or snail in the road and wait for a car to run over the treasure and crack its hard shell, a kind of large-scale tool use. We know crows are smart when we see them play with falling flower petals, with found feathers of another bird, with sticks they drop to swoop and catch. We know it when they speak — in one of the hundreds of individually meaningful vocalizations making up crow language — to one another (*I am here! Food! Predator! Assemble! Good night, my small chick…*); to our cats and dogs (tormentingly, and probably disparagingly); to hawks, owls, raccoons, and even robins that approach their nests; and yes, to us (we all know the call that means *Get away from my nest!* or, if we have been regularly feeding crows, *More food now!* —

with nary a *please*). We know crows are smart when we realize that they recognize a particular human, and when they scold and dive-bomb this person — only this person — whenever he passes, even picking him out of a crowd, sometimes for years on end. We know crows are smart when we come upon them observing their own dead, standing in utter silence over the bodies of family members.* We know crows are smart when we see them lined up on the electrical wires over our heads holding urban-planning meetings to which we are not invited, with subject matter to which we are not privy.

Crows are one of the most insistent animal presences in the urban bestiary, avian or non-. Their population growth in general mirrors human population growth; the upward-swinging graphed curve of human and crow numbers over time overlie each other almost perfectly. Many of the other birds — the house sparrows, pigeons, and starlings — that thrive alongside human habitations have been introduced to this country. Crows are native, wild. Yet they have shown a startling adaptability to human presence and ways, attracted to human towns once by our agriculture, and now by our refuse. We give crows plenty of roosts and nesting places in our gardens and street plantings, provide warmth in the heat sink of urban environments, and although crows (though they appear bold) are wary of humans and would prefer to avoid us, the easy food sources provided by urban and suburban ecologies are irresistible. We remove swaths of native trees and replace them with open, easy,

---

* *Thousands of people have witnessed crow funerals over the years, but the first serious mention of such activity in the academic literature came in the summer of 2012, when researchers at the University of California, Davis, described scrub jays, corvids closely related to crows, recognizing and gathering around the dead of their own species.*

wormy lawns. We leave our cat and dog food outside, and convenient water dishes beside it. We fill our trash cans with bones and pizza crusts and old pieces of berry pie, but we don't fasten the lids. We toss fries and popcorn outside McDonald's and Target. We attract smaller songbirds to our homes with food-filled feeders, and these birds' nests provide eggs and — even better — moist nestlings to round out the urban crow's diet. If it weren't for us humans and our dogs and cars disturbing them (crows build their nests higher in urban trees than in rural ones, to keep away from us), these birds would find themselves in a veritable crow heaven.

Crows are a polarizing force in the urban wild. Some people love them, some fear them, some hate them. Some dream them, some keep them as pets, some know them as totems, and an astonishing number choose to permanently ink the crow's image onto their bodies in soaring tattoos.* All agree that they are uncannily intelligent. I argued in my book *Crow Planet* that observing and learning to understand the crows among us is an ideal way to deepen our sense of place in the urban landscape. They show us the movements and behaviors of a fascinating bird species, yes, but also those of other creatures. A crow ruckus is the surest way to a wild story. When I opened the front door to gather mail the other day, there was a crow on the wire, scolding madly. Looking around, I spotted a nearby squirrel, but surely that wasn't enough to upset a crow (they tend to have the upper hand with squirrels), and the

---

* When I started doing Crow Planet readings, I was pleasantly surprised at how many people from the audience would stand in line afterward, not just to have a book signed but also to share with me their crow ink — some of the tattoos rendered on body locations they could have bared publicly, some not. Depending on where I was reading, I learned to venture a question: "Does anyone have any crow tattoos they'd like to share?" This would go over with great success at, say, Powell's bookstore in Portland, Oregon; with less success at the local Rotary Club.

Crow Tracks and Sign

Most urban passerines are too small and light to make tracks in anything but the lightest dust or snow. Crows are unique in that they are just heavy enough and just big-footed enough to make tracks in everyday substrates like garden soil or a bit of mud at the sidewalk's edge. Their tracks will be the largest of the classic bird tracks you will find (gulls' are bigger, but webbed). Notice the somewhat pronounced toe pads and the lightness in the center—the metatarsal, or middle of the track, barely registers. Next to a stubbier pigeon track, a crow's track will appear longish and elegant.

Other indicators of crow presence and activity include:

Crow pellets. Owl pellets get all the glory, with their fur and tiny skeletons, but many other birds, including crows, also cast pellets. Crow pellets are full of grains, seeds, and sometimes bits of gravel. In season, they are berry red. They are not as tightly formed as raptor pellets and often fall apart when they hit the ground, amorphous—we are stepping over them all the time without knowing it. Watch for crow pellets beneath your neighborhood crows' favorite perches.

Nutshells. Crows are expert at excavating the meat from acorns and other shells. A crow will wedge the nut into a crack on a log or some other crevice to keep it in place, or hold it tightly under one foot while pecking at it with its dexterous bill. Jays and some mammals will open acorns as well, but look for the crow's large, jagged, messy holes. The punctures will often go through to the other side of the shell. If the crow is excavating an acorn weevil (a favored prize) instead of the nut meat, it is typically just the cap side of the shell, the opening to the top of the nut where the weevil resides, that is pecked.

Feathers. Many bird feathers become a mystery once separated from the bird, very hard to identify. But crow feathers are big and black and difficult to mistake. In autumn, after the young are fledged and the adults are finished with the energetic task of nesting, much of the population will molt, and over the course of a few evening walks around the neighborhood, you might find enough feathers to make a whole crow! We collect them and keep them on the table inside the front door during this season, picking out the primary and secondary wing feathers and arranging them in order.

squirrel was anxiously chattering too. Even a little Anna's hummingbird perched near the crow was protesting. Finally I looked down to see a young raccoon just a few feet below me, at the bottom of my porch steps, exploring my front garden. "Hello," I said, half-heartedly attempting to shoo him away. He just stood on his haunches staring at me with a nonchalant stillness, and I wondered how it had taken me so long to notice him. Crow, squirrel, hummingbird, human—clearly I am the dullest animal in the bunch.

With practice, you can pick out crow alarm calls or the less urgent scolding calls from the baseline crow language. Always follow — they bring news of the universe. But the presence of crows cuts two ways. A planet on which urban crows are thriving in such numbers is a planet with too much concrete — a substrate to which very few nonhumans can adapt. It is a place where we can be informed by the wild creatures in our midst even as the rich diversity of wild animals is replaced by a few dominant, resourceful species. Crows render both wonder and warning.

Because of their size, crows are not thought of as songbirds, but they are in fact a large passerine in the corvid family, which includes jays, magpies, nutcrackers, the rooks and jackdaws of Europe, and ravens. It might appear on the surface that a crow is simply a smaller version of a raven. In addition to size, there are several other physical differences between crows and ravens. Ravens have bills that are proportionately larger than crows', their bodies are bulkier, and the edges of their tails are diamond-shaped, whereas crows' are more or less straight. In flight, ravens are "heavier," not as winsome and agile as crows. All of this takes some experience to pick out in the field, but one big help is that in most of the places that humans densely congregate, the big black corvid we commonly see will in fact be a crow, not a raven. Crows live socially and in cities; ravens are more solitary, and in general more rural (there are exceptions, and as anyone who lives in Seward, Alaska, will tell you, there are towns where ravens gather in numbers).

But physical differences are just one part of the equation. For a long time, the common narrative ran that while both crows and ravens are intelligent birds, ravens have bigger brains and are smarter. It's true that ravens can often problem-solve at a higher level, and even their play can be more complex. But the advanced social structure of crows has endowed them with a social intelligence that may in some ways surpass that of ravens. The vocalizations that crows use to communicate among themselves are more numerous and nuanced, and crows appear to have a more refined awareness of the death of their kind (particularly of family members), and even a sort of "crow justice"—attacking or ousting crows that are physically or socially aberrant. Crow nesting is more intricately social, often involving a helper, typically young from a previous year that are not ready to breed (crows don't nest until they are three or four—late among songbirds, most of which breed in their first year). If you are observing a neighborhood nest and regularly see three adult crows in attendance rather than two, the third bird is likely one of these helpers. The helper will function as a kind of crow nanny, keeping the nest in good repair, helping to guard and feed the female as she broods and later the young after they hatch. It was hypothesized that such helpers increased nesting success, but field studies proved otherwise—crow nests with or without helpers fledged the same number of young. What researchers did find was that crows that had been helpers fledged more young of their own when it came their turn to nest! Evidently the practice and observation makes them more successful parents. So yes, crows and ravens are similar and closely related species but also unique, exhibiting the wondrous capacities of corvid intelligence in their own lives and ways.

Recent scientific observations of captive corvids (and the YouTube videos accompanying them) have spurred our collective imagination. Betty, the New Caledonian crow who quickly fashioned a piece of wire into a hook with which to retrieve a small bucket of food in a deep plastic tube, is the most famous. New Caledonian

Baby Crows in Our Midst

"Why do I never see baby crows?" is a common crow question. In truth, it is likely that we have all seen plenty of baby crows, but we are misled by the human tendency to conflate baby-ness with smallness. A few crows will jump from the nest before they are grown and when they cannot yet fly. Such precocious chicks are quickly hidden beneath shrubbery by their parents, and we seldom see them, though occasionally we might run across one of these fat, round, wide-eyed little fluff balls. Normally, though, when a baby crow leaves the nest, it is about the same size as its adult parent, and fully feathered; in the peak of baby-crow season—late spring to early summer—they will be everywhere. Physically, baby crows can be recognized by their bills, which may have a fleshy grayish-pink gape left at the base; their feathers, which are a duller matte brown-black, rather than the iridescent purple-black of the adult crow; their eyes, which are typically gray-blue rather than the dark amber of adults'; and perhaps their tails, which may be slightly stubby. Occasionally there will be a bit of downy fluff left above the eyes.

But the best way to tell a baby crow is by its behavior. Baby crows are not dumb; they possess all the native intelligence of their species. But they are naive. They sit quietly, looking slowly all around. They are approachable and believe that just about anything—a bicycle, a giant cat with a bell around its neck, a raccoon, an SUV, you or me—is a strange, wondrous, and probably even friendly thing. They have hesitant takeoffs and rather bad landings. They look sweet. They are loud, begging for food from their parents with an annoying *waaaaaaaahhh* call. If you see a crow, and you instinctively think of it as a baby, you're probably right. Watch for them—they are all around us, a pleasure to observe.

An aside: Ornithologists and even hard-core birders do not call young crows babies. "Humans have babies, birds have young," we are told. True, true, but I believe it is a harmless colloquialism, and it comes so naturally to our tongues, an example of the easy empathy that is one of our own species' loveliest qualities. Still, if you want to be orno-hip, you can call these babies hatch-year birds through the fall, after which it becomes harder to identify them. By autumn, most young of the year will have grown their first adult flight feathers—their wings and tails will be shiny and new, but their backs and heads will still be a dull matte brown.

crows have since demonstrated the use of meta-tools — they will use a small stick to retrieve a bigger stick that will allow them to reach a piece of food. And after the Betty sensation, scientists for the first time observed New Caledonian crows constructing tools in the wild (though presumably native Pacific islanders were well aware of the practice). The crow will carefully choose a stick, pull leaves and bark selectively off the end (in effect sharpening it), then use it to evict grubs and insects from their hiding places or to outright stab them. The tool-use tendency is strong in this species, and evidently heritable — New Caledonian crows hatched in captivity will choose to use tools to perform simple food-extraction tasks, sometimes even if they don't need the tool to do it. English rooks in captivity have also learned to make wire hooks, and they can solve other complex problems, such as choosing exactly the right size stone among several options to drop down a plastic tube and force the release of a food morsel. Rooks do not appear to use tools in the wild. But as far as rocks go, I have seen a crow in my neighborhood constructing a tiny crow cairn, attempting to create a small stack of stones (it got only one stone to balance on another but tried for a third for over half an hour as I watched with binoculars, bemused, from my open study window). A friend of mine saw another crow doing the same thing, this one close to the Seattle Art Museum's downtown sculpture park; perhaps the bird was inspired by the Claes Oldenburg. Captive magpies are the only nonprimates known to exhibit self-recognition when shown a mirror. When a yellow sticker is placed on the magpie's feathers and it is shown its reflection, the bird will attempt to get the sticker off. Most animals, including those we consider to be the most brilliant (such as our own dogs), will not make this connection.

When crow intelligence is described, it is most often measured against human intelligence or, more generally, primate intelligence. Crows are "as smart as some lower primates" or "approach the intelligence of some higher primates" or demonstrate certain behaviors and ways of knowing that are "amazingly" or "uncannily" or "disturbingly" like our own. These three words come up frequently. *Uncannily* and *amazingly,* I suppose, because we have so long believed that we primates possess the only real intelligence. *Disturbingly,* I imagine, because we prefer that this be so. We have been willing to grant the higher intelligence of remote creatures, such as dolphins in the depths of the oceans or safely exotic elephant tribes. But crows? Dirty, loud, ultra-common birds we see every day, watching our every move and shitting on our SUVs?

Animal behaviorists at Cambridge University evaluated a vast collection of scientific papers and research on crows and other corvids with an eye to cognitive processes, and they reported their findings in *Science.* They concluded that crows share the same "cognitive toolbox" as humans and other primates. Living in close social groups and striving within these groups to find food and secure bodily safety in the face of similar social and ecological challenges have led us all—crow, primate, human—to develop the same complex cognitive pathways, including *causal reasoning* (as in the

A Murder of Crows versus Crow Murder

No one knows for certain why a group of crows is referred to as a murder; the term has been around since the fifteenth century, and its origin in this context is a mystery, lost in time. The *Oxford English Dictionary* speculates that it may have to do with the bird's cultural association with death, or perhaps its "harsh and raucous cry." It is unlikely to stem from a notion of crows themselves as murderers, though there are thousands of anecdotal reports of violent skirmishes between crows, some of them resulting in death. I have never seen a crow murder, but I have observed some vicious attacks. Crows are highly social and live in extended family groups, where there are bound to be occasional skirmishes. Intragroup disagreements are typically solved with symbolic posturing and vocalizing, or a few pecks. But if there is a territorial interloper from outside a crow's social group or a crow seeking access to another crow's mate, then the fights can be more brutal. And like many other birds, crows will attack and sometimes kill a bird with aberrant coloring or one that is sick or injured. This may be to keep the standout or vulnerable bird from drawing the attention of predators, which would put the other crows at risk. In the case of injured crows, though, I rarely see them attacked; it is far more common, in my experience, to observe crows standing guard over an injured family member, attempting a measure of care.

development and use of tools); *flexibility* (the ability to generate rules from past experiences that provide a varied repertoire of potential responses to novel stimuli, as opposed to rote learning); *imagination* (where situations and scenarios not presently experienced can still be conceptualized in the mind's eye); and *prospection* (the ability to imagine future events).

Prospection in particular marks advanced mental acuity. Envisioning the future allows us (both crows and humans) to play out various scenarios, weigh consequences, avoid dangerous or unproductive actions, and take calculated risks. It is key in the practice of deception. There is a crow nest in the big hawthorn tree in front of my house. One spring day, while the nest was in progress, I saw a crow fly toward it carrying a large twig. When she spotted me standing there on the sidewalk, she landed on the electrical wire over my head, regarded me sidelong for a few seconds, then flew purposefully away with her stick, not to her nest, but to an abandoned crow nest across the street, where she actually pretended to go to work, nestling her stick among the others. I quickly scampered inside and up to the blind provided by my study window. With binoculars, I saw the crow emerge from the tree and sit again on the electrical wire, scanning the block, presumably looking for me. Satisfied, she flew to her real nest, but not before retrieving her fresh twig from the sham nest! Such deception at the nest is common among crows and is far more complicated than rote forms of avian distraction, such as the killdeer's famous broken-wing predator-distraction display (where an adult killdeer flops on the ground as if injured when a potential threat nears her ground-scrape nest).

Neurobiological studies round out the picture of crow intelligence. We know by simple weight and measurement that corvid brains are relatively large — given the size of the birds, their brains are bigger than we would expect (as a percentage of body mass, some corvid brains are even larger than ours), and this is one indicator of mental potential. Yet new research shows that it is not just the size of the crow brain but its structure that accounts for the birds' storied intelligence. It's not just any old part of the brain that is enlarged in crows, it's the forebrain in particular — the segment having to do with behavioral responses to sensory stimuli, problem-solving, causal reasoning, and the integration of memory with sensory and motor signals, and even emotion. This means that while crows do react to the world by instinct or by what they've learned through mimicking other crows or by rote (as do most vertebrate animals), they also respond through imagination and experiment and experience and whim. Novel situations may invite play, engagement, or perhaps a seemingly studied disinterest. More than most birds, crows make up their lives; they do new things, nutty things, really, really smart things all the time, and if we watch, we will be privileged to observe them.

It is wonderful that we have come to a time when we are beginning to speak openly in stringent scientific circles about the rich consciousness of a bird, something that was nearly unheard of in the last century. With this realization, we enter into an empathy and intimacy that is as instructive as it is instinctive (to recognize the consciousness of animals comes naturally — it is often *unlearned* in our formal education, and then relearned in our experience of the world). But acknowledging the ways that avian intelligence can be like ours is just a start. I believe that crows are asking something even more of us. For so long we have mistaken human intelligence for all intelligence, limiting our understanding of the wild, of

Dive-Bombing Crows

Dive-bombing of humans by crows is a seasonal occurrence, linked to the most vulnerable stages of crow nesting. Even if we don't actually see the young, the adult birds in spring and summer may be protecting a nest with eggs, a hidden nest with freshly hatched chicks, or chicks that have left the nest and are tucked away in the branches or shrubbery. In a couple of months, when the young are grown and self-sufficient, the dive-bombing will stop.

Being so large and loud and bulky, crows are at a disadvantage as nesters. Think about it: Most of the urban tree-nesting songbirds are so small. Robins, chickadees, sparrows, finches—they can build sweet little nests tucked into shadowy corners, well camouflaged and difficult to find. Their young are small too, and easy to hide. Crows have no such luck. They are stealthy for their size, but it's hard to hide a big nest full of baby crows, all of them cawing in that baby-crow way, sounding like ducks. As large, unpredictable mammals, we are rightly perceived as a threat.

Here's what to do about dive-bombing crows: If a crow is cawing at you during nesting season, just cross nonchalantly to the other side of the street, ignoring it completely, as if that's what you meant to do anyway. Continue on your way, enjoying the day. If you are dive-bombed anyway, just keep going—the farther away you get, the better. Think kind thoughts for the well-being of the crow young. (Why not? Crows are sometimes good at perceiving intent, so cultivating a benevolent attitude might help you seem less threatening.) If a crow has already determined, fairly or not, that you are a threat and is dive-bombing you on sight (not ideal—other crows will think that this crow has a good reason to hate you and might join the fun), then avoid the area for a while. If that's impossible, walk through the area waving your arms slowly over your head, or, since we know that crows recognize human faces, consider a disguise—for real! A wide-brimmed hat that hides your hair and face, some sunglasses…

Crows attacking hawks and owls is another common occurrence, and that happens year-round. Many hawks and owls prey on both adult crows and their young, so crows are proactive about discouraging these birds' presence. It's amazing to watch a few small crows attacking a huge hawk or eagle. The crows that seem so large on our city sidewalks suddenly become tiny next to a bald eagle.

I'm not a crow apologist, but I do think it helps to consider matters from the complicated standpoint of an urban-nesting crow parent. And I think it's delightful that, no matter how urban our lives, we can witness firsthand the circle of life from our home places.

nonhumans, and of ourselves. The next step in the evolution of our own natural intelligence might be for us—as individuals, naturalists, scientists, just folks going along our day with creatures of all kinds in our path—to allow the depth of animal minds and cognition to exist apart from a human yardstick, to recognize a plethora of intelligences that possess richness and value apart from how much or how little they resemble our own.

What is flight intelligence? Flock intelligence? What is learned when there is a breeze in your feathers, when your voice is shaped by a syrinx, when you can see the ultraviolet spectrum glow upon the wing of another bird?

Darwin was able to hold this duality lightly. Though the science of which he is the supposed father has dismissed the anthropomorphizing of animals as sentimental and inappropriate, if Darwin recognized an expression or emotion in an animal, he never hesitated to call it by the name that made sense. Whereas modern scientific journals would never use such language, Darwin freely referred to animals as happy, peaceful, distressed, or displaying any other emotion that seemed to make common sense. For him, continuity in human and animal consciousness was a given, one so basic to his understanding of evolutionary continuity (why should it be morphological only, with consciousness suddenly sprouting in the human animal? — this made no sense whatever) that he took it as a baseline given, one he never even sought to defend. But Darwin did not see animal minds as little, more limited human minds. We all know the famous depictions of Darwin's Tree of Life, with multifarious branches leading from the insects to the fish and reptiles, up to the birds, the squirrels and skunks, the giraffes, the small primates, the great primates, and perching at the top of the tree, in a final, gloriously intelligent (if slightly precarious) leaf: *us*. But this was never Darwin's vision. Darwin's tree was really more of a shrub — a Shrub of Life, where all the tiny branches tangle together, not strictly stratified. We spring from a root intelligence that develops uniquely and in the span of evolutionary time, in the manner fit for each species. Thus crow intelligence is *crow intelligence* (residing alongside coyote intelligence, chicken intelligence, butterfly intelligence, the strange knowing of trees that exists without even a brain), not an inferior form or approximation of human intelligence.

Story is an entrance to this middle way. In storytelling we recognize human-animal similarity and allow the mystery of uniqueness at the same time. And there is no better guide into the world of wild story than the ever-present crow. Everyone has a crow story. If you find yourself seated at a boring dinner with conversation flagging, just bring up crows — "The other day I saw a crow do the craziest thing" — and the party will leap to life, with guests proclaiming that they have seen crows chase falling leaves, play in the snow, climb a ladder for fun, pester the cat by imitating her meow, practice aerodynamic maneuvers in the wind, follow the mail carrier, befriend the kitten, steal from the squirrel, daintily eat french fries out of the trash can as if dining on haute cuisine.

These stories come alive for us in the noticing and gain something more in the telling. In story, we feel less compelled to impose ourselves, our interpretations, our beliefs than we do in other ways of information-sharing. (Beatrix Potter teaches this well: the ill-fitting human clothes worn by her animals keep falling off.) We report what we objectively see, more or less, and yet nearly all crow stories end, eyes wide, with the same questions: What was that bird doing? What was it *thinking*? We pause. It is this lovely, restive uncertainty that makes the story wonderful.

In the Coast Salish mythology from my own corner of the world, there is a famous tale in which a crow or raven returns light to a darkened world:

Grandfather kept the sun hidden in a cedar box, and
Crow — desiring the sunlight and being the consummate

trickster shape-shifter — found a way to seduce Grandfather's daughter, journey into her as a seed, and become born as a beloved grandson. Unable to deny the boy anything, Grandfather one day gave in to his grandson's begging and let him play with the secret sun box. When he did, the boy shifted back into Crow form and flew through the smoke hole in the ceiling, spreading light across the world.

There are many other tales of crows and ravens and light retrieval among First Peoples in North America, but I was thrilled to find a similar myth far across the globe, among the Ainu stories of northern Japan:

In the early days, a scaled monster fed his incessant hunger by swallowing the sun. The earth grew shadowy, and the people were cold, afraid, and hungry as their crops began to fail in the darkness. Only a crow named Pashkuru Kamui had the audacity to fly at the monster. Pashkuru Kamui pecked the monster's forked tongue until the beast panicked and regurgitated his prey, the sun. Light and warmth returned to the earth and the people.

It is no longer "the early days," but we are inhabiting this myth now, in our way, as crows guide humans toward a new kind of light. Our crow stories bring the fullness of another animal's intelligence into our sphere — that which we see, that which we know, that which we recognize, that which science proclaims, and that which we can never know. In allowing this fullness, we allow our own intelligence to come to life — wild, rangy, riverine, sunlit.

Hawk and Owl

The Seen and the Unseen

B
etter not get too close." *Claire and I were out on an autumn stroll in*
the neighborhood, and this advice was proffered by a round,
baseball hatted gentleman, arms folded atop his belly. "It's a red-
tailed hawk, and it's got a pigeon," he reported, nodding toward the
sidewalk. "No telling what it will do." We spotted the birds on the
grassy parking strip, a Cooper's hawk with a lifeless pigeon beneath his
bright yellow feet. Claire looked at me sidelong with big, slightly anxious eyes. She was not worried a whit about a hawk attack, but she'd
heard my Why-is-it-that-the-only-hawk-name-people-know-is-the-red-
tailed-so-they-call-anything-resembling-a-hawk-a-red-tailed
speech often enough to know that the innocent group of five or so folk
that were gathering around this unfolding urban-wild drama might be
in for a lecture. I winked at her and held my tongue. I loved this misguided but well-intended advice, spoken with such authority — the

Which Hawk?

In the *Aberdeen Bestiary,* there are two kinds of hawks: wild and domesticated. Domesticated birds would have been falcons or accipiters whose legs were fitted with leather jesses held by the falconer's hand. The lack of further differentiation is singular. In the urban wilds, many species of the various hawk tribes are possible—v-winged falcons, eagles, the fish-eating ospreys, soaring buteos, and forest accipiters. Of these, Cooper's, sharp-shinned, and red-tailed occur in most neighborhoods.

Sharp-shinned hawk   Cooper's hawk

Cooper's and sharp-shinned hawks are stunning bird-eating hawks that regularly grace the urban wilds, visiting our gardens and perching near our feeders, preying on passerine birds. They are not common in terms of numbers, but individual birds turn up consistently and dramatically. Both belong to the accipiter tribe—long-tailed birds with shorter wings for navigating forest corridors in pursuit of smaller birds. These little hawks fling themselves from trees and into the air with thrilling abandon. Adults of both species have blue-gray backs, darker gray heads, buff and orange breasts, orange-red eyes, and long yellow legs. Younger birds remain streaky brown with yellow eyes until they are about two years old. Both sometimes make a sweet, quizzical expression. While Cooper's are generally larger, size is difficult to judge in the field. Female raptors of all species, both hawks and owls, are substantially larger than males, but this is especially true of the sharp-shinned hawk, where females are up to 57 percent larger than males. This means that a large female sharp-shinned might be bigger than a small male Cooper's. Even so, if you see one of these hawks alongside a crow (which is where you typically see them, as crows come in to chase a hawk away the second they spot one), you can make a good guess as to which hawk you are looking at—the body of a sharp-shinned hawk is decidedly smaller than a crow, about the size of a robin (they look bigger, because their tails are so long and their heads are larger, and maybe also because they are so aggressive). A Cooper's hawk's body is about crow-size.

Red-tailed hawk

Red-tailed hawks are common urban raptors in the buteo tribe— soaring birds with nicely proportioned wings and fanning tails. Perched on branches or highway lampposts, red-tails are shaped just like footballs and are shades of brown, with a buff-ivory breast, typically with a necklace of brown feathers across the belly. In flight, the red of the tail shows through, though young birds will have brown-striped tails until they are about three. Unlike the accipiters, red-tails are not fussy about their diet, one of the things that make them the most ubiquitous raptor in North America. They eat snakes, lizards, mice, rats, rabbits, chipmunks, squirrels, opossums, smaller skunks and young raccoons, ducks and any other birds they can manage to catch (buteos are not as speedy or agile as accipiters and falcons), grasshoppers, cockroaches, even butterflies. They will eat domestic pets, particularly cats, but also puppies or smaller dogs. A fat little backyard chicken is just right for a red-tail.

worry that this little hawk, overcome with possessiveness over its pigeon, might attack a human. An elderly couple now came out of their house, smoking, and the "Stay back" guy, who, with his posture and substance, had taken charge of the situation, kept yelling "Shut up!" at the barking retriever tied up on his porch. Crows dive-bombed the hawk mercilessly, and more were coming in—a couple dozen of them. The thin young Cooper's could almost speak with his eyes: *Oh, please, please, just leave me alone, just let me have my pigeon.* But it was too much for him—humans, retrievers, cigarettes, crows—and he finally fled sans pigeon (a heavy bird for a Cooper's to carry in flight) to a high branch in the near birch. He was wild-eyed and fearful now, turning from the dog to the onlookers to the crows, straggles of downy pigeon feathers hanging from his bill and feet. We stood together, none of us, including the hawk, ready to give up the moment. I was about to suggest that we quietly leave, let the bird have his meal, but then I gasped, along with the rest of the human onlookers, all of us unprepared for what happened next. The still cloud of feathers in the grass that was the dead pigeon burst into flight and was gone.

There is much to entice a raptor in the city—structural complexity (built, if not botanical), abundant prey in a concentrated place (rats, mice, pigeons, huge flocks of starlings, grasshoppers, cockroaches), water sources, and moderate temperatures (with their heated buildings, most cities run several degrees warmer than neighboring rural places). Birds of prey lace our cities—the edges, parks, cemeteries, and backyards. Red-tails roost on highway corridor lampposts, where snakes, rats, rabbits, and mice populate the grassy medians; bird-eating sharp-shinned and Cooper's hawks dart through our yards or perch stealthily in our garden trees, waiting for a chance to snatch a sparrow or starling meal from our feeders; peregrine falcons nest on skyscrapers and bridges, feasting on pigeons. In watery places, ospreys, like the peregrines recovering from plummeting populations before the banning of DDT, respond favorably to nesting platforms and make themselves at home in urban parks. A merlin flew overhead during my neighborhood walk the other day, a small falcon whose uncommon presence warranted a call to my birder neighbors. And though owls in general are not known for their love of bathing, in the secret darkness, screech owls splash in our suburban birdbaths, snatching a moth or mouse on the way back to their roosts. Great horned owls roost in the largest trees at a city's leafy edges eating rats, skunks, and cats and calling, hooting, dueting with their mates all night long and into the Yeatsian dawn.

Some researchers believe that urban environments exist as an ecological sink for many raptors, that is, as a poorer-quality habitat in which the population could not be self-sustaining without an influx of birds from a higher-quality habitat. Most raptors that nest in cities suffer far less depredation upon their nestlings than raptors that nest in rural places—probably because in the watered-down urban ecosystem, there are fewer predators to eat them. But there are unique urban hazards that may balance out, or even offset, this benefit: electrocution, malnourishment, illness from eating diseased birds who have picked up infections at ill-kept feeders, disturbance by human presence causing nest abandonment, and, more than all of these, cars. One study of Cooper's hawks indicates that birds that become accustomed to humans when young don't live as long as others, for reasons yet unknown.

Both hawks and owls are present in far fewer numbers than most other avian species that populate urban areas; as carnivorous predators, they are at the top of the food chain. Just as there are more squirrels than coyotes, there are more robins than red-tails. Though there are fewer of them, these birds somehow take up a greater quantity of our psychic space and inspire disproportionate excitement when seen, capturing our imaginations and our hearts. The red-tail Pale Male and his various mates in Manhattan were made famous nationwide by the book *Red-Tails in Love,* and when the hotel they nested on decided it was done with the whitewash mess flung down its stone sides, public outcry kept its owners from removing the nest, and Pale Male claimed a full front-page spread in the *New York Times,* with an illustrated genealogy of his mates and descendants. Here in Seattle we had the peregrines Stuart and Belle nesting famously on the Washington Mutual Bank–cum–Chase Tower, spectacularly dispatching pigeons, raising their black-eyed chicks, and starring in a beautifully photographed children's book. We fix owl-cams, eagle-cams, hawk-cams upon their nests and spy at all hours on the busy engaged parents, the fluffy, playful, vulnerable young.

This heightened attention to raptors has surfaced in all cultures over the course of history, always and everywhere. The presence of a raptor is *meaningful.* We catch them at the edge of our peripheral vision, our own animal viscera responding instinctively to the shadow of a predator spiraling overhead.* These are birds that fly between the

---

* *I once had a guinea pig named Tazmania who sometimes roamed loose in my apartment, along with Ani the cat and three parakeets. (I'm truly not a Crazy Pet Lady; this was just a random interlude in my single days.) An odd little peaceable kingdom it was — given half a chance, Ani would sneak onto the lanai when I wasn't looking and quickly snatch a wild house finch, but she would never touch "her" parakeets, even when they sidled up to her and playfully picked at her whiskers, and she would actually lick and snuggle Taz. But whenever one of the parakeets flew over the guinea pig, poor Tazzie would flatten against the floor. This was an inbred pet-store rodent who had never been outdoors in his life, acting from an instinct buried in the DNA that links him to cavy ancestors in Peru. I think of him (RIP, Tazmania) whenever I feel that involuntary, prehuman rush at the presence of a hawk in flight.*

worlds of life and death and then, with a silent, unexpected rush, they bring these worlds crashing together. There are other birds, the avian scavengers—crows, ravens, vultures—whose biology draws them into real and symbolic association with death. But our response to scavenging is very different from our response to the capture of prey. The awareness of death called up at the sight of a hawk or owl is fresh, careening, near. If we chance to see a raptor with its prey, the victim is so new, so *suddenly* dead. This death is no flattened roadside opossum; it's visceral, pressing, the victim so recently alive that we can feel it living still, must look twice to be sure, and even then cannot help but wonder with a hopeful, irrational compassion rising unbidden from a shared biological frailty: Did I see it move? Might it still live?

It is rare to see a raptor actually catch its prey; birds of prey are fast, secretive, stealthy, eat only once or twice a day, and, in the case of most owls, hunt in the dark night when we are tucked in and dreaming. But we can sense the possibility—the immediacy of a hunt—in their physiology, in every turn of sinew and feather, made for this preying. The rich cross-cultural mythology surrounding these birds rises, as all good myth does, straight from their bodies, their hunt-and-kill-adapted physiology. Regarding the red-tailed hawk on the highway lamppost, the great horned and screech owls on our city edges, we see that Darwin's truth (adaptations of eye, talon, feather, piercing bill) and the insights of ancient myth (from Egypt to the North American plains, where hawks and owls are spiritual conduits from life to death) meet and blend.

Biologically, the two groups are not closely related. Hawks and owls share physical adaptations like big brains, clutching feet, curling talons, and binocular vision as a function of convergent evolution—they both have similar physical/lifestyle requirements, resulting in separate lineages evolving similar traits. (Convergent evolution regularly crosses larger biological gaps than the span between owls and hawks — flippers in both penguins and dolphins, for example, or dorsal fins in porpoises and sharks, or long sticky tongues in woodpeckers and armadillos.) But it makes sense that hawks and owls are entwined in both our psychic and ecological landscapes. Mythologically, these birds have always evoked power, vision, wisdom, the hunt, transition, death. Hawks represent the solar aspect of these themes, owls the lunar. Most large predatory animals claim an absolute spatial territory, but for hawks and owls, there is a temporal dimension as well. They hunt in the same place and share a similar prey base, but they are separated by time and light, with some species in particular forming layered, territorial pairs. Red-tailed hawks and great horned owls are linked in this solar/lunar way, as are, sometimes, the small falcons (kestrels and merlins) and screech owls. There is a bit of safety in this arrangement, as the individual birds and their territories are afforded some protection by the vigilance of the one predator while the other is asleep. Unless we are trying hard, we see more hawks than owls, so I love to keep this eco-poetical truth in mind: When a hawk shows herself beneath the light of the sun, somewhere nearby her lunar owl sister sits, bark-plumage invisible against the trunk of a park tree, feathered lids closed against the intrusive daylight. The seen and the unseen, equally real and present among us.

Most owls are not the least inclined to build nests. They prefer to purloin the nests that others have made and touch them up a very little bit, if at all. Smaller owls, like the common urban screech owls, nest in small cavities made by woodpeckers, found in natural hollows, or provided by nest boxes. If other birds are already in the hole, they will chase them away, cover their eggs with grasses, and blithely lay their own clutch on top of them. Large owls will take over the used stick nests of hawks, and great horned owls in particular are known for happily reusing the old nests of their daytime counterpart, the red-tailed hawk. And while the red-tails somehow leave perfectly serviceable nests behind after fledging their young, when the owls and their big-footed, trampling chicks are done with it, nothing will be left but tatters, a nest beyond repair.

To find owls, dream and hope.* To find hawks, look up. Seeing a raptor is always a thrill. But in daily urban life, it happens as often by chance, happenstance, or luck as by effort or desire. Unless you have been studying a place with some consistency, finding a hawk at will or whim is an uncertain endeavor. Nearly all of my urban hawk sightings occur in the moments I happen to look up—from my writing, my coffee, my navel—and there will be a sharp-shinned, shooting flat across the yard, a kettle of vultures rising on a late-morning thermal, a red-tail circling high. Some study and watching, developing a sense of what to look for, learning to discern a raptor from the ranks of the crows and ducks and robins all of this will help, as will a readiness to see. I always find that if I am in a raptor-study mood—reading up on the latest research, studying

---

* When I find an owl in the city, no matter how circuitous the trail that led me to it, it seems like an accident and a miracle. Even when an owl is present, it can be difficult to discover. Owls sleep during the day against tree trunks, wrapped in their soft camouflaged feathers, looking themselves like textured bark strewn with lichens. Even when I know exactly where to look for an owl, and I know the owl is there, I can't always find it right away, or at all. Daytime hooting is almost always a dove or pigeon, no matter how owlish it sounds. The best way to observe owls is to go on an owl walk with your local Audubon Society or to ask someone who knows about such things. This is more complicated than it sounds—expect scrutiny! Birders are secretive and don't want "their" owls disturbed. You may have to speak in hushed tones, proffer a bribe of home-baked bread, or otherwise prove yourself owl-worthy. Once you have found an owl, remember that owls have a fair bit of fidelity to their roosts, and you may be able to visit the same bird day after day.

Raptor Brains, Bird Necks, and the Trouble with Owl Eyes

Raptors look smart because they are. The brains of both hawks and owls are proportionately large, as birds go, in part because survival by aerial hunting requires a scrappy plasticity of behavior and the intelligence that accompanies it. The consciousness of hawks and owls has been little studied, but, like crows, ravens, and parrots, both owls and hawks appear to play, a category of behavior associated with high intelligence. Red-tails drop sticks and catch them on the wing, just as crows and ravens do. Accipiters appear to fly more often on windy days, enjoying aerial acrobatics for no good, "practical" reason. Fledgling owls of various species, including the western screech, have been observed pouncing on inanimate objects or dead prey very much like kittens. And my physician friend Bob called one morning to report that a great horned owl in a nearby park had chased the yellow tennis ball he threw over and over for his big dog, Molly. The owl would swoop over dog and ball and then lift at the last minute, letting the dog catch her toy. With her precise vision, it was unlikely she mistook the ball for prey. The question of play among the raptors is a relatively new one. The truth is, we don't know, and we likely underestimate, the breadth of their interior lives, as is true for our knowledge of most nonhuman animals, including, as Darwin showed us, earthworms.

Owls cannot turn their heads all the way around, as is commonly believed, but they can rotate their heads 270 degrees in either direction. Owls have fourteen cervical vertebrae, twice as many neck bones as humans possess (and with seven cervical vertebrae, we can turn our heads only eighty to one hundred degrees without injury), but not that many for a bird; even the shortest-necked birds have eleven cervical vertebrae, and longer-necked birds like grebes or geese have up to twenty-five, which gives them all a good range of motion in the neck. And in all birds, including owls, the large carotid artery runs along the middle of the neck vertebrae, rather than alongside them as it does in humans. This keeps the artery from being pinched and damaged during rotation, allowing even more cervical mobility. So why don't we see all the birds contorting their necks in that trademark owl fashion? Well, what *is* unique to owls is the *need* to turn their heads so far, a need that has as much to do with their brains and eyes as it does their skeletons.

An owl's skull must fulfill many competing requirements. It must provide space for a brain big enough to accommodate the intelligence and versatility of behavior required by a successful predator; have room for eyes large enough to be keen in the night; maintain a structure that sits proportionally atop the bird, not becoming too top heavy; and remain light enough for the bird's agile flight. In all of this, an evolutionary compromise has been wrought. With the owl's big brain and sharp eyes squeezed into the skull, there is no room for anything else, not even a bit of space around the eyeballs. There is some variation among species, but in general the owl eyes we see looking out at the world in that startling owl way are fit so snugly within their sockets that they cannot move. Owls have to turn their heads, sometimes dramatically, in order to see anything other than what's straight ahead of them. Though other birds might have the flexibility for extreme neck rotation, most of them cannot pull it off too often or for too long without injury.

New research published by an interdisciplinary team at Johns Hopkins finally explains the mystery of how owls are able to turn their heads so far, so frequently, and for such extended periods of time without damaging their arteries, or cutting off the blood supply to their brains and having owl strokes. To conduct the study, the researchers infused an x-ray enhancing dye into the cervical blood vessels of dead barred, snowy, and great horned owls (all had died of natural causes). Imaging the owl's necks during movement, they were able to discern that the holes in owl neck bones through which major arteries travel are much bigger than they are in other birds, and they are buffered with air sacs; the space and the cushioning protect the arteries during rotation. In addition, the blood vessels nearest the head and jaw are expandable—they can fill with reservoirs of pooled blood. These little balloons of blood supply the owl's brain during extreme movement. "There's no real clinical relevance here," quipped one of the scientists, "other than don't try this at home." But it's wonderful that in this age of techno-science, there are still basic physiological secrets to be told by the creatures we thought we knew best.

taxonomy or identification secrets, or just thinking about hawks on a given day — I will see more of them. Always. It is a spiritual/psychological corollary, one that I cannot explain but that is absolutely true. Quiet expectation, along with experience and luck, all help in the finding and observation of any wild animal.

Besides watchfulness, preparation, and fate, the best way to find city hawks is to have the other birds, crows in particular, tell you where they are. If crows are making a ruckus, it is always worth checking out. Typically, they will be tormenting some poor hated (by the crows) creature, perhaps a canine, feline, human, or raccoon, but most often a hawk. Because both hawks and owls prey upon crow nestlings and even on adult crows (in the case of adult crows, it is often an owl in the night, swooping upon a female crow hushed upon her nest), crows indiscriminately mob all raptors at all times of the year.

It's effective. While mature hawks and eagles will seem to ignore the mob, young hawks can be at a complete loss in the face of crow attacks, and while observing such mobs, I find that my sympathy runs both ways. Crows have reason to fear. I have seen a Cooper's hawk calmly eating a barely fledged crow as the parent birds shrieked in a rare vocalization that I can only describe as horror tinged with the crow version of sorrow. But very often there is no immediate danger, and the hawk being mobbed is young and likely hungry, one of the birds that, like most hawks, will not live to its first birthday. When the young hawk is pelted by crows, the look in its eyes will sometimes change from that aloof self-possession that raptors exude to thin desperation. In any case, when crows are in an uproar, always check it out. It is a good habit, and a simple one, to follow the messages of birds. We will so often be led, in the middle of a day that was otherwise normal, into an unexpected urban circumstance, magical in its wildness—the things that fly, literally beneath (or above) our typical human radar.

But we must remember too that, as is true for coyotes, moles, and mice, there are more raptors among us than we see or even know. We love to see the bird itself, but glimpses are hard-won. To follow the storied presence of raptors in our urban lives, we watch for more than their feathered bodies. We find the presence of hawks and owls in their whitewashes, in their pellets, and in the trail of their sustenance—the bits and pieces of prey animals they leave behind.

The first thing I noticed when I went out for a morning walk the other day was that the patch of earth beneath the big cypress in front of my house had been sprinkled with a circle of glitter. I knelt down and scooped some of the sprinkles into my hand they were the gold-tipped edges of adult starling feathers. The more I searched, the more I found, and I was eventually led to the hapless bird's head, separated from the missing body and stuck bright yellow beak first into the soil at the base of my tree. Well, this was a singular and unnerving scene, even for a self-proclaimed urban naturalist. I decided to leave the head where it was, just to see what would happen next. (The following morning the feathered skull was entirely gone, but the yellow beak was still stuck in the ground!) Walking to the library later that day, I spotted a Cooper's hawk and imagined it to be a bit extra-plump, perched there on an electrical wire, with a satisfied I-have-just-consumed-a-starling look about it. Like many bird-eating raptors, Cooper's hawks often behead their prey before defeathering and eating it. I have read in several natural science and track/sign treatises that such-and-such hawk species always eats the head, such-and-such owl species never does. But in

Bats, Creatures of Air

No, bats are not raptorial birds. But in the *Aberdeen* and other medieval bestiaries, they appear alongside the birds, typically the owls. Just as I was about to dismiss this in my mind as a quaint medievalism, I recalled that over the years, several well-educated people have said to me something along the lines of, *You study birds, right? So, I have this question about bats...* I'll mention as gently as possible that bats, of course, aren't birds, after which there is a startled and embarrassed pause. Obviously, the questioner knows this. We all know that bats are mammals, the only mammals with true, powered flight. Most of us know that they are beneficial mammals in the urban landscape, each eating about two thousand mosquitoes every night. I used to wonder over such bird/mammal confusion, to see it as an ill-thought-out muddle stemming from inconsistent exposure to good natural history training, but now I see it differently. We humans seek to categorize, to put things into a kind of order. One valid order is the scientific/taxonomic—in some circles, it is the only valid ordering for the organismic world. But another tendency that seems to inhere in us is a penchant for understanding things elementally. The bat and the bird, whatever their taxonomic grouping, are creatures of air. When Claire was very young, I scolded Tom on a boat in Alaska when he pointed to a breaching gray whale and said to our impressionable and toothless young daughter, "Honey! Look at the big fishy!" *Fishy?* (After all these years, he hasn't lived down the comment, and I haven't lived down my overreaction!) But again, this is a common parental utterance, one that may be based more on an intrinsic bond with elemental nature than on a misunderstanding of biology. There is something beautiful here—a wild, immediate sensibility that appears to be innate, bodily, and unarguably true.

Bats live among us, largely unnoticed. Of the several species that have adapted to urban places, the most common are the little brown bat, which hibernates in the winter, and the big brown bat, active year-round. All species hang upside down by their feet, typically with their wings wrapped around their bodies, and if startled, they can drop into sudden flight. Females like protected places with consistent temperatures for their nurseries and come into conflict with humans when they gather in attics, and people complain of noise, guano, or just being creeped out by bats. Autumn is the best time to seal potential bat entrances—young bats will be grown and flying, and hibernation will not have begun. Bats have flourished in North America since the time of dinosaurs, but in the last five years, the skin disease known as white-nose syndrome has killed millions of bats. Sick bats were first discovered in New York City, and since then the disease has devastated populations in the Northeast, spreading swiftly to at least sixteen states. Putting up bat houses on human-approved sections of our houses might assist bats while keeping them from congregating in our attics.

practice, there seem to be no hard-and-fast species-specific rules about head-eating and head-leaving, so the presence or absence of a head seems to me a dubious who-ate-this-bird clue. Nearly all bird-eating raptors *will* eat viscera first, then sinew, discarding the legs and the wings (there is some dissonance in seeing a pretty little kestrel or saw-whet owl with its foot wrapped around a mouse, the mouse's entrails dangling indelicately from the bird's bill like spaghetti). Some raptors slurp out the skull's contents but leave the skull itself, as with my starling.

Watch for feathers, wings, leftover heads and feet. A cat-kill site will be a random mess; hawks tend to stand in the middle of a "faerie ring" of plucked feathers, like the starling-glitter in my yard. You can tell whether the bird was scavenged or killed fresh by examining the feather pile. A freshly plucked bird will leave no flesh sticking to its feather tips, but bits of flesh come off with the feathers of a cold bird. This is messy and perhaps unwelcome information, but poetic in its way. We learn to read the world, the wild trails among us, to know it as biology, as story, as *shared* life.

The legs and feet of both hawks and owls are endowed with an involuntary clutching mechanism that allows the bird to ratchet tightly about its prey and pull it close to its body. I learned this viscerally one day when, years ago, I was interning as a raptor rehabber and needed to change the bandage on a red-tailed hawk's wing. When handling red-tails, we normally wore thick leather gloves that reached up to our elbows to protect against the talons and the clutching (it's different than handling, say, a small falcon, like a kestrel or merlin, where garden gloves suffice). This day, I wanted my fingers free to do a nice job with the delicate bandaging and heedlessly believed myself beyond harm from this beloved hawk. I pulled my Carhartt jacket down to my wrist, then picked up the bird with my bare hands. Like most birds, red-tails are funny about being

Barred Owls and Urban Attacks

The barred owl is a beautiful bird, closely related to the northern spotted owl, an ecologically sensitive species, dependent on deep, ancient forests. Barred owls are larger, more adaptable, and more aggressive than the spotted, and where the two species overlap, it appears that barred owls disrupt the smaller owls' nesting process, compete with them for food, and sometimes even attack or kill them. Unlike spotted owls, barred owls can adapt to scrappier forest and disturbed forest edges and urban parks. In recent years, its range has expanded dramatically westward and now includes the beachside park near my home, where a pair of owls have been attacking hapless joggers who venture too near their nest. (Conjecture on the neighborhood blog has run wild. Perhaps the owls thought a certain jogger's bald head was a rat?) Such incidents are not at all the norm, but similar reports are turning up across the country. Barred owls have just recently begun nesting so close to human habitation, and they are protecting their nests from a large, unfamiliar, strangely bipedal mammal. People associate nesting behavior with springtime, but owls begin setting up territories in the darkest winter. It is a delight to have owls among us, but defensive parent owls can terrify. Give them a wide berth, and if your daily walk or jog takes you in their path, then walk with your arms over your head, waving them gently as if you are a human willow tree, or carry an umbrella and put it up in owl territory. Consider working with park or city officials to create an educational sign to help protect both humans and nesting owls. (The U.S. Fish and Wildlife Service continues to contemplate killing barred owls to protect spotteds, but disturbed urban parks are a perfectly good place for barred owls, and heroic preservation of ancient forests is the only workable long-term protection for the spotted owl.) From a respectful distance, owl watching is perfectly safe.

held; if you have their wings pinned, they don't really think they can get away and tend to relax, especially if everything else around them is calm. I tucked the seemingly mellow bird under one elbow so I could work on her with both hands. In a moment of inattention, I carelessly reached across her belly, and she got me. Two hawk feet were clasped more deeply and tightly than I ever thought possible around my spindly forearm. The talons didn't penetrate my skin, but within a minute, my hand began to feel stiff, then went numb. The hawk seemed totally relaxed. Clearly this was costing her no effort whatsoever, and I was sure that if I dangled her from my arm and shook madly, she still would not have budged. Eyes beginning to bulge from my skull, I wandered the grounds with the injured, clinging bird until I finally found a friend to help me. "I'm a loon researcher," he deadpanned, "I don't do hawks." Funny. He had to peel the hawk's toes, one by one, from my arm. No blood, but I had an impressive blue bruise in the treelike shape of a hawk's foot, new respect for raptorial feet, and deepened empathy for their prey.

In the early decades of the twentieth century, Cooper's and sharp-shinned hawks were persecuted as "vicious bird killers." Men and boys would set up with rifles at migration routes to drop as many of the birds as possible, day after day. Even avian conservation organizations joined in sanctioning the slaughter to protect songbirds, and tens of thousands of hawks were killed. As science and conservation took a more ecological turn, the role of predators came to the fore, and the mass killing for the most part stopped by midcentury, giving the accipiter populations time to recover before their numbers were again decimated later in the century by DDT (though not to quite as perilous a brink as peregrines, ospreys, and bald eagles).

Surely it is natural to feel compassion for songbirds or prey animals in any instance. Who doesn't root for the gazelle, at least on some level, in all those nature documentaries? And of course, no one is obligated to love birds of prey in particular. But one of the strangest incidents of irrational hawk hatred involves the revered ornithologist Alexander Skutch, author of some of my most treasured natural history volumes, including the massive *Field Guide to the Birds of Costa Rica,* which I carried around every second of my honeymoon in spite of its size and my poor groom's slight jealousy (shouldn't I be paying at least as much attention to him?). Before his death, in 2004, Skutch penned some of the most observationally patient treatises on the behavior and consciousness of neotropical birds ever written, and his treatments combine a poetico-spiritual absorption with watchful scientific detail— indeed, it is possible that he observed these birds more thoroughly than anyone else on earth. So I was shocked when I eventually learned that on the sanctuary he kept and conserved for neotropical birds, he not only discouraged birds of prey, but actively hunted and killed them. He exempted the laughing falcons that nested near his hut from this sinister regime because they killed snakes, another hated predator! Dr. Skutch's activities were fueled in part by the evolution of his increasingly delusional philosophy that earthen nature should exist in a state of blissful harmony; predators were out of step with this vision. For years I have sought a way to reconcile Skutch's rare insight into animal ways and avian consciousness with this astonishing gap in his ecological understanding. But to this moment I remain bewildered, and for now must live with this tension, Skutch's books always within reach on my study shelves.

Just yesterday I looked randomly, without expectation, out my kitchen window and witnessed the split second that it took a small

Raptor Trails: Wash and Pellets

We all recognize white splat as an indicator of bird presence, but raptor leavings are unique. Most birds excrete all their waste—solid and liquid—in one swoop; depending on the bird's diet, we see the solid waste as a dark color, brownish or green, and the uric acid is white. Mammals defecate and urinate through different passageways, so if you see a tubular scat and aren't sure whether it was made by a mammal or a large bird, maybe a goose, the coating of white uric acid is a good clue to avian origin (unless the scats are quite old and dried up, in which case the whiteness can disappear). In most birds the solids and white uric acid remain clearly distinct, but many groups, including the herons, gulls, crows, hawks, and owls, just excrete mainly white uric acid through their vents and egest most solid waste by coughing up a pellet full of the indigestibles—feathers, bones, fur, seeds, occasionally the thick skins of fruits. Thus, wash of hawks and owls is pure liquid-white, and waterfalls of whitewash down the side of a tree can indicate a favorite owl perch. Always search when you see such sign—look up for owls and below for pellets or feathers or even bits of dead prey animals. Hawks leave such wash too, but they tend to be less committed to a single perch than owls, and they lift their tails and spray their excreta farther, making less of an obvious stream down the side of a tree.

Raptor pellets may contain seeds and cellulose from the birds' stomachs, but they are famous for being full of fur and bones, which intrepid naturalists can often identify to species. You can tell hawk and owl pellets apart—hawks tend to have stronger digestive juices, so small bones don't usually make it into the pellet. A hawk pellet may have fur, and just the largest, most indigestible bone, but owl pellets might contain entire skeletons, including the pellet explorer's prize—perfect tiny skulls.

The formation of pellets is a fascination. After the bird swallows prey, a kind of pellet-making compartment is created when the sphincters between the stomach and the gizzard close. After a few hours, the indigestible remains of the prey are squeezed into an ever-tightening space, and within about ten hours, the pellet is fixed. There it sits until egestion begins. For most raptors, the meal-to-pellet interval (yes, the MPI in the scientific journals) is between thirteen and twenty hours. One good meal per day.

The owl pellets that schools obtain for student study have been sterilized, and on top of this, students are usually made to wear gloves when examining them. The advice from one popular biological supply catalog reads, "Handle owl pellets, even sterilized ones, as though they could be a source of bacterial or viral contamination."

I find such counsel a bit prudish, feeding a recent and unnatural fear humans have developed about brushing anything at all that has a biological origin against our own skin. Owl stomachs are so acidic that any virus or bacteria is unlikely to make it back up in the pellet. If you are fortunate enough to find a wild owl pellet, then just examine it with care, delight in the tininess of the bones, and wash your hands.

sharp-shinned hawk to dive low and flat into the rhododendrons by the back fence. In another second she was standing on the ground beneath the cherry tree, breathing hard, as I was. In the diving of a hungry hawk there is a purity of physical intent that is seldom experienced by humans, except in the most rarefied moments of athletic achievement. My response—immediate, heightened, unsettled excitement—was involuntary. I thought the hawk had missed, that she was just recovering from her effort, but in a second glance I saw a varied thrush on its back beneath the hawk's thin yellow foot. Varied thrushes are one of my favorite birds, and this year I have been delighting in their backyard presence. We usually have just one or two visit occasionally, but this autumn a half dozen have been here every day. The thrush's upturned feet were moving on their hinges as the hawk went to work defeathering her catch. Bird-hunting hawks typically use their bills to pluck most feathers from their prey, so I was surprised to see this sharpie using her feet in quick jogging motions to remove the light breast feathers. Soon the two birds were shrouded in a cloud of down. I felt my body move forward and realized that it was going to rescue the thrush. Even after I saw that it was futile (not to mention ecologically unenlightened), my mind and body remained in involuntary dissonance on this subject (forgivably so, I think — the impulse to compassion is not objective, not scientific, but remains one of our most beautiful human capacities).

This matters, this winding of story, this intimacy with the predatory, with the very viscera of our home place. All of us together, the creatures we see and those we don't, partake of this struggle. Paying attention, *attending,* we begin to live more creatively, compassionately, brightly, fearfully. *Fearfully* in the beautiful archaic sense — the complex yet natural twining of dread and reverence. We take our place in the difficult balance of earthen grace.

Chicken

The School of Lost Borders

One midsummer morning, I looked out the window over the rim of my coffee cup and spotted a Cooper's hawk perched on the edge of our garden shed. Even through the glass I could see this bird's glowing yellow legs and orange eyes. Like any good birdwatcher, I rushed to get my binoculars. But in the next breath I realized, oh my Lord, that hawk was eyeing my six-week-old baby chickens! I ran out to the coop like Ma Ingalls, barefoot in the wet grass, pink flannel pajamas dragging around my feet, waving my arms and yelling, "Shoo! Bad hawk! Go away!" The hawk eyed me coolly before lifting over the shed roof, and I gathered my feathered girls into a corner of the kitchen for the day.

I'd always been critical of farmers who bait so-called vermin such as coyotes, wolves, and cougars because they are a perceived threat to livestock. As a graduate student in eco-philosophy and environmental ethics, I penned youthfully strident papers that preached about the need for keepers of agricultural animals to protect their holdings through improved husbandry practices rather than lethal control of predators. But this hawk episode threw me right out of my ivory tower.

My family and I belong to the growing contingent of urban dwellers who keep small flocks of backyard chickens. We began raising chickens about fourteen years ago, and we do it for many reasons: because we are seeking a deepened sense of connection in our food lives; because you can't beat delicious fresh eggs laid by birds that are part of the family; because hens produce lush fertilizer for the garden; because it aligns us with the local, sustainable food movement; and because chickens are so darn cute. But what if I really were Ma Ingalls? What if those chickens were not my hobby but my family's livelihood and my children's sustenance? What if all this were true, *and* I had a shotgun hanging over the door? When there is a conflict between food (eggs and garden) and wildlife (raccoons, hawks, squirrels), is it a given that the human activities claim priority? And if not, then how are such questions to be navigated?

I write today against the background sound of constant sweet cheeping — three baby chicks now inhabit a corner of our mudroom, just off the kitchen. They are buff Orpington chicks, my favorite heritage breed, the quintessential golden Beatrix Potter chicken, like Henny-Penny, whose three-toed stockings the hedgehog laundress Mrs. Tiggy-Winkle despaired over: "They are very bad to wash." Buff Orpingtons are wonderful hens; good layers; sweet-tempered; great for family flocks; and their chicks are a classic fluffy yellow. When we first started raising chickens, it was still something of a curiosity in the city. Now urban chickens are so hip they're almost passé. Neighbors are comparing breeds and coop plans, local Tilth organizations can't offer enough City Chickens 101 classes to meet the demand, and that nice clucking sound is becoming more common on walks through urban neighborhoods across the country.

We recently spent two months traveling in Kenya and Tanzania, staying a fair bit of the time in small, off-the-track villages. There, nearly everyone keeps chickens, and they roam free in the dirt roads, alleys, fields, and schoolyards. Most homes have a shelter for their chickens, with a roof and a nest box, but the hens and chicks are never fed or locked away from dogs or predators. They scratch for their sustenance and get by (or not) on their chicken wits. So it is with a measure of self-directed irony that I tell you that until our chicks are about five weeks old, we raise them in the kitchen, where, like most other urban chick moms, I hover over them and cater to their every desire as if they were newborn humans.

So many urban chicken people respond blithely when I ask them their reasons for keeping hens. Something along the lines of *We want our food lives to be in line with the rhythms of nature.* Sure, chickens lay eggs, so in tending them, both kids and adults remember that food originates in a place, and with work, and through other creatures, rather than materializing preboxed from the store. But here is a singular paradox: the most essential way that urban chickens draw us into "nature's rhythm" is by putting us *at odds* with nature. Inviting chickens into our lives, we also invite raccoons, bird-hunting hawks, and, depending on where we live, perhaps also coyotes or foxes. Certainly we invite rats.* We intentionally bring into

---

* *Chickens don't really attract more rats to neighborhoods. The rats are already there. But they do bring rats to the nice coop you built, with its warm shelter and ever-full food and water dishes. If they get a chance, chickens will actually corner and kill rats.*

our yard and under our care flesh-and-blood birds that are prone to diseases and health crises that city folk in their right minds never have to think about.

Today, Ethel the barred rock continues her recent spate of broodiness. She will not leave the nest box, and the other hens cannot get in the box to lay their own eggs. She is hostile toward anyone who might threaten her imagined clutch of eggs — her future, impossible brood of chicks. (We keep no rooster. It is one of the most common questions I field from urban people regarding chickens: How do you get eggs with no rooster? Using their own human bodies as an analogy, most people can figure it out quickly enough — you need a rooster to get *chicks,* not eggs.) And so I write with a timer on. Every hour it rings, and I take a break to go outside and chase Ethel off the nest, remind her of life beyond her small pile of straw, hope that she will recover herself and rejoin life in the chicken yard. The common home remedy for broodiness in the chicken-keeping lore is to dunk the hen in cold water and hold her there long enough to lower her body temperature, which has been raised by the creation of a highly vascularized brood patch. But the chasing method has always worked for me before, and I am going to give it a shot before traumatizing young Ethel in the dunk tank.

This little drama falls on the heels of Adelaide the buff Orpington's medical emergency. Just a month ago, she was near death, starving due to an impacted crop that prevented her from swallowing. I did some fancy chicken nursing, using a long eyedropper to squeeze mineral oil down her throat, massaging the crop, then holding poor Adelaide upside down by her feet as I stroked her esophagus, and the mucusy blockage poured out. What on earth is a nice city girl like me doing in a situation like this? Worrying about broody hens and chicken-eating raccoons and icky impacted crops? But I love it. *Love* it. I am enlivened, lively, in love with the creativity I feel in this life of lost borders, the preconceptions of urban-rural-wild breaking down around me.

Below are my reasons for bringing domestic chickens, a traditionally rural beast, into the urban bestiary and my own backyard. The first few points echo lists that are proliferating through countless magazines, newspapers, and blogs discussing urban-sustainability issues. The others are a little different. I am not suggesting everyone run out and get chickens. Far from it. I am concerned about the current trend being just a trend ("Chickens are the new black," claim an infinity of blogs) rather than a well-thought-out way of life. But it can be the latter, and whether individuals choose to keep chickens or not, the presence of chickens in the urban landscape rouses and educates us.

Chickens are lovable. I love how they look, how they walk, and how they tilt their heads to look you in the eye. I love their funny, fluffy shape. I love their unique chicken intelligence, which constantly surprises me. I love the soft, calming *cluck-cluck* sound they make. I love how, if you choose the right breed, chickens are sweet, docile, and friendly. I love how when you plop them onto an urban lot their expression says, *Yeah, I can do this,* as if they own the place, as if there is no question that they belong just where they are.

Chickens lay gorgeous fresh eggs. There are few things more satisfying than gathering your own eggs, especially when they are the most beautiful, golden-centered, delicious eggs you have ever tasted. There have been various attempts to question the nutritional value of eggs. We have been told that the cholesterol in eggs will clog our arteries; followers of macrobiotics claim that as a highly *yang* food, eggs will unbalance our systems; there is even an alternative-health notion that eating chicken eggs might mess with our human reproductive systems. But none of this is consistent with the traditional wisdom about eggs. Eggs produced by healthy, happy chickens fed a nourishing diet are among the most nutrient-dense foods on earth. There is a reason that eggs from domesticated chickens are a part of every major cuisine in the world, from Japanese egg-noodle soup, *miso nikomi udon,* to Nicaraguan red beans with poached eggs, *sopa de frijoles.* It might seem like your dearest friends and family couldn't possibly love you more than they already do, but just try giving them a bowl of your homegrown eggs. Backyard chickens breed more love in the world.

Children can take a great deal of responsibility for raising chicks and keeping chickens, and this is good for them. When Claire was tiny, she would go out with her eggs basket, words she could barely pronounce, and gather the eggs to make blueberry muffins while Genevieve the Polish hen perched on her shoulder. Now that she is fourteen years old and both a food activist and a baker in her own right, I believe sharing our household with food-producing animals helps to grow a sense of self-sufficiency, a broader sense of home, an expansive sense of kindness, and a deepened relationship to *huevos rancheros* and french toast.

Chickenomics. There is another dimension to chicken-keeping that plays into the modern psyche. I read a quote by the editor of *Backyard Poultry* magazine, Elaine Belanger, which said that whenever the economy tanks, their subscriptions soar. This doesn't make *common* sense—after all, unless you are supremely resourceful, it takes some money to get set up for a backyard chicken flock. The ongoing cost of chicken food isn't that much less than the cost of eggs, and anyway, it's certainly not buying eggs that is making or breaking us. The current popularity of chickens might have to do with the economy, but it can't be just about *money*. Wondering over this, I picked up the phone and gave Belanger a call. "You're right," she told me. "On the surface, there is a myth that growing our own food will save money, and I get calls from editors in New York who are covering the economy, and they think that's what it's all about. But if you've raised chickens, you know that it's something else." In troubled times with multiple crises—economic collapse, ecological distress, global violence, swine flu, bird flu—there's a longing for independence, self-reliance, security, food safety, and a desire to bring a dimension of the earthen "idyllic" into our daily lives. Chickens give us a hands-on, tangible sense of satisfaction on all of these levels—it's both a practical and *emotional* satisfaction. But Belanger points out that the current resurgence in homestead-style practices, including chicken-keeping, predates the economic crisis by a couple of years. I believe we are in the midst of a long political cycle in this country that is leaving us feeling empty and desperate for authenticity. We are finding, and creating, meaning in the most truly grassroots of actions—those that begin with our own household grass.

Speaking of which—chickens are adept at removing grass and tilling garden beds.

Increased understanding of intraspecies intelligence, and the attendant compassion such understanding brings. I often hear that chickens are dumb, and surely the best-ever articulation of this position comes from Werner Herzog, who in his famous and oft-parodied intonation expounds on chicken stupidity with such a singular combination of gravity and passion that you'd think he was lecturing on a beloved topic in medieval philosophy. In a brilliant forty-second video by filmmakers Siri Bunford and Tom Streithorst, Herzog sits enthroned in a dusky room upon a heavy upholstered chair, surrounded by macabre examples of mammalian taxidermy. Imagine it in Herzog's accent:

> The enormity of their flat brain, the enormity of their stupidity is just overwhelming. You have to do yourself a favor when you are out in the countryside and you see chickens. Try to look a chicken in the eye with great intensity, and the intensity of the stupidity that is looking back at you is just amazing. By the way, it's very easy to hypnotize a chicken. They are very prone to hypnosis, and in one or two films I've actually shown that.

So wonderful! I have studied chicken-hypnosis techniques but haven't yet succeeded in hypnotizing my own chickens (I'll keep trying). And though I've watched this little video over and over, and love it more every time, of course I disagree with Herzog. New research sides with the chicken. In his extensive studies, Dr. Chris

Evans, a psychology professor at Macquarie University in Australia, has found that chickens have a stable and sophisticated social organization (maintained by an established pecking order); they have at least twenty-four vocalizations with which they communicate a wealth of information to one another, including separate alarm calls for different kinds of predators; they have remarkable problem-solving skills. And of course, they are good and watchful mothers. Anyone who has paid attention to her own backyard or barnyard flock knows that every chicken has a distinct personality — a sign of plasticity in behavior that is also an indicator of intelligence. Chickens do not possess human intelligence, certainly, but they have a unique chicken intelligence in abundance, and it never fails to surprise me. I observed their problem-solving skills this winter during our once-a-year Seattle snowfall. This was the first time these chickens had ever seen snow, and they were thoroughly unimpressed. At the far end of their yard is a perch, and there is a wooden crate in the middle. It took some trial and error, but the hens figured out how to get from place to place and back into the coop without their feet ever touching the ground (even Tom, a chicken-intelligence doubter, had to call this crafty).

I find a kindred spirit in one of my most beloved authors, Flannery O'Connor, who was on television when she was six years old because she had taught her cochin hen to walk backward. In the 1932 film clip, there is a grainy black-and-white shot of young Flannery, then called Mary, with chickens jumping on her shoulders, and a knit beret on her blond head. She raised poultry her whole life and always found in the birds a source of peace and artistic inspiration. She later said famously of the backward-walking-chicken-on-television event, "I was just there to assist the chicken but it was the high point in my life. Everything since has been anti-climax." And ethologist Margaret Morse Nice, one of my greatest personal inspirations in avian observation, had a flock of brown leghorns as a girl, "all named and cherished," which she studied intensively. Margaret and her sister told their family that chicken observations taught them about bird behavior generally, but also about human psychology, a position their parents took to be anti-Christian!

Chicken time. In a culture that promotes microtasking, multitasking, and an obsessive adherence to schedules and time-based accomplishment, the chickens offer a way to step out of the rush of human-measured minutes and seconds and into a rhythmic sense of time based on light and warmth and the turning of the earth.

Chicken time runs daily. To prevent visits from raccoons and rats, our chickens get closed up in their coop every night, and then let out every morning. I can't tell you how often I rebel against going out into the damp cold, only to feel blessed by the fresh air, the dampness in my hair, the glimmer of moon, the last moments of shining Venus that I would not have experienced otherwise. Even in deepest winter, I am drawn outdoors by my chicken duties every night and morning. And on the nights that I forget until it is so dark I can't see into the coop, I reach in and count the lumps of feathers by feel, making sure everyone is tucked in. Always there is a soft gentle clucking. Nighttime clucking, whisper clucks. A sweet sound to take to bed.

Chicken time also runs seasonally. In colonial America, the full moons of early spring were called Egg Moons. The longer days and increased light of the season stimulated the pituitary glands of the hens in the chicken yard, and as the hours of sunlight increased, so did egg laying. Those of us with chickens in the backyard know this cycle well. Though our first-year hens may lay every day during the winter, by year two or so the number of eggs gathered in the dark months dwindles. Then, just as we feel our own spirits rising with the light and green of spring, we watch the hens' natural response to the season spill forth from their little coop.

As we move from summer back to the season of darkness, I have observed that my own impulse to cozy down into an early bedtime is mirrored by the mood of the chickens. Starting in late summer, the girls put themselves to bed earlier and earlier every night, following the earlier sunsets, and on dark autumn mornings they look at me like I'm crazy if I open their door too early — *Why would we come out into all that cold, wet darkness, thank you very much?* In the summer, my house-sitter wondered about corralling the hens into the coop at night, and I told him not to worry — "They put themselves to bed at nine, and you can just close the door." That winter we left the chickens in the care of the same friend. "Nine o'clock, right?" he asked. "Oh dear, no, now they go to bed at five thirty!" I love how their little bums look, all feathery, settled in to roost for the night. And I love following the seasons in chicken time.

Livestock lineage. Chickens bring us into sympathy with the round of life, death, and food that follows humans across time and cultures. When we were in Tanzania, we walked with our young Masai guide up to his village in the Usumbara mountains. Once there, we sat with some of the women in his family in their dark, windowless home of mounded earth. We loved seeing Melubo's simple home, the *boma* where he was born; we sat there in the smoky dark (they cook on an indoor fire, but there is no chimney), and as our eyes adjusted, he translated his aunt's questions to us. You have only one child? (Peals of laughter; she has eight!) Do you have cattle? When do you plant your corn? Claire told them we had chickens, and I realized that this could lead to misconceptions, as if all urban Americans raise chickens alongside their one, fetishized, REI-outfitted child. But it seemed too much to convey, and too silly. Back at home, though, I think of the chickens in Africa and the families that rely on them. I think again of Ma Ingalls, so grateful to the neighbor who started a flock for her at the new homestead in De Smet. I think of the adult Flannery O'Connor, sick with her progressing lupus and standing on crutches near her birds at the Savannah estate. And I think it is good. Good to stand in this lineage, to know something about the lives of all these people that I couldn't have comprehended without hens of my own.

Tricking ourselves. For modern urban people, Chicken becomes as much a modern trickster figure as Coyote, turning our preconceived ideas and limitations on their heads, inviting us to rethink the normal rules of urban life. We live in the tidy, slick-built city, and suddenly here are chickens —*farm* animals —turning up. And if we feel inspired by this and decide upon chickens for our own urban plot, we are pitched into another kind of upheaval. We want eggs and snuggly chicken sounds, but we get raccoons and rats and sharp-eyed hawks. In keeping chickens, we are drawn into a more vivid awareness of the home wild, and we are required to respond creatively, brightly, and sometimes with life-or-death consequences (for the chickens or their predators) to this presence. This meeting of practicality and intimacy is uncommon in urban life; even gardening doesn't throw us in this deep. Domestic chickens make us wilder ourselves.

Though they have been bred into all manner of sizes, shapes, colors, and personalities in the past several hundred years, chickens are all one species, *Gallus domesticus,* members of the gallinaceous order of birds that includes pheasants, quail, partridges, peafowls, turkeys, guinea hens, and grouse. There is general agreement that humans have been domesticating chickens for somewhere between six and ten *thousand* years. Domestic chickens were even raised on Easter Island as early as 400 CE and appear to be the only animals intentionally brought there (Polynesian rats were probably stowaways). The islanders built great stone-fortress coops for their flocks.

Symbolically, female chickens are associated with fertility and fierce-but-gentle maternal protection. As she lay dying, Saint Thérèse of Lisieux found comfort and sacred solace in observing the hens and chicks that wandered the cloister grounds, taking direction from the words of her divine spouse: *O Jerusalem ... how often would I have gathered your children together, as a hen gathers her chicks under her wings.* Even more than this, chickens and eggs are linked in the classic and cross-cultural symbolism of rebirth, renewal, creativity, and regeneration. In their dawn wakening, they are creatures of transition and enlightenment—messengers from the magical, liminal moments of dark into-light; the break of day; the moments we ourselves awaken into newness and possibility. When I think of the supposed conflict that urban chicken farming brings up, I want to reframe it in light of this symbolism.

As we work to keep the raccoon (rat, hawk, coyote ...) out, the ways and needs of the raccoon itself come into relief. Why is it here? Not to vex us, and not because it is a violent beast (though anyone who has viewed the bloody aftermath of a raccoon's visit to the henhouse knows it is hard not to think so). The raccoon's interest in the chickens is exactly the same as our own. Food and, more broadly, sustenance. The henhouse brings us into the lively, sharp, live-by-our-wits creativity that is the essence of evolutionary adapt-edness. This is not conflict but *participation,* and within it we grow not just eggs but the deepest kind of renewal — an ability to glimpse new possibilities for what our urban homes can mean for ourselves, our community, the more-than-human creatures, the earth.

PART IV

The Branching and the Rooted

Tree

The Branching Beast

When *Ann Linnea was forty-three years old, in 1992, she set off on a* ten-week kayak trip, exploring the perimeter of Lake Superior, upon whose shores she made her home. Near the end of the first week, she listened to the weather report on her little marine-band VHF radio, calculated that she had several hours to find shore and shelter before the predicted rain hit, and set out in her plastic Aquaterra sea kayak. Within fifteen minutes, the wind picked up, the lake jumped in foot high chops, fog and heavy mist enveloped her. On Lake Superior, which makes its own crazy-dangerous weather, Linnea read these signs for what they were — serious; she paddled like mad for a landing place. But the North Shore is rimmed by rock, cliff, and cobble — to land her kayak in these conditions, Linnea needed a smooth shoreline of sand or small stones. After paddling wildly for two hours in the freezing damp, her strength all but gone, she spotted a thin gray line in the distance, used the last of her energy to paddle toward it, and, to her delight, landed the kayak. She managed to struggle out of her spray skirt and mitts, tie the boat, and put up a tarp with bone-numb hands before she was seized by muscle spasms that froze her belly and legs into a fetal position and racked her with excruciating pain. Linnea was frozen, unable to move, unable to breathe, fearing hypothermia as her mind lost its grip on the situation and any possible solution. In this pitiful state, Ann looked up to the slender aspen trees to which she had cinched her tarp. They moved in the wind and seemed to simultaneously feel and transcend the cruelty of the storm. To Ann, their branches appeared to incline toward her in a gesture of sympathy. "What should I do?" she addressed the trees nonverbally. "Please help me." And immediately, she felt a response. The trees said to her, *Breathe.* The first breath was so painful, she dreaded another, but there, as Linnea tells it, were the trees, breathing in their own way, and she knew — as she had not known minutes before — "I am not going to die."

"Finally I could relax my stomach, and slowly straighten out my legs. I lay on my back under the tarp and looked at the trees. 'Thank you,' I whispered aloud. *Keep breathing.* I lay on the cold, wet ground for what seemed a long while, afraid to sit up for fear the cramp would return. But I was calm. Among these aspens, I was a lone human, but I was not utterly alone."

I fancied this bestiary might be the first to include an entry about an organism without a central nervous system and that it might be an edgy sort of thing to attempt, making readers say to themselves, *Tree? A tree is not a beast.* But it turns out that a thousand years ago, trees were given a long account in the *Aberdeen Bes-*

tiary itself; we are informed, with that volume's usual suspect etymology, that "a wood, *nemus,* gets its name from *numina,* deities, because the heathen consecrated their idols there; for woods contain large trees, whose boughs give deep shade." But the question remains: Do trees have a place in the modern bestiary?

A couple of years ago, Ann asked me to write the foreword for her book *Keepers of the Trees: A Guide to Re-Greening North America.* It's a beautiful project, full of human-tree stories from people who make their lives working with and protecting trees: a sustainable-furniture craftsman, a conservationist, a forester, a pruner, a community organizer, a wilderness researcher, a totem carver, and even a logger. Linnea crisscrossed North America gathering stories, interviewing these disparate people, and I read the tales of their lives with a sense of inspiration and gratitude for the opportunity to be included in this wonderful project. In the end, Ann—under gentle pressure from many of the other interviewees—added her own story to the collection, and she titled it "The Botanist Grandmother." In the twenty-some years since the kayak incident, Linnea's sense that trees are relational, have a kind of sentience, and can speak to us has only deepened. "*Relationship,*" she writes, "is commonly defined as a connection, association, or involvement. We humans generally view relationship to mean a connection with other humans or animals—beings that look back at us. I believe the possibility for relationship also exists between humans and trees." It took me a couple of readings to understand that Linnea wasn't equivocating on the meaning of *relationship,* as we do within the flexibility of the English language. One has a relationship with another person, or perhaps a dog—a thing with eyes, and brain, and nervous system—and we know what we mean by the word. In another sense, one has a relationship with, say, a landscape. Here, there is a response that is cultivated over time in the presence of a particular place, one that is personal and meaningful. We know the landscape, have grasped something in it toward which we lean—*relationship* is an appropriate word, albeit different from the sort a human has with another vertebrate creature. But Ann does not mean it differently. After the counsel of the aspens, she continued to study and cultivate her friendship with individual trees. Energy-field practices such as healing-touch therapy and Reiki, as well as traditionally scientific studies of botanical energy flow, deepened her rational belief in the possibility of the relationship she intuitively felt. "The more I learned," she told me, "the more I came to understand the commonalities between trees and all other life forms, including humans."

Claire and I joined Ann Linnea on a forest walk near her current home on Whidbey Island, the trail populated by western hemlock, Sitka spruce, Douglas fir, and western red cedar, some of them ancient, old-growth "grandmother trees." Ann is slender and athletic, with short graying hair and eyes that are simultaneously sharp and sparkling. She's twenty years my elder, but I have no doubt that on a serious hike, she would drop me in the dust. Linnea walks meaningfully (though not always slowly) through the forest. When you ask her something, instead of babbling back to you as she walks like most of us do, she stops and looks at you as she speaks. She didn't flinch a bit when I asked questions about her story that anyone might secretly want to ask: Don't hypothermic humans tend to have visions when there is a dearth of oxygen reaching the brain? Or, when the aspen told her to breathe, could it not have been her own inner voice, the desperate wisdom of an endangered biological body, projected onto this tree in a moment of desolate loneliness and physical danger? Even for someone deeply sympathetic to the consoling and healing presence of trees, these seem fair questions to ask in relation to Ann's experience with the aspens on the North Shore. Don't we commonly project our own needs, or desires, or even wisdom onto organisms of all sorts? Is that not why the pretty vine maple in my backyard said to me this very afternoon, *My dear, you deserve a nice glass of pinot and a shard of dark chocolate?*

But Linnea is clear on this. The answer was not her inner response to the healing beauty of the trees; it originated in the trees themselves. The language of trees is not English or Urdu or any kind of spoken human language. Nor is it barking or chirping. Tree language, says Linnea, lies in energetics. The constant, biokinetic flow of energy from earth to heavens, and the resulting energetic presence, something humans share, is a dimension in which we can respond to trees, *and they can respond to us* — in actuality, not just in our imaginations, or our inner visions, or even in our summoning of mythic and symbolic traditions.

Ann Linnea is not the only otherwise sane, high-functioning, articulate human to have claimed relational possibilities for trees. Far from it. In his comprehensive study *The Tree: A Natural History of What Trees Are, How They Live, and Why They Matter,* Linnean Society of London fellow Colin Tudge speaks frequently of trees that he has "met" and writes that while trees are not aware in the same way as animals, as they do not have brains, "they are sentient in their way; they gauge what's going on as much as they need to, and they conduct their affairs as adroitly as any military strategist." The 2010 poet laureate W. S. Merwin, who has spent decades reclaiming the forested property where he has made his home in

The Life Within Trees

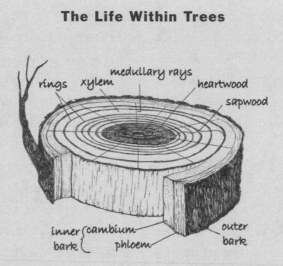

Basic tree biology offers a model for the energetic movement Linnea speaks of. In all the plant world, broadleaf trees and conifers have the most subtlety in the growth and functioning of their trunks. Beneath the outer bark lies a layer of inner bark made of generative stem-cell tissue, called the cambium. On its inner side, the cambium produces xylem, a substance made up of thick-walled woody cells that provide support for the tree while transporting water up and down, from the tips of the roots to the leaves. The cambium produces another substance called phloem on its outer side. Phloem is more thin-walled and viscous; it moves energy in the form of sucrose through the tree. As the cambium generates more phloem on the outside and xylem on the inside, the trunk grows thicker year after year—perhaps for centuries—while remaining supple and functional. As the cells that form the xylem die, they leave behind their stiff cell walls, which are pressed to the center of the tree, becoming heartwood and, closer to the outside, sapwood (truly full of sap)—the ever outwardly growing trunk. The crushed phloem is pushed to the perimeter, where it is incorporated into the bark that provides so much of the tree's external protection (an analogue to human skin, and in fact, the *Aberdeen*

Bestiary refers to the bark as the corium, or hide). Most trees grow seasonally, and the production of xylem is intermittent, so in a cross-section of the tree, the differences between the xylem laid down in the spring (wide but thin-walled) and the summer (narrow, but thicker-walled) is easy to observe in the concentric growth rings, typically one per annum. Good growing years and drought years can be discerned by the thickness or thinness of the rings. The medullary rays—the sun-like lines that move from the center of the trunk outward—work like capillaries, carrying nutrients throughout the trunk, so while a living tree is more supple toward the exterior, it is alive throughout.

Maui, planting thousands of native palms and ferns, says of the trees, "They are ancient and very wise creatures." Even the prickly John Fowles wrote that far more than ourselves, trees are "social creatures," and he spoke of their woodland groupings as "societies." Environmental studies professor and Buddhist teacher Stephanie Kaza wrote an entire essay collection subtitled *Conversations with Trees,* and she introduces the book with a description of how she "meets" a tree, approaching each one with calm respect and an openness to the tree's own response. "My primary orientation in the book is not to tree as symbol," she writes, "but to tree as Other, as one party in an I Thou relationship ... my effort here, awkward as it feels at times, is to try to speak directly with trees." Buddhist teachers from ancient times and in a variety of modern schools commonly include trees in their lists of sentient beings for whom, and *with whom,* we are to cultivate connection and compassion. And of course, many First Peoples include trees in their creation stories, ask permission of trees for certain activities, and continue to speak of trees as elders, grandmothers, ancestors.

Sentience, meeting, creatures, ancestors. We are not being asked to believe that trees have literal brains. We know they do not. Instead, we are speaking again of an expansive way of knowing, of relating, of a plethora of intelligences. We thought opossums and crows and chickens and pigeons challenged us. Now, here, all of these human mentors ask us, beautifully, expansively, with a rare and exquisite trust in our capacity as humans, to respect the singular intelligence of trees.

In *The Tree,* Colin Tudge spends hundreds of pages elucidating the biological activities of trees, all of which we humans easily recognize, as we ourselves are biologically occupied with the same activities: growth; the gathering of light, water, and nutrients; reproduction; preparation for seasonal heat and cold; regeneration after injury; death. Trees, of course, accomplish all of these things without moving, or without moving *much.** They grow directionally, limbs toward the light, roots toward the dark earth. They grow in climates that accommodate the unique biology of their species. They grow in proximity to other individuals of the same species with whom they share chemical and biological communication, climatic cues, and pollen. Without brains, without legs, without defense against human whim (and ax), they grow as best

---

* *This lack of movement extends to the dying of trees. Humans are whisked quickly away after death. Other animals fall to earth and decompose, or desiccate with natural efficiency. But dead trees often remain standing, sometimes for years, their bodies living a life beyond themselves as continued shelter and food for grubs, birds, mammals, and epiphytic plants. When they do finally fall, their horizontal beings remain. Here in the moist Pacific Northwest, rich red cedars become "nurse" or "mother" logs, lying on a ferny earth as young honeysuckle, hemlock, and fir grow from their rich, decomposing bark. Far more than most animals, a tree maintains a presence and a life beyond itself that few humans will know. I heard Gary Snyder speak when he had just turned sixty years old and was feeling that at this age, he could officially be called wise. He speculated on how it would be if humans remained standing after death, as many trees do. "Did you hear?" quipped Snyder. "Thoreau finally fell over."*

they can in places that make sense for themselves as individuals and species.

In urban places, we have tampered with all of these natural tree tendencies dramatically. We plant trees one at a time, as garden specimens, natives and nonnatives mixed up together, rarely in large groups of a particular species the way the trees themselves often prefer. We plant them in an environment full of tall buildings, protected from limb-strengthening wind; in a world of concrete and runoff, with no organic soil replenishment; and with a dearth of native pollinators. We have left the trees confused. Blossoming early or late, new growth stunted, fruits ripening early or failing to ripen at all. And as urban dwellers, we, in turn, experience a confused, topsy-turvy relationship with trees — our elemental connection to trees near and native has been dismantled. Until very recently in human history, the trees we lived with were the *same* trees that sustained us physically in the form of heat, fuel, shelter, furniture, and food. The connection to close-to-home trees was a given. Like many of our parents and grandparents, Ann Linnea remembers heating her childhood home with birch and pine from the local forests. Today we might glean some fruits from our own small circle of garden trees or those of our neighbors, but for the most part modern urban people no longer rely on the trees we live with to provide our basic human needs.

Even so, our dependence on trees remains absolute. We need wood from trees for shelter, furniture, fuel, ships, fences, poles. We need trees for food in the shape of fruits, nuts, and fodder for agricultural animals. We need trees as sources of varnishes, resins, oils, glues, dyes, pharmaceuticals, poisons, incense, unguents. We need trees for our musical instruments — pianos, violins, guitars, oboes.

We need trees to cleanse the air we breathe, absorbing carbon dioxide and many other pollutants while releasing fresh oxygen. We need trees, of course, for paper. But instead of most of these things coming from the trees that grow among us, they come from trees that we will never see, and can barely imagine. We depend on trees whose forests we don't understand, whose locations we do not know, and whose species names most of us have never learned.

My point here is not that we are ignorant and disconnected (as true as that may be), but something much more heartening: while we are kept physically alive by trees that grow far away, we are sustained on different but still profound and beautiful levels — psychological, spiritual, emotional, even intellectual — by the odd collection of trees in our urban midst. Our dependence on these close-to-home trees is real, essential, but more difficult to quantify. We know, both from experience and now from published scientific studies, that being among trees, or simply viewing trees through a window, makes people calmer, and even happier. Trees counteract the psychological and physical stresses of urban life. Views of trees from school or home will decrease ADHD symptoms in all age groups. Studies at a public housing project in inner-city Chicago showed that girls who could see trees out the window had higher concentration levels and more self-discipline than girls who couldn't, and their mothers were better able to cope with major life stresses; even *one tree* can make a measurable difference. The presence of trees in cities lowers human blood pressure, decreases anxiety, and may help prevent disease. Postoperative patients recover more quickly when they have a view of trees, and women who live near big trees during pregnancy are less likely to birth underweight babies.

It is good to be able to say, "Scientific research shows..." But we do not really need to be told that trees bring us calm and happiness, do we? We know these things as if by heart, and we know other things about trees and through trees, things that have yet to be proven by science. We know things about connection and wildness and life. We know that we have, at some time in our lives, felt watched over by a tree. We know that we have, even if it is a child-hood memory, at some time felt the hair on our heads and arms as leaves in a breeze. (*The Aberdeen Bestiary* says, "The highest parts of the tree are called flagella, whiplashes, because they catch repeated gusts of wind.") We know that tree time is not human time. Who has not felt the peculiar, exquisite lostness of tree time, a time mea-sured in light and spaciousness and a suspension of minutes or hours, rather than their swift passing? In Shakespeare's *As You Like It,* when Rosalind asks Orlando, "I pray you, what is't o'clock?" he answers, "You should ask me what time o' day, there's no clock in the forest." And in fairy tales, we all know that when the child steps into the forest, we might as well throw our watches to the wind, as tree time is about to reign absolute. We know, too, that when we stand openly beneath overhead branches, we can be lifted into our own wildness—out of our heads, our places, our little lives; or, no, more deeply into all of these things. And who has not, lying beneath a tree, felt her own body rooted, and earthen—the invitation to horizontal gravity that only trees offer? And giving in to this gravity, to this moment of lying in that space between the spread of roots and the spread of branches, a recognition that yes, the world can make do without us, and in the not-too-distant future will do just that.

Are trees beings? Creatures? Sentient? Relational? Proper resi-dents of the urban bestiary? I know that people of science and

Birds and Trees

For many urban birds, the presence or lack of a tree means the difference between the birds' flourishing and dying. In tremendous part, the trees that are with us determine what animals are with us. In the first study of its kind, research by scientists at Australian National University showed that urban trees were vital, "urgently needed" for sustaining biodiversity for all animals, and birds in particular. We have long known that large native trees are keystone structures for wildlife in forest or agricultural settings. But the new research shows that even in cities, more trees correlates directly with higher numbers of birds and more bird species, including species that are considered woodland-dependent. This is especially true for big trees, and parks or even backyards with more large trees have more bird species than those with only smaller trees. Study author Karen Stagoll is not above stating the obvious: "It takes decades for a newly planted sapling to grow into a large tree. We need to think and act early." The removal of large trees has to be reconsidered in this light— public concerns about the threat posed by older trees might be managed by fencing, education, and protective landscaping.

There is no one way to plan for trees and wildlife in urban places, no one philosophy for all occasions. For decades, the wisdom from conservation biology has involved the preservation of large forest fragments—the bigger the better—and this was viewed as the most important thing. And it's true—leaving remaining woodlands undisturbed is essential. But we're learning that there are other elements at play— when we decrease impervious surfaces, increase the number of trees (especially native trees, including conifers, where appropriate), and work to create a multilayered botanical structure, more native forest bird species turn up, even in the denser urban matrix. By the work of our own hands, we can turn city neighborhoods that host mainly crows, starlings, pigeons, house sparrows, robins, and flickers into places that also support more sensitive birds that can flourish alongside human habitation when attention is paid to their requirements: migratory warblers, various woodland thrushes, western or scarlet tanagers, downy or hairy woodpeckers, Pacific or winter wrens, and many others.

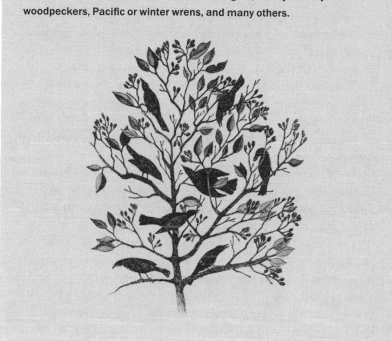

literature and possessing the wisdom of age have said so. I know that some trees themselves seem to have said so too. I know that I love certain trees as much as I've loved almost anything. My argument is not for the sentience of trees, not necessarily — it is for possibility. What if? What if we live in a constant and mutual relationship with trees, and all this while — while we have admired, loved, and worshipped them, lived off their fruits and in the shelter of their forms — what if we modern humans have not yet properly understood the dimensions of tree-human *interbeing,* as Thich Nhat Hanh calls "the interconnection of all things"? Imagine what

An Appointment with an Oak

American naturalist John Burroughs was enamored of Henry David Thoreau's commitment to natural observation and immersion: "He would go any number of miles to interview a muskrat or a woodchuck, or to keep an 'appointment with an oak-tree.'" Never mind that it wasn't an oak. Thoreau wrote: "I frequently tramped eight or ten miles through the deepest snow to keep an appointment with a beech-tree, or a yellow birch, or an old acquaintance among the pines."

There are many ways to become more conversant with the trees we live with, to "keep appointments" with our own versions of Thoreau's beech. One suggestion I have heard is to choose a "year tree," a tree in your yard or neighborhood, and commit to visiting that tree each day, sketching it or making notes about the goings-on in its limbs, leaves, and roots. I undertook a different kind of experiment during the writing of this chapter—I decided to make my own appointment with a huge bigleaf maple in the wooded park near my home. I would spend the entire day in the company of this sprawling tree, from dawn to dark. I chose the tree on a walk before the day of the appointment and packed my bag with a mixture of simplicity and opulence. On the simple side, I brought no books, no devices, no phone, nothing to occupy myself except a wooden pencil and a notebook. On the deluxe side, I brought my favorite tattered quilt upon which to spread an inspiring picnic of farmers'-market cheeses, strawberries, baguette, chocolate, and one of those tiny bottles of red wine. Certainly Thoreau would not have objected, even though there would, thank God, be no trudging through snow. This was a sunny, dappled, late-summer day. I confess to hoping for some kind of botanico-philosophical revelation during my many hours of tree immersion, maybe

life-giving delight may be in store for us, walking about, knowing of our true relationship with trees. Are the trees branching beasts? If the poets, visionaries, botanists, Buddhists, and even the trees themselves are proclaiming their unique sentience, then why on earth would any of us argue?

the kind of direct communication that Ann Linnea had described. But these expectations dissolved early on as I found I was receiving something much better: nothing in particular. Hours passed, chickadees and kinglets gave way to Steller's jays and quick rushes from overfed park squirrels, up, down, up. The shadows moved across the grass, and I moved my quilt to follow them. I watched, leaned against the tree, napped extravagantly. I wrote—small thoughts, tree thoughts. I wished for everyone such a day with a tree.

Human
Home Practice for a Person-Size Animal

Human mammals are funny-looking. Think of us, walking along in our human animal skins. Notably, when compared to other mammals, we are standing upright on two flat feet, fully bipedal without bending to rest, ever, on our knuckles. Almost as strikingly, we are furless. Naked and cold, sparsely covered with hairlets, topped with a shock of thicker hair but no undercoat. Other than a slightly protruding nose, the human face is flat and singularly snoutless. Female humans, unlike any other mammal, have breasts that are swollen year-round, and men's penises hang down, the genitals fully exposed (even in species that display the genitals, such as East Africa's bright blue–testicled vervet monkeys, the penis is rarely so vulnerable). Physically, we are virtually defenseless—more so for our size than any other mammal, including a mouse. The skin on our hands and feet is a little callused, but not very. We are not hoofed or protectively padded. We have no sharp teeth, no claws, no armor, no plates, no scales. We have no venom, no bitter taste or mild toxicity in our skin, no chemical defenses. All that we have done to create beauty; to raise culture; to dominate the earth, other species, and one another, we have done with little to recommend us but the play between our thumbs and fingers and our wondrous human brains.

Giving humans a place in the bestiary is not an original idea — the author of the *Aberdeen Bestiary* gave a full section to the creation and functioning of man. As usual, Isidore finds both philosophical and scientific explication in the Latin words for his subjects' names and parts. "Man, *homo,* is so called," he writes, "because he is made from the soil, *humus,* as it says in the book of Genesis: 'And the Lord God formed the man of the dust of the ground.'" (The etymology is false, of course. *Homo* is self-defining, from the Latin for "man," though in this same myth, the human's Hebrew name, Adam, is derived from *adamah,* earth.) But the notion is a lovely one, an early statement of our absolute continuity with the soil, with the earth.

This story in Genesis 2 is from the creation mythology of ancient Israel and may have been penned by J, one of the four main authors of the Pentateuch, in the ninth century BCE. In this myth, animals are not created before the man, as in the first chapter of Genesis, but after him, as his companions. The Genesis 2 story echoes a common thread in human creation stories from around the globe: people are brought forth from the stuff of the earth.

In one Norse myth, the first man and woman are formed out of an ash tree and an elm tree. They reside with their descendants in Middle Earth, created for them by the god Odin — the whole universe is propped up by Yggdrasil, the world ash (so even the first humans have to deal with troubles from squirrels like Ratatoskr).

The Quiche Maya of Guatemala's ancient highlands tell of people created by a trio of gods: Maker, Heart of Sky, and Feathered Serpent. After forming humans of wood, the gods disconcertedly realize that though the people can move and speak and look as people should look, the wood people have no minds, and no hearts, and do not remember their makers. So the people are re-created out of a more supple medium — yellow and white corn, fruits, and vegetables, all fixed together with honey and flowers. The bodies and minds of the first true people are gardens.

In one telling of a myth from the Yoruban people of West Africa, the god Olorun is dismayed by the mess of chaos beneath him — scattered mud and stone and smoke. He orders his good lackey Orisha to make something of it, and to help Orisha along on the task, Olorun provides him with the most helpful of things: a shell full of magic earth, a pigeon, a five-toed hen, and, to oversee it all, a very particular chameleon. Orisha spills the magic earth upon the chaos, and the birds go to work, pecking and scratching, until they have separated the mess into masses of earth and sea. They continue working until the chameleon inspects their work and calls it finished. Rain falls, and forests flourish. Orisha forms people from the mud of the beautiful new earth, and Olorun, pleased, breathes life into them.

I love the frugal practicality of such myths — we were created from what was at hand, as a pioneer woman would have pieced a quilt. And I love the continuity these stories spell: no wonder we are capable of feeling such residence upon this earth, such interconnectedness with its processes, stones, and soil. Of course we do. We were born from these things.

But something strange has happened to our earthen human-animal selves. We have grown large, much larger than our individual physical bodies, spread farther in the world than we can perceive. In the past few years, I have been in conversation with Dr. William Catton, a provocative environmental sociologist and the author of *Overshoot,* the seminal work on the relationship between human population and the earthen biosphere. In considering the force of modern urban humans, Catton has adopted the medical concept of a prosthesis, a manufactured object that extends the ability of the human biological form — a fabricated substitute for something damaged or missing. Typically, we think of prosthetics as replacements for lost limbs or organs or as devices to enhance limited abilities. A false hand, or a glass eye. A prosthetic does not have to be physically built in; it can also be carried. Canes are a variety of prosthetic, as are eyeglasses. But Catton has begun to view the other built apparatuses we use in our daily lives — structures and devices that enhance the efforts of our physical bodies, or actually do things for us — as another kind of prosthetic. Phones are a prosthetic for communication, allowing our voices to carry farther; cars take us beyond the places we can easily walk, and they take us there faster. These are obvious examples. But once we start seeing everyday objects as prosthetic intermediaries for our own physical activity, it is difficult to stop seeing them, and there are far more of them today than when Catton began thinking of such things just a few short decades ago: we now unlock car doors with buttons rather than our hands; we manage our television screens with remotes instead of getting off our bums and walking the few feet to change the channel. I've been embarrassed to find myself, purportedly a nature writer, checking the current temperature and weather conditions on my iPhone weather app rather than taking a step out the door to feel the elements on my own face.

All animals need things beyond their bodies (food and oxygen at the very least). Ecosystem studies teach us that energy, as it wends its way through the food web, is lost, and only about 10 percent of food energy passes from one trophic level to the next. Thus it is normal, it is *natural,* to take up more energetic space than the simple physical space of our biological bodies. It is true of all animals. But the prostheses of modern human life, all of which must be manufactured, obtained, maintained, and eventually disposed of, have made this space we as humans take up—our "outside-the-body metabolism"—a great deal larger than it has ever been. We know that our fuel-based way of life reaches into the past for petrological sustenance, using energy stores from long before humans evolved; it touches the air and soil of the present; it spreads toward the future via waste products that are visible (physical refuse to be dumped— our cell phones, plastic pens, outworn shoes, demolished buildings) as well as via invisible heat, held in the diminishing atmosphere where it will affect future generations of human and nonhuman lives. The energetic and physical refuse of our lives stretches across the earth—elsewhere, but also, Catton writes, else*when*—inviting an understanding that is as poetic as it is bio-geological. Our current activities are rich with meaning beyond the moment in which we enjoy them. The most striking detail of Catton's prosthetic thesis is the specific diagramming of the extra-body, or "exo-somatic being," as he calls it, of the ecosystemic space we each require. A modern urban human moves in the landscape with the physical shadow of a sperm whale or a large dinosaur.

I want to be a human-size animal. As human-size as I can be, an animal with a just-right shadow, appropriate to my body and place, with awareness of the other bodies, near and far, human and

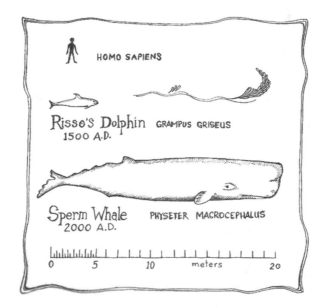

In 1500 ᴄᴇ, a human took up as much ecosystemic space as a Risso's dolphin. Today, an urban human is more like a sperm whale.

more-than-human, those that share my neighborhood and those I will never see. Thinking of myself walking out the door in the shape of an apatosaurus is enough to make me ride that pretty bicycle of mine in spite of all the hills in Seattle. I do not want to move through the world as a dinosaur. I do not want to displace a sperm whale's worth of seawater when I dip my toe into the sandy shoreline waves at the Puget Sound beach near our home, holding my daughter's hand and watching an osprey dive again for salmon smolt, no larger than her own feathered self.

No one is advocating for a return to pretechnological existence, and I would not suggest it even if it were possible (though if the peak-oil folks have it right, we won't have much choice). I live richly and gratefully amid the blessings of the modern world — its travel, its medicine, its art, its science. I love the technological elegance of my iPhone almost as much as I love my fountain pen. This isn't about regressing into primitivism, but rather about choosing thoughtfully how we live and what we use, and living *closer to scale*. In his classic book *Small Is Beautiful: Economics as if People Mattered*, E. F. Schumacher suggested "a lifestyle designed for permanence" and "technology with a human face." I want to remember that as many blessings as my beautiful prostheses confer, it is often without them that I enter my own multifaceted intelligence most deeply.

We live in a farmhouse that was built in the 1920s. Over the decades, the fruit orchards that surrounded it were replaced with houses — most of them in the 1940s, some in the 1970s. When my family and I walk through the neighborhood, we find other houses that look like ours farm-distance away, and I enjoy imagining the inhabitants of these houses, our historical neighbors, their apple trees cross-pollinating those that surrounded our house. In the 1938 Seattle city census photograph of our house, there are not just fruit trees, but a chicken coop out back, long-buried dirt roads leading to the front drive, and a whooping cough-quarantine sign on the door.

The interior of our house has suffered many bad remodels over the decades and was restored several years ago by the previous owner, just before we moved in. He lovingly scraped away layers of paint to reveal the original grain in the thick molding of local Douglas fir. Glued-down linoleum was peeled back, and the floors beneath it — more fir — were sanded and oiled. The kitchen was gutted and replaced, and the exterior cedar lap siding was painted a pleasing shade of green.

We are grateful for all this effort, as none of it sounds very fun to us. Turning to the kind of work that better suits our family, we have embarked on what I like to think of as Home Restoration, Phase II. According to my treasured copy of Eric Partridge's etymological dictionary, the word *restore* comes from the Latin *restaurare,* meaning "to give back something either lost or removed," an apt and lovely origin in this context. It is in this spirit we have returned a chicken coop to the backyard of this home that once produced so much food and sweet fruit. A plum tree has been added, an Asian pear, and two little columnar apples. A sweet gum was removed, given to a local monastery's memorial garden, and replaced with an Asian pear tree. We've drastically (perhaps insancly) removed grass and expanded the vegetable garden, and we have added cold frames for the chill Seattle spring. We removed a tangle of escallonia shrubs along the side fence and replaced them with northwest native vine maples, sword ferns, lady ferns, flowering currant, and huckleberry. We referred to the permaculture manual, remembering that we can both provide natives for wildlife and feed ourselves by paying attention to even this small-scale plot of land as an ecologically complex place. In the current "victory garden" movement, it seems the impulse is to construct a few rectangular wooden raised beds, then fill them with soil and rows of plants. Permaculture asks us to approach gardening with more heart, to first take a step back and ask two questions. What is it that we, the human inhabitants, require of our bit of land (food, a place to play, herbs, peace for the soul)? And then, *What does the land, and the region, need from us* (soil rejuvenation, removal of invasive plants/grass, space for native plants and their pollinators, varied dimensions to provide habitat for birds)? So often we think of restoration as an aesthetic endeavor, but expansively, it can be so much more. Even our small yards constitute land, and we can begin to give back to this land its "lost" innate fertility.

The sustainable-homes movement emphasizes that while human-designed homes can never be biologically complex enough to be fully analogous to a natural ecosystem, many home systems, such as gardens, are comparable to natural systems. As true as this is, I want to say something different. Our homes — no matter how we live in them, how ecologically inspired or ecologically unenlightened — are *functioning parts of ecosystems,* and in creating a home, so are we. This is not just poetic analogy. From our homes, we exchange food, water, waste, and energy with the living organisms that surround us in our neighborhoods and beyond. These are the cycles that make us ecosystemic creatures, that bring us into conversation with land, air, plants, and animals. It is a beautiful, ominous realization, when we allow it to sink in. How we live matters, and matters wondrously. It doesn't make any difference where we dwell — a house, an apartment, a tent, urban or rural — we are caretakers of the place from which we make our home — not just its physical walls, but the myriad ways in which it spills beyond itself. It is our homes that connect us, deeply, ecosystemically, to the wild earth, and all creatures near and far.

This realization is inciting a whole movement, as urban dwellers across the country choose to practice some subsistence habits from home — growing food and making some of our household goods — because it makes us feel healthy, happy, and creative; because it throws us into the round of wild nature; and because it allows us to disengage, even if just a little, from the crazy-manic consumer economy. Urban homesteading and urban farming are the vogue labels for the movement; these are inspiring and playful epithets, and I have nothing against them, but they make me a little self-conscious (true homesteading and farming are deep and challenging lifestyles, both historically and today, and I just can't claim to be doing either one seriously). For my own household, I prefer to adopt the older English word *smallholding*. A smallholding is just what it sounds like — a bit of land upon which a few people grow some of their food and make some of their living from home. Sometimes there is enough to sell at a small market or more typically to share with friends or neighbors. In my appropriated use, a smallholding can be *very* small — an urban apartment, even — while still bespeaking a responsible and responsive interaction of humans, plants, native trees, fruit trees. Plots of cultivation and corners full of tendrils run feral. Adults and children. Domestic animals and wild creatures. Chickens and chickadees.

I believe that living mindfully in the bestiary is primarily a matter of creating homes that make sense, what Thoreau called common sense: a home that allows both appropriate boundaries and appropriate permeability; that provides opportunity for observation and interaction but permits wild creatures to maintain their wildness; that keeps us safe while enabling the animals that co-inhabit our urban places to flourish. Urban planning and the transition to eco-cities that integrate appropriate wildlife habitat are essential, and the most necessary steps will vary geographically; we need to be involved in this dimension of our communities and our cities. This will include everything from creating highway overpasses for wildlife and restoring urban parks to decreasing car dependence and increasing community-based agriculture. But daily, as creatures, as humans walking in the bestiary, we act from home. So often we take steps to change our habits out of guilt — we know about global climate change and that we ought to reduce our footprint. We feel guilty when we don't recycle, when we eat too much beef, when we compare our consumptive lifestyles to those of people who live so much more simply around the world. But I absolutely believe that guilt cannot be the highest or even the most efficient motivator. Attending the world more closely, we are inspired to act instead from a sense of love, interconnection, and a recognition of mutual strength and frailty.

There are many home practices that allow us to cultivate continuity and empathy with the wild earth — with more-than-human life near and far. Here are some of my favorites, the ones I consider essential in my own household, the ones that make our home rounder, our psyches wilder, our bodies closer to their perfect human size.

Grow something to eat. In their fun book *The Urban Homestead*, Kelly Coyne and Erik Knutzen encourage our gardening efforts by telling us that "nature is standing by, ready to help." Just as often, though, I resonate with Michael Pollan, who writes in his literate meditation *Second Nature*, "Nature abhors a garden." As far as life in the bestiary goes, nothing makes us more aware of the animals among us than arguing with them over the food we are trying to grow for ourselves. We are supposed to be smiling there in the sun, planting seeds, feeding our souls, and thinking how pretty nature is. But here is a complex beauty. There are birds eating the berries. Squirrels uprooting the bulbs and stealing the sunflower seeds from the chickadees. Moles doing the horrible things moles do. Our well-intentioned, lovingly tended, sweat-built gardens are being nibbled by everything from robins and rats to skunks and cabbage butterflies.

Yet this tension can be enlivening. Our awareness of the wild creatures in our midst is elevated, and in our response, we find the creativity that is the core of evolutionary adaptedness. We find empathy for all things that eat, earning a sense of what other animals have to deal with daily—the knowledge that food is risky, never a sure thing. We find an animal vigilance that we might never have discovered in ourselves but that is strong and original and beautiful, and grows right from our wild roots.

I confess that I am subject to infrequent but powerful periods of melancholia, the "long walk with the black dog," as Samuel Johnson called it. Usually I am very well, but during the occasional stretches that leave me barely able to get out of my pajamas, I've found that if I can somehow find my way into the garden and get my hands dirty, I will be lifted for a time out of the downward spiral. We know that natural light and physical movement are good for mental health, but we are now learning that there is so much more going on. There are somewhere between one hundred million and one billion bacteria in about a teaspoon of productive garden soil. These are participants in the soil food web, related to the plants and plant-root exudates, and though we know that some of these bacteria have to do with nutrient cycling, water dynamics, and disease suppression in plants and soil organisms, the specific roles most of these soil bacteria play remain a scientific mystery. But in 2007, studies in London and Bristol led by Christopher Lowry (now at the University of Colorado) and published in the journal *Neuroscience* show that one specific common soil bacteria, *Mycobacterium vaccae,* appears to act upon the neurons in the human brain that produce serotonin, which helps to regulate metabolism, sleep, anger, mood, anxiety, motor activity, and coping responses to stress. The bacteria can have the same effect as the class of drugs known as SSRIs, selective serotonin reuptake inhibitors, such as Prozac and Celexa, that are prescribed as antidepressants, though the bacteria acts on the brain more specifically than these medications and without negative side effects. And though the mechanisms aren't fully understood, we know that gardening reduces the release of cortisol, the steroid hormone related to stress, and acts in other ways to calm the nerves and reduce anxiety. The implication is that more time spent with soil, from wilderness walks to planting a backyard tomato, can actually prevent depression and improve mental and physical health. How elegant, when things we feel to be true are borne out by modern science. By liberating us from the need to work the soil, modernity has separated us from a source of everyday joy and health. Even if all you have space or energy for is a pot of thyme on the windowsill, the wild participation is there. The herbs must be watered. The fragrance of soil rises. We cultivate a lovely multisensory attentiveness, something not sold in the plastic-boxed herbs at the grocery.

Dry your clothes on a clothesline. A few years ago Tom, Claire, and I traveled in Kenya and Tanzania for two months. Our first stop was a volunteer stint at the Colobus Trust on the coast of Kenya, where we worked on Colobus monkey conservation, and lodged in the organization's simple rooms. Our packs were light, with few extra clothes, and it was the cusp of the rainy season. When our freshly washed clothes were hung in the open-air windows, they sometimes took days to dry, even though they were under cover — the air was so thick and moist. Midway into our first week there, I'd been wearing my only dry shirt for a few days and was starting to feel quite funky. "Do you think they'll ever dry?" I lightly asked one of the staff, who lived in a village nearby. "Oh, sure," he told me, "when the sun comes out, they'll dry right away." "Well, you know how impatient we Americans are," I joked, "used to just popping things in the dryer!" "The what?" "Um, the clothes dryer," I said meekly, suddenly remembering that I was speaking to a man who'd lived his whole life with several other family members in a one-room house the size of my daughter's bedroom made of simple earthen materials and without power.

Many of the people we talked to in the villages of Kenya and Tanzania know that Americans' houses are too big and that they own cars, but the thought of clothes dryers was inconceivable. Using an expensive machine to do something that the air does naturally came across as profligate, idiotic, and I suppose even indecent. At the Colobus Trust, my Kenyan friend started to laugh, and I was about to laugh along when I realized that this was a private laugh, tinged with bitterness—a laughter I was not invited to join. I resolved in that moment to sever my dryer dependency.

Rainy Seattle isn't the most intuitive place for a clothesline, and Tom was not the least inclined to help me build one, so I rigged up a retractable line that runs from the corner of our raised deck all the way across the yard to the cherry tree. For rainy days, I have a line strung across the ceiling of the basement, where our washer is. Of course, hanging laundry on the subterranean line isn't as delightful as hanging clothes outside on a sunny day, but it is still meditative, and I find it pleasant. Occasionally, I multitask: while pinning clothes to the line, I sing or listen to recorded French lessons with headphones (a clothesline Luddite with an iPod).

I'm lazy and still use my dryer sometimes. Ah, the clothes come out so soft and warm, and so fast! I think of William Catton's work—what a monstrous prosthetic is the clothes dryer, and the clothesline is such a sweet, human-size technology. But more than this, I think of my grandmother Carrie Anna Attleson-Haupt. My dad grew up in Iowa just after the Depression, dryer-less, of course. He tells me about how his mother would bring the clothes in from the winter line, the shirts frozen solid as boards. I like to remember her, my grandma Carrie, as I hang my family's clothes on our own makeshift lines.

Keep track, and carry a pencil. Writing is a way of knowing. When I bring a pencil and notebook with me on a walk, my mindset instantly changes without conscious effort on my part. The pencil is a signal to ourselves—we are prepared to see. And when we are prepared, somehow more is given. It is good to inhabit the bestiary with some sort of nature diary at hand—a place where observations, avian encounters, sketches of animal sign, thoughts that occur during urban-wild rambles and encounters, can be captured. We are in good company; Leonardo da Vinci, Charles Darwin, Mary Oliver, Henry David Thoreau, Edith Holden, and innumerable others never ventured forth without a small notebook.

The act of writing and sketching not only embeds an observation into our minds but also preserves it for future access. Memory is notoriously fickle, not to mention unreliable, lazy, and sometimes nonexistent. As the beloved naturalist Bernd Heinrich shares, "I've been keeping journals of one sort or another since I was a teenager, and if there is one thing I can now confidently say about all this scribbling and note-taking, it is that if it wasn't written down, it didn't happen."

Keeping a nature notebook is personal; there is lots of advice out there, but no rules, no one way. Use whatever size notebook attracts you and is practical for carrying about. I use a middle-size hardcover book with blank sheets, sketch with a mechanical pencil, and narrate or take notes with a fine-nib fountain pen filled with Noodler's brand brown ink. These days, my nature diary is one and the same as my personal diary, my "commonplace journal," as Darwin would have called it. In the past, I have kept these two records separate, but that was a bit problematical (which notebook should I carry?) and, I eventually decided, artificial. For one, I would look back at my earlier nature diaries (predominantly birds in years past), and wonder — what was going on in my life? What underlies these observations? What moods? What human visitors? What interior joys and struggles? What was I wearing, carrying, and what did I have for lunch? These simple details of life intertwine with our watching, and I felt that without them, my notes seemed a little bereft. When researching my book about Darwin, it was a revelation for me to overlay his ornithological notes with his diaries and letters, discovering how his moods, worries, and physical state mingled with his natural history observation. The scientific notes never mentioned his homesickness, for example, and on days when it was clear from the diary that the homesickness had lifted, he seemed to engage with his surroundings more deeply in his scientific notes, perhaps vividly recording an encounter with a particularly wonderful new bird, something he might not have had the enthusiasm for on his down days. How beautifully the two — life and science — entwined.

And so in my current diary, my personal life and naturalist notes mingle in one wild, earthy tangle. The sketch of a squirrel's paw sits next to the memo *Overcaffeinated and cold*. More squirrel sketches follow a page of worries about my current manuscript and a passage reflecting on whether it's finally time to get Claire a cell phone. In the margins next to the cell-phone pondering are sketches of the

Bewick's wren I can see from the bench where I write, hopping, singing, causing far too much ruckus for such a tiny bird. This is my current method, but there is certainly something both romantic and useful about keeping a separate nature journal. Do what sounds most appealing and practical for you. Just carrying a little pocket notebook can be enough to enjoy the benefits of nature diarizing.

Be an amateur phenologist. In addition to a personal diary, I advocate the keeping of a household phenology notebook. Phenology is the study of the outward signs of natural, seasonal change. The birds that come and go, the nests being built, the first butterfly, the larval hatching, the changing night sky, the first blooming trillium, the depth of snow, the first frost, the first thaw. The ever-changing, always-moving rhythm of life as it unfolds daily throughout the year. Paying attention to such things locates us in nature, grounds us in our own lives, our homes, our rhythmic bodies. With artificial light, heating, cooling, and the year-round abundance of imported, unseasonal fresh foods from the grocery store, it is easy for us to become severed from these cycles, a disconnection that breeds a vague anxiety, a mental lostness and physical uprootedness.

Right after graduating from college, I worked as a naturalist at an environmental learning center in Minnesota, where all staff meetings began with phenology announcements, a practice that influenced the rest of my life. One of us would sit with the phenology notebook open on the table and ask what everyone had seen that week. The hooded mergansers on the lake were spotted with tiny "merganserlets." An emerging lady-slipper orchid was discovered. The last patch of snow in the north field had completely melted. I imagine corporate meetings beginning in this same lovely, grounded way: The glaucous-winged gull is laying eggs on the ledge of the eleventh-floor office. The Anna's hummingbird finally found the window feeder suction-cupped to the sixth-floor window. The starlings that everyone has noticed from the bus stop are flocking up for the winter, moving in those fantastic cloud formations they create out of wing and feather. Then to business.

Keeping a phenology notebook is a beautiful home practice. All that is needed is a way of noting things down that is accessible to everyone in the household. We've developed our own, slightly idiosyncratic method. Before my grandmother became so old that she stopped writing things down altogether, she kept a perpetual diary—not a personal diary, but a simple record of daily happenings. Who visited, what the weather was like, and, maybe, if it was really yummy, what was for dinner. For this she used a giant spiral-bound notebook, with one page for every day of the year and the date written across the top. She would take a few lines per page for each day, then the following year start the same notebook again at the beginning, writing under the previous year's entry for that date, so that as she filled in her lines for the day, she could see what happened the year before, and the year before that. I loved hearing her say, for instance, as we sat down to a family dinner, "Oh, Lyanda, you were in Japan this day eight years ago. Why on earth did your mother let you go all that way?" The opinionated verbal commentary was inevitable, but the diary held just the fact. I used this as the model for our own family's phenology notebook, but instead of just keeping a list of phenological observations for the day, I decided to follow my own philosophy about diaries and create a phenology record that reminds us how personal life and wild life twine and inform each other, unfolding side by side. Thus the "what happened today" section occupies a few lines on the left side of the page, and the phenology a few lines on the right. We call this *The Book of Everything*. Instead of a spiral notebook, I use a large three-ring binder with filler paper, so I can add and remove garden notes in the back. I also keep a few pages in the back for our home wildlife list — what birds, mammals, conspicuous insects, arachnids, and "bugs" have visited our yard. Almost magically, knowing that this receptacle for our observations exists and that what we see will be shared, we become more alert, notice more, and it seems that there is actually more to see.

There are good web sites that will help organize phenological observations and that make it easy to contribute your notes to national citizen-science efforts. Citizen science has never been so important, and it is absolutely true with no exaggeration that the kinds of daily observations each of us is making, small and disjointed as they seem, are contributing to a new sense of what is unfolding on the earth, and how deeply we are all a part of it.

It is largely through citizen contributions to phenological studies that people have become aware of how organisms are responding to climate change: many flower species are blooming earlier, and the pollinators are correspondingly confused; some avian migrations are occurring earlier, following rises in temperature trends and subsequent changes in insect hatchings. Thoreau was an obsessive phenologist and started keeping track of the wildflowers in the Concord woods nearly 160 years ago. His notes are being compared with modern records to track the impact of climate change on the flowering plants in the area. Overall, there has been a general rise in temperature since Thoreau's era of 2.4 degrees, resulting in a flowering time that is about a week earlier for species that are able to respond to temperature changes. But many species have a set flowering time that is not responsive to temperature, and it is these species that are facing serious declines: the dogwoods, violets, saxifrages, roses, lilies, bladderworts, orchids, and others. Without Thoreau's notes, we would not have this knowledge, and it is not impossible that our own small efforts will have similar significance.

In October, I looked out into my backyard to see a scrub jay perched boldly on top of my opened cold frame, looking for all the world as if he belonged there. The blue on his back glowed — brighter than the blue of our local Steller's jay, which is normally found in shady, leafy places, where brightest blue is not as useful as it is for a bird of open scrubby places. But if you look at a species-distribution map for the scrub jay, you will see that, officially, it doesn't belong here at all. Birders and some wildlife officials know that for the past decade, scrub jays have been turning up in parts of Seattle, unbidden, and even unwanted (between crows, Steller's jays, and the occasional raven nesting in a forested park, there is enough corvid mischief around here). Do these scattered sightings indicate that the jays are expanding their range, and if so, why? For the naturalist, the sighting of a creature in the wrong place is both exhilarating and disorienting. We keep track of all these things.

Sleep outside. Every summer, we move our sleeping quarters outside into a tent. I love crawling out through the tent door at midnight (admittedly, to pee in the grass) and finding myself in the night world — sky, moon, stars, the rustling of night creatures real and imagined. It always feels new and surprising. And being something of an insomniac, I love that I sleep so much better out there, tucked into a big flannel sleeping bag, cool air on my face, and stars through the screen overhead.

Stars, moon, breeze. Sounds so sweet and calm. But it can be mayhem out there. *Mayhem.* Some nights we wake to opossums rustling, or raccoons trilling, or who knows what manner of creature grunting and sniffing. Every morning, I fully expect to step out of the tent and see the yard in a shambles, with benches overturned and shrubbery uprooted, but somehow the daylight garden is tranquil, just as I'd left it. One night early in the season, a raccoon climbed the cherry tree above our tent to gather the farthest reaches of the harvest—the berries we couldn't reach on our ladder. The tree swayed over our heads, and we could see the ringed tail hanging in the shadows. Then the pits started falling on our tent. They left red marks that wore off only after several summer rains.

Last summer Tom and I opened the tent flap to investigate some particularly suspicious sounds and found a small raccoon a few feet away, chewing on Tom's shoe. It was so close—even though the clock read 2:00 a.m., we woke Claire to have a look before Tom crawled out in his skivvies to chase the little thief away and retrieve his nibbled sandal. Once Claire woke me up to listen to a gull she heard in the dark of morning. But it wasn't a gull, I whispered to her (Tom was sound asleep), it was a western screech owl, a small owl that doesn't actually screech; its voice sounds like a muffled bouncing ball. Later that day, I found a screech-owl feather a block from our home, and on that same walk, just one block farther, I discovered fresh coyote scat right on the sidewalk. I have never seen one of the coyotes that inhabit the nearby greenbelt venture into our yard, but in the middle of the night, amid all the noise of the urban wilds, I am always grateful we took the effort to make our chicken coop so snug and impenetrable.

We sleep in the tent because it's cozy and fun, of course, but also because I love being reminded that the "urban wilderness" is more than just an expression—that we live in a more-than-human world filled with creatures who have no regard for the City Limits sign. In recent years, we've started leaving the tent up longer — into late October if we don't get too cold — and in these weeks, I love knowing that Claire heads to school each morning with not only a backpack of completed assignments but also visions of wild creatures in the night, an owl in the morning, and stars over her dreaming head. When we eventually do move back into the house, we remember the wild stories unfolding all around us as we sleep, even when we're not out there in their midst.

Cultivate a still spot. In childhood, most of us had a small space outdoors that we claimed as our own, a place of sweet secrecy outside the walls of home that cradled and comforted us. A place we gravitated to like the laps of our mothers. A place we would sit, outside of time, not hearing calls to dinner, knees drawn to our chests, eyes skyward.

My absolute favorite book on nature practices is the *Coyote's Guide to Connecting with Nature,* published by the Wilderness Awareness School and holding decades of wisdom gleaned by the school's founders and teachers. In the book are hundreds of activities drawn from human cultures across time and place. These are not lessons, we are told, not knowledge, but *"things people do* to learn nature's ways." They are habits, *practices.* The sit spot is the center, the magic pill of their core routine, and the instructions are minimal: find a place outdoors that speaks to you, and visit this place in a spirit of observant quiet. (I prefer the term *still spot,* which I am borrowing from nature writer and dear friend Lynda Mapes.) Do this frequently, preferably every day, and bring nothing more than your notebook and pencil, if you bring anything at all, and stay there as long as you like. In this place, we stretch the boundaries of our comfortable built dwellings and find a home in nature where we experience all the wild tendrils we normally strive so busily to exclude: darkness, weather, bugs, the technologically unmediated thrum of the natural world. There is no rule for finding a place, but ideally it would hide us a little, offer some shade or shelter, and put us in the potential path of wild things (they don't have to be "fancy" wild things — we aren't going to be seeing coyotes every day in our backyard still spot — but perhaps there will be birds sometimes, spiders, an occasional rainfall). I have two still spots — which might be cheating a little, but frequency is key, so I have a place in the backyard that is my special place of meditation, observation, and retreat, and I have another place in Lincoln Park, the urban woodland near my home. The Wilderness Awareness School teachers envision us in a traditionally wilder place, but urban still spots might include patios, the bases of fruit trees, shaded corners of grass and leaves not far from a birdbath.

In sitting still, we are both inviting and invited. The insects, birds, and possibly hidden mammals are always disturbed by our arriving, our initial sitting. They bristle, stiffen, become quiet, turn motionless, fly away. As we sit in stillness, they begin to realize two things: that we are not going away and also that we are not going to be moving about. They go back to what they were doing, to their more-than-human lives, and we are given the opportunity to become attendant upon these lives. The more often we come here, the more quickly this return occurs; the more easily we shed our housebound skins, the deeper we are allowed to enter. Sitting still in one place, outside, is the essential activity for humans in the urban bestiary. How lovely, how necessary, how simple and difficult, how thoroughly countercultural. Here is what Thoreau wrote, sitting in his cabin doorway:

There were times when I could not afford to sacrifice the bloom of the present moment to any work, whether of head or hands. Sometimes, in a summer morning, having taken my accustomed bath, I sat in my sunny doorway from sunrise till noon, rapt in a reverie, amidst the pines and hickories and sumachs, in undisturbed solitude and stillness, while the birds sang around. I grew in those seasons like corn in the night, and they were far better than any work of the hands would have been. They were not time subtracted from my life, but so much over and above my usual allowance.

In stillness, outdoors, we are dislodged from the human economy and dropped into the natural wild economy. We are made for this. I do not want to pretend that we should be sitting about in our skins all day every day. We have other things to do, good things. But it is this stillness that is in danger in the modern economy, and it will refresh and restore us, as it schools us in another kind of knowing. It is no wonder this is something so many of us have done on our own since we were children — the Wilderness Awareness School teaches that we are rediscovering what the Haudenosaunee people call our original instructions, our evolved, innate aptitude for awareness and delight in nature. Our wildness.

This list is short and personal, and it is meant to be an invitation, more than anything. We are all called to imagine and cultivate our own practices, daily habits that bring us to life, bring us to intimate presence with the wild among us. Walk more. Wear flowers in your hair to attract hummingbirds to your head. Bake bread. Study field guides. Sketch birds. Eat dandelions. Celebrate the seasons with abandon. Plot with neighbors, save trees, share lettuce, invent cottage industries, create a life that makes sense. *Write your own besti-ary,* and allow the creatures around you to contribute to its pages with their own tracks, words, roars. We don't have to wait for government funding, or scientific research, or political platform, or academic approval. We can think things up and carry them forth, on our own, with intelligence and heart, in the community of neighbors and all beings. We move forward with a mature optimism, one that recognizes fully the daunting ecological outlook for the earth, while maintaining our human obligation to live with awareness, and respect, and joy. We are learning to inhabit this new nature, and finding our way as we go. We are humans in the besti-ary, a blessed, privileged, weighty, beautiful thing to be.

Acknowledgments

Many thanks to the wildlife professionals, scientists, scholars, naturalists, writers, friends, and family who contributed so much to this project, including Stan Gehrt, Brian Kertson, Dennis Paulson, David Moskowitz, John Marzluff, Sean Met, Chris Anderson, Russell Link, Tracy Record and the West Seattle Blog, Rand Johnson, Jane Geddes, Maria Dolan, Kathryn True, David Williams, David Laskin, Lynda Mapes, Douglas MacDonald, Langdon Cook, Andrew Emlen, Karen Kuhar, Nancy Stillger, Tauna Evans, Phil Evans, Maggie Hooks, Jerry Haupt, Irene Haupt, Kelly Haupt, Jill Storey, Ginny Furtwangler, Al Furtwangler, Ann Copeland, and Delilah. Thank you, Unspeakables. So much gratitude to artist Tracie Noles-Ross, whose gorgeous work graces these pages. I'm grateful to my editor, Tracy Behar, and my agent, Elizabeth Wales, for their abiding patience, enthusiasm, and skill. Thanks to Tracy Roe for her intrepid copyediting. Thanks to the good folks at Whiteley Center and the University of Washington Friday Harbor Labs for providing a glorious writing desk at the edge of the Salish Sea. I'm indebted to the Benedictine sisters at St. Placid Priory for their hospitality and peaceful inspiration. As always, I'm beholden to the librarians at the University of Washington's Suzzallo and Allen Libraries, and the Seattle Public Libraries. Love to all the relations who share my home and inspire my days: the two-legged, four-legged, feathered, and finned. And, as ever, thank you with my whole heart to Tom and Claire Furtwangler.

Select Bibliography

The Aberdeen Bestiary Project. University of Aberdeen. www.abdn.ac.uk/bestiary/.

Armstrong, Karen. *A Short History of Myth.* New York: Canongate Books, 2005.

Bekoff, Marc. "Coyotes: Victims of Their Own Success." *Canid News* 3 (1995): 36–40.

Benton, Janetta Rebold. *The Medieval Menagerie: Animals in the Art of the Middle Ages.* New York: Abbeville Press, 1992.

Boyd, Brian. *On the Origin of Stories, Evolution, Cognition and Fiction.* Cambridge, MA: Belknap Press of Harvard, 2009.

Canfield, Michael R., ed. *Field Notes on Science and Nature.* Cambridge, MA: Harvard University Press, 2011.

Caspari, Elizabeth. *Animal Life in Nature, Myth and Dreams.* Wilmette, IL: Chiron Publications, 2003.

Catton, William R., Jr. "Understanding Humanity's Damaged Future." *Sociological Inquiry* 79 (2009): 509–22.

Clark, Willene, and Meredith T. McMunn. *Birds and Beasts of the Middle Ages. The Bestiary and Its Legacy.* Philadelphia: University of Pennsylvania Press, 1989.

Comer, Gary L., and Amanda D. Rodewald. "Effective Mole Control." *Ohio State University Extension Fact Sheet.* Ohio School of Natural Resources. Accessed February 28, 2013. http://ohioline.osu.edu/w-fact/0011.html.

Comstock, Anna Botsford. *Handbook of Nature Study.* Ithaca, NY: Cornell University Press, 1939.

Coyne, Kelly, and Erik Knutzen. *The Urban Homestead: Your Guide to Self-Sufficient Living in the Heart of the City.* Port Townsend, WA: Process, 2010.

Curtis, Odette E., R. N. Rosenfield, and J. Bielefeldt. "Cooper's Hawk (*Accipiter cooperii*)." In *The Birds of North America Online*, edited by A. Poole. Ithaca, NY: Cornell Lab of Ornithology, 2006.

Davis, Wade. *The Wayfinders: Why Ancient Wisdom Matters in the Modern World.* Toronto, ON: House of Anansi Press, 2009.

Dawson, William Leon, and John Hooper Bowles. *The Birds of Washington.* Seattle: Occidental Publishing Group, 1909.

DeStefano, Stephen. *Coyote at the Kitchen Door: Living with Wildlife in Suburbia.* Cambridge, MA: Harvard University Press, 2010.

Diamond, Jared. "Easter Island's End." *Discover* (August 1995).

Ditchkoff, Stephen S., Sarah T. Saalfeld, and Charles J. Gibson. "Animal Behavior in Urban Ecosystems: Modifications Due to Human-induced Stress." *Urban Ecosystems* 9 (2006): 5–12.

Donnelly, Roarke, and John M. Marzluff. "Relative Importance of Habitat Quantity, Structure, and Spatial Pattern to Birds in Urbanizing Environments." *Urban Ecosystems* 9 (2006): 99–117.

Donovan, G. H., Y. L. Michael, D. T. Butry, A. D. Sullivan, and J. M. Chase. "Urban Trees and the Risk of Poor Birth Outcomes." *Health and Place* 17 (2011): 390–93.

Ebenkamp, Paul, ed. *The Etiquette of Freedom.* Berkeley, CA: Counterpoint, 2010.

Elbroch, Mark. *Bird Tracks and Sign: A Guide to North American Species.* Mechanicsburg, PA: Stackpole Books, 2001.

———. *Mammal Tracks and Sign: A Guide to North American Species.* Mechanicsburg, PA: Stackpole Books, 2003.

Environment Canada. *Area-Sensitive Forest Birds in Urban Areas.* Downsview, ON: Canadian Wildlife Service, 2007.

Estes, Wendy A., and R. William Mannan. "Feeding Behavior of Cooper's Hawks at Urban and Rural Nests in Southeastern Arizona." *Condor* 105 (2003): 107–16.

Faber Taylor, A., and F. Kuo. "Children with Attention Deficits Concentrate Better After Walk in the Park." *Journal of Attention Disorders* 12 (2009): 402–9.

Faeth, Stanley H., Paige S. Warren, Eyal Shochat, and Wendy A. Marussich. "Trophic Dynamics in Urban Communities." *Bioscience* 55 (2005): 388–407.

Feinstein, Julie. *Field Guide to Urban Wildlife.* Mechanicsburg, PA: Stackpole Books, 2011.

Fowles, John. *The Tree.* New York: Harper Collins, 1979.

Gehrt, Stanley D. "Ecology of Coyotes in Urban Landscapes." In *Proceedings of the Twelfth Wildlife Damage Management Conference,* edited by D. L. Nolte, W. M. Arjo, and D. H. Stalman, 2007.

Gehrt, Stanley D., Justin L. Brown, and Chris Anchor. "Is the Urban Coyote a Misanthropic Synanthrope? The Case from Chicago." *Cities and the Environment* 4 (2011).

Gibeau, M. L. "Use of Urban Habitat by Coyotes in the Vicinity of Banff, Alberta." *Urban Ecosystems* 2 (1998): 129–39.

Gleiser, Marcelo. *The Dancing Universe: From Creation Myths to the Big Bang.* New York: Penguin, 1997.

Gross, Liza. "Mountain Lions Straying into More Urban Areas." *San Francisco Chronicle,* November 28, 2010.

Grynbaum, Michael M. "Seen It All on Subway? Look Under This Seat." *New York Times,* January 17, 2012.

Hamilton, Virginia. *In the Beginning: Creation Stories from Around the World.* New York: Graphia, 1991.

Hansen, Kevin. *Cougar: The American Lion.* Iron River, MI: Northland, 1992.

Henderson, Robert F. "Moles." *Prevention and Control of Wildlife Damage.* Institute of Agriculture and Natural Resources, University of Nebraska, 1994.

Herzog, Hal. *Some We Love, Some We Hate, Some We Eat: Why It's So Hard to Think Straight About Animals.* New York: Harper, 2010.

Holmgren, Virginia C. *Raccoons in History, Folklore, and Today's Backyards.* Santa Barbara, CA: Capra Press, 1990.

Hutton, C. Stuart, Dwight G. Smith, and Christoph Rohner. "Great Horned Owl (*Bubo virginianus*)." In *The Birds of North America Online,* edited by A. Poole. Ithaca, NY: Cornell Lab of Ornithology, 1998.

Kaza, Stephanie. *The Attentive Heart: Conversations with Trees.* New York: Fawcett Columbine, 1993.

Kellert, Stephen. "Ordinary Nature: The Value of Exploring and Restoring Nature in Everyday Life." In *Proceedings of the Fourth International Urban Wildlife Symposium,* edited by W. Shaw et al., 2004.

Koenig, Walter D. "European Starlings and Their Effect on Native Cavity-Nesting Birds." *Conservation Biology* 17 (2002): 1134–40.

Lee, Jeanne. *I Once Was a Monkey: Stories Buddha Told.* New York: Farrar, Straus and Giroux, 1999.

Leslie, Clare Walker, and Charles E. Roth. *Keeping a Nature Journal.* North Adams, MA: Storey Publishing, 2003.

Levy, Sharon. "Rise of the Coyote: The New Top Dog." *Nature* 485 (2012): 296–97.

Link, Russell. *Living with Wildlife in the Pacific Northwest.* Seattle: University of Washington Press, 2004.

Linnea, Ann. *Keepers of the Trees.* New York: Skyhorse Publishing, 2010.

Louv, Richard. *The Nature Principle: Human Restoration and the End of Nature-Deficit Disorder.* Chapel Hill, NC: Algonquin Books of Chapel Hill, 2011.

Luniak, Maciej. "Synurbization—Adaptation of Animal Wildlife to Urban Development." In *Proceedings of the Fourth International Urban Wildlife Symposium,* edited by W. Shaw et al., 2004.

Mapes, Lynda. "Of Moles and Men." *Seattle Times,* February 8, 2011.

Marzluff, John, and Tony Angell. *Gifts of the Crow: How Perception, Emotion, and Thought Allow Smart Birds to Behave Like Humans.* New York: Free Press, 2012.

McGinnis, Mark. *Buddhist Animal Wisdom Stories.* New York: Weatherhill, 2004.

McGowan, Kevin. "Demographic and Behavioral Comparisons of Suburban and Rural American Crows." In *Avian Ecology and Conservation in an Urbanizing World,* edited by J. Marzluff, R. Bowman, and R. Donnelly. Boston: Kluwer Academic Press, 2001.

McKibben, Bill. *Eaarth: Making a Life on a Tough New Planet.* New York: Henry Holt and Company, 2010.

McLoughlin, John. *The Animals Among Us: Wildlife in the City.* New York: Viking Press, 1978.

Meloy, Ellen. *Eating Stone: Imagination and the Loss of the Wild.* New York: Pantheon Books, 2005.

Mortimer, Ian. *The Time Traveler's Guide to Medieval England.* New York: Touchstone, 2008.

Moskowitz, David. *Wildlife of the Pacific Northwest: Tracking and Identifying Mammals, Birds, Reptiles, Amphibians, and Insects.* Portland, OR: Timber Press, 2010.

Newman, Peter, and Isabella Jennings. *Cities as Sustainable Ecosystems: Principles and Practices.* Washington, DC: Island Press, 2008.

Nice, Margaret Morse. *Research Is a Passion with Me.* Toronto, ON: Amethyst Communications, 1979.

Nicholls, Henry. "The Royal Raccoon from Swedesboro." *Nature* 446 (2007): 225–26.

Nilon, Charles H., Alan R. Berkowitz, and Karen S. Hollweg. "Understanding Urban Ecosystems: A New Frontier for Science and Education." *Urban Ecosystems* 3 (1999): 3–4.

Noss, Reed F. "Can Urban Areas Have Ecological Integrity?" In *Proceedings of the Fourth International Urban Wildlife Symposium,* edited by W. Shaw et al., 2004.

Parker, Tommy S., and Charles H. Nilon. "Gray Squirrel Density, Habitat Suitability, and Behavior in Urban Parks." *Urban Ecosystems* 11 (2008): 243–55.

Parrish, Susan Scott. "The Female Opossum and the Nature of the New World." *William and Mary Quarterly* 54 (1997): 475–514.

Partecke, Jesko, Ingrid Schwabl, and Eberhard Gwinner. "Stress and the City: Urbanization and Its Effects on the Stress Physiology in European Blackbirds." *Ecology* 87 (2006): 1945–52.

Partridge, Eric. *Origins: A Short Etymological Dictionary of Modern English.* New York: Greenwich House, 1983.

Pollan, Michael. *Second Nature: A Gardener's Education.* New York: Grove Press, 1991.

Prentice, Jessica. *Full Moon Feast: Food and the Hunger for Connection.* White River Junction, VT: Chelsea Green Publishing Company, 2006.

Rezendes, Paul. *Tracking and the Art of Seeing: How to Read Animal Tracks and Sign.* New York: Harper Collins, 1999.

———. *The Wild Within: Adventures in Nature and Animal Teachings.* New York: Tarcher/Putnam, 1998.

Royte, Elizabeth. "Canis Soup." *Outside* (March 2010).

Schwarz, Naoki. "L.A.'s Urban Cougars Under Siege." Associated Press, October 2, 2011.

ScienceDaily. "Eavesdropping Nuthatches Appear to Understand Chickadees in Distress." *ScienceDaily,* March 19, 2007.

Smith, Susan M. "Black-Capped Chickadee (*Poecile atricapillus*)." In *The Birds of North America Online,* edited by A. Poole. Ithaca, NY: Cornell Lab of Ornithology, 2010.

Snyder, Gary. *The Practice of the Wild.* San Francisco: North Point Press, 1990.

Stiles, Gary F. "In Memoriam: Alexander F. Skutch, 1904–2004." *Auk* 122 (2005): 708–10.

Thoreau, Henry David. *Walden.* Boston: Beacon Press, 1997.

Todd, Kim. *Tinkering with Eden: A Natural History of Exotics in America.* New York: Norton, 2002.

Tudge, Colin. *The Tree.* New York: Three Rivers Press, 2005.

Turner, Jack. *The Abstract Wild.* Tucson: University of Arizona Press, 1996.

Ulrich, R. S. "View Through a Window May Influence Recovery from Surgery." *Science* 224 (1984): 420–21.

Weisman, Alan. *The World Without Us.* New York: Thomas Dunne Books, 2007.

Weitzel, Norman H. "Nest-Side Competition Between the European Starling and Native Breeding Birds in Northwestern Nevada." *Condor* 90 (1988): 515–17.

Young, Jon. *What the Robin Knows: How Birds Reveal the Secrets of the Natural World.* Boston: Houghton Mifflin, 2012.

Young, Jon, Ellen Haas, and Evan McGown. *Coyote's Guide to Connecting with Nature.* Shelton, WA: Owlink Media, 2010.

Index

Note: Italic page numbers refer to illustrations.

About the Author

Lyanda Lynn Haupt is a naturalist, eco-philosopher, teacher, and speaker whose writing is at the forefront of the movement to connect people with nature in their everyday lives. She has worked as education director for Seattle Audubon, in raptor rehabilitation, and as a seabird researcher for the U.S. Fish and Wildlife Service in the remote tropical Pacific.

Haupt is the author of the award-winning books *Crow Planet* and *Rare Encounters with Ordinary Birds*. Her work has appeared in many publications, including *Orion* and the *LA Times,* and she blogs at *The Tangled Nest.* She lives with her husband and daughter in Seattle.